MASSACHUSETTS, COLONY TO COMMONWEALTH

DOCUMENTARY PROBLEMS IN EARLY AMERICAN HISTORY

The Great Awakening
Documents on the Revival of Religion, 1740–1745

Edited by Richard L. Bushman

The Glorious Revolution in America
Documents on the Colonial Crisis of 1689

Edited by Michael G. Hall, Lawrence H. Leder, and Michael G. Kammen

Massachusetts, Colony to Commonwealth
Documents on the Formation of Its Constitution, 1775–1780

Edited by Robert J. Taylor

Prologue to Revolution
Sources and Documents on the Stamp Act Crisis, 1764–1766

Edited by Edmund S. Morgan

Massachusetts, Colony to Commonwealth

DOCUMENTS ON THE FORMATION OF ITS CONSTITUTION, 1775–1780

Edited by
Robert J. Taylor

W· W· NORTON & COMPANY· INC·
NEW YORK

This volume is published for the Institute of Early American History and Culture at Williamsburg, Virginia. The Institute of Early American History and Culture is sponsored jointly by the College of William and Mary and Colonial Williamsburg, Incorporated.

This edition first published 1972
by arrangement with The University of North Carolina Press

SBN 393 09396 4

Published simultaneously in Canada
by George J. McLeod Limited, Toronto

PRINTED IN THE UNITED STATES OF AMERICA

1 2 3 4 5 6 7 8 9 0

CONTENTS

Chapter V. THE CONSTITUTIONALISTS DEMAND ACTION

Chapter VI. THE CONSTITUTION OF 1780

The Ratification of the Constitution of 1780

Reactions to Ratification

INTRODUCTION

THE POLITICAL development of the United States has always interested other peoples and has inspired emulation on more than one occasion—events of our own day being but the latest instance. The written constitution has been one of our most important exports—and one of our older ones. On constitution-making in America, Madison once wrote: "Nothing has excited more admiration in the world than the manner in which free governments have been established in America; for it was the first instance, from the creation of the world—that free inhabitants have been seen deliberating on a form of government, and selecting such of their citizens as possess their confidence, to determine upon and give effect to it."

Of the many constitutions drafted in this country that of Massachusetts, adopted in 1780, is one of the most important. "If I were called upon to select a single fact or enterprise which more nearly than any other single thing embraced the significance of the American Revolution," said President Andrew C. McLaughlin of the American Historical Association in 1914, "I should select—not Saratoga or the French alliance, or even the Declaration of Independence—I should choose the formation of the Massachusetts Constitution of 1780, and I should do so because that constitution rested upon the fully developed convention, the greatest institution of government which America has produced, the instituton which answered, in itself, the problem of how men could make government of their own free will." Stated thus grandly, the action of Massachusetts calls up visions of dignified ancestors in knee-breeches solemnly laying the foundations of government by consent. In actuality, "the fully developed convention" with all that it implied about free government came after a prolonged and sometimes bitter struggle of six year's duration. Massachusetts men came only gradually to the idea that a special convention was needed for drafting a constitution and that its handiwork required the direct assent of the people in every particular.

The story of the maneuvering and deliberating that preceded final adoption of the constitution is recorded in hundreds of documents, offering abundant material for the historian to ponder. The sources chosen for this book are designed to point up problems that will enable the student to approximate the task of the historian—the sifting and weighing of evidence in the effort to get closer to the actuality of past events and their meaning. Close study of the documents will not demean but rather magnify the achievement of which President McLaughlin spoke, for the student will have a greater appreciation of the courage, patience, and dedication of those who sought to establish a lasting government suitable for free men.

Further, study of these documents will point up the significance for ordinary men of some of the constitutional issues underlying the American Revolution. In their town meetings and conventions simple farmers and artisans, some of them barely literate, grappled with fundamental principles and problems, stressing such basic ideas as no taxation without representation, the equality of men before the law, the superiority of fixed constitutions to legislative enactments, and the exact nature of the liberties of free men. Massachusetts people did not always agree on how problems should be solved, nor on the principles that should prevail. But anyone tempted to dismiss the appeal to principle as merely a cover-up for economic or other motives in the Revolution must consider carefully the language of simple men addressing not posterity, but their own work-a-day representatives. Of course, all the debates were not on the exalted plane of principles; these were men, not heroes. Class animosities, provincial distrust of Boston, and political rivalries played their parts, too. Yet the town meetings and their leaders did rise above petty concerns to hammer out a workable system of self government; both in content and in method of adoption the Massachusetts Constitution underscored the constitutional significance of the American Revolution.

Although all the states except Rhode Island and Connecticut adopted written constitutions during the Revolution (Rhode Island and Connecticut merely modified their royal charters), many of these organic instruments were hastily drafted and soon replaced. Massachusetts, the last of the states to adopt a constitution, ended up with a carefully constructed fundamental law which has lasted, though much amended, until the present day. Besides a bill of rights, an important part of every state constitution, the specially called convention of Massachusetts provided a genuine system of checks and balances: a two-house legislature, each house elected by a somewhat different electorate; a strong executive with veto power; and a judiciary with life tenure. In these features the Massachusetts constitution anticipated the United States Constitution adopted eight years later.

In selecting documents to illustrate the course of events in Massachusetts, I have emphasized the material in the State Archives, the official record of documents received from the town meetings and also from persons, groups, and conventions that sought to persuade the legislature to one course of action or another. The Archives do not contain a complete record of the returns of the towns, but I have chosen to limit myself to returns available there on the grounds that those actually received in Boston presumably counted for something. Sometimes individual towns acted too late to be effective or even failed to send in a record of their action. Undoubtedly some returns that did arrive in time were not preserved, but it is impossible now to make such determinations. In addition to archival material I have included a few representative pieces from pamphlets, diaries, memoirs, etc., to help round out the picture. Although I have also used the newspapers for supplementary matter, I have done so sparingly because arguments published in them usually found expression in the returns of the towns.

It is my hope that the documents selected will not only interest students but also be of use to scholars. Many of the documents have never before been printed, and others have been out of print for some time. As much as space limitations will permit, I have sought to give documents in full; where I have made excerpts, I have done so to allow comparisons to be made on a single point or two. I have expanded abbreviations, but I have retained the spelling and punctuation of the originals, both for historical accuracy and because in some instances they offer a clue to the educational level of the authors. In the few cases in which I was unable to find the original manuscript, I have relied upon printed versions with modernized orthography.

I want to acknowledge here my thanks to the following persons and institutions for permission to print documents in their possession: Mr. Joseph D. Ward, Secretary of the Commonwealth of Massachusetts, for the material from the State Archives; Mrs. H. W. Edwards, Curator of the Local History Collection, Berkshire Athenaeum, Pittsfield, for the material from the William Williams Collection; and the New York Public Library for letters from the Hawley Papers. Thanks are due also to the Old South Association for permission to reproduce its printed version of the Constitution of 1778, a carefully done text based on collation of a pamphlet and a newspaper text with the version in the Archives. The following deserve my gratitude for assisting me in getting documents reproduced: Mr. Malcolm Freiberg of the Massachusetts Historical Society, Mrs. Graham D. Wilcox of the Stockbridge Library, Mr. Leo Flaherty of the Massachusetts Archives, and the Library of the State Historical Society of Wisconsin.

Finally, I express my deepest appreciation to Mr. James M. Smith, Editor of Publications for the Institute of Early American History and Culture, whose many suggestions and wise counsel have been invaluable; and to Miss Sonya Dowrey, one of my students, for helping in the tedious work of recording votes and transcribing from microfilm. To some degree I accepted her suggestions in picking returns from the towns that would be interesting to readers.

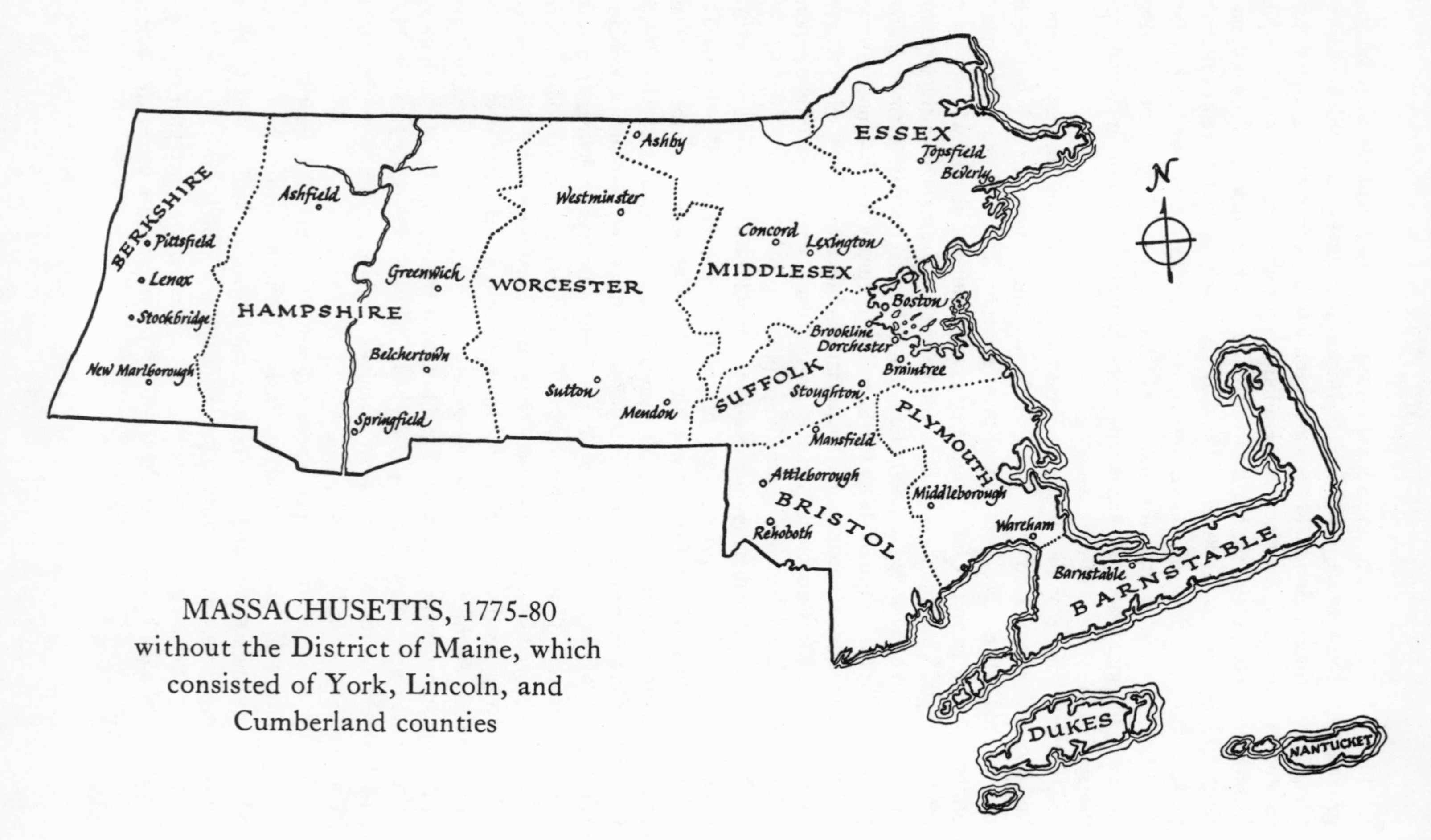

MASSACHUSETTS, 1775-80
without the District of Maine, which
consisted of York, Lincoln, and
Cumberland counties

CHAPTER I

TAKING UP THE POWERS OF CIVIL GOVERNMENT

LONG BEFORE the Declaration of Independence proclaimed that "these United States are, and of right ought to be Free and Independent States," American colonists had been forced to confront the problem of governing themselves. To go from regulated and protected colonies to self-governing commonwealths or states was a big step; and not surprisingly, Americans disagreed on both the timing and the method of taking such a step.

Although the Revolutionary troubles began in Massachusetts with the Boston Tea Party, the Bay Colony was more deliberate than any other in institutionalizing the constitutional change from colony to commonwealth. Until the Coercive Acts of 1774, the royal province of Massachusetts-Bay was governed under a charter, granted in 1691, which sought to leaven royal government with some measure of local control. The governor was appointed by the king, as in all royal provinces, but the Council was elected annually by the House of Representatives and the outgoing Council in May. Each of the twenty-eight councilors had to meet the approval of the governor, for whom the Council acted as an advisory body. With the advice and consent of Council, the governor appointed military and judicial officers at all levels of government, their commissions running in the name of the king. The Council also functioned as an upper branch of the legislature, its concurrence being necessary for all laws and joint resolutions. The governor had an absolute veto over the acts of the legislature, or General Court as it was usually called. The legislature appointed officials like the Treasurer and Receiver-General; and by its control over the purse, including the appropriation for the governor's salary, the General Court in time came to hold the upper hand. The governor frequently sought to win political support by naming men who were loyal to him to the various lucrative postions in his gift; quite commonly one man held several official places at the same time.

According to law every town with forty or more freeholders had to send a representative to the General Court, those with 120 or more freeholders could send two, and Boston was allowed to send four. Each town paid for its representatives' travel and attendance, the amount being collected from the town as part of the provincial taxes. Many towns neglected to avail themselves of their right to representation because they found the expense burdensome; such towns were sometimes fined by the General Court. During the eighteenth century the British had decreed that to keep the size of the House of Representatives limited, new towns created should not have the right to send representatives; such new towns were known as districts. By an act passed in August 1775, all districts automatically gained the right of representation.

The charter of 1691 left unchanged the system of local government which had evolved during the seventeenth century. In their town meetings the freeholders assessed town rates, made regulations, declared themselves on public questions, and elected a great variety of town officials as well as representatives to the General Court. Town by-laws and the actions of town officials came under the purview of the General Sessions of the Peace, a county court known more familiarily as the Quarter Sessions. Its bench was made up of all the justices of the peace for the county, who might number a dozen or even two dozen. In its administrative capacity this court assessed county taxes, licensed tavern-keepers, and saw to the laying out of county roads and bridges, as well as overseeing town government and handling other matters on the county level. The Quarter Sessions also functioned as a criminal court which heard cases beyond the competence of a single justice of the peace. The latter fined violators of the peace and heard petty suits against debtors. If a civil suit involved land titles or sums over forty shillings, the case would be heard by the Inferior Court of Common Pleas; most of its litigation involved debtors. The judges of Common Pleas were almost always justices of the peace as well and thus sat on the Quarter Sessions bench along with the other justices. Those brought to court paid a multiplicity of fees established by law, but fees paid for lawyers' services were additional and were not fixed by statute. The expensiveness of legal proceedings caused many a debtor to plead for a "confession act," by means of which he could simply confess judgment before a justice and thus save fees for writs, witnesses, and the like. If he could not pay his debts, he went to jail, where his creditor could keep him indefinitely.

This pattern of local and provincial government was rudely wrenched out of shape by action of the British Parliament in 1774 in the aftermath of the Boston Tea Party. It will be recalled that the British, wanting to mollify the colonists and yet wishing to keep intact the principle of Parliamentary taxation, had repealed all of the Townshend taxes except that on tea; moreover, the Parliament had given the East India Company the privilege of exporting tea directly to the colonies instead of selling it first to middlemen in England. This privilege gave the Company a competitive advantage with respect to colonial merchants that seemed to threaten outright disaster. If the Company could eliminate the profits of middlemen on tea, it might in the future obtain the same privilege with respect to other goods. In short, the buying of East India tea meant acquiescense in taxation by Parliament; the selling of it meant losses for colonial merchants. The Boston patriots solved the problem by dumping the hated tea into the harbor on December 16, 1773, their example setting off a series of tea parties in other colonies. And after 1773, the Sons of Liberty exerted considerable pressure on their compatriots to give up tea altogether lest one inadvertently drink taxed rather than smuggled tea.

The wholesale destruction of valuable tea brought irresistible demands in Parliament for punishment of the offenders. Boston had long been regarded as intractable, even seditious, and Parliament promptly passed the Coercive Acts in 1774 to make an example of the colony. One act closed the port of Boston to all commerce, and another prohibited town meetings throughout the colony without the governor's permission, except for the purpose of elections. The Massachusetts Government Act summarily replaced the annually elected Council with a royally appointed body of thirty-six members, each to hold office during the king's pleasure. Another act allowed magistrates, custom officials, or soldiers indicted for capital offenses within the colony to transfer their trials to England or Nova Scotia, where their cases would not be heard by hostile local juries. A final act provided for the quartering of troops in Boston. In addition, General Thomas Gage, commander-in-chief of British forces in North America, was commissioned as governor of Massachusetts and was given greater power in appointing and removing judges, sheriffs, and other officials without the consent of Council. Juries were to be chosen by sheriffs.

When the people of Massachusetts flatly refused to accept these alterations in their government, Governor Gage dissolved the General Court in June 1774. During the summer and fall, county conventions vigorously condemned the Government Act, some demanding the closing of the courts for as long as judges were to be merely creatures of the governor. Action soon replaced resolutions and prevented the courts from sitting. In short, the answer of Massachusetts to what it regarded as the despotic acts of King and Parliament was a suspension of government through intimidation of the courts.

Acts of violence caused Governor Gage to cancel the scheduled meeting of the General Court for October, although he had issued writs for electing representatives. But a number of men who had been elected met anyway at the designated time and place, and then adjourned to Concord, where they joined others who had been elected by various county conventions. Together these men formed the first Provincial Congress of Massachusetts. Three Provincial Congresses, wholly without legal status, governed Massachusetts between October 1774 and July 1775. It was these bodies that elected delegates to the First Continental Congress, which assembled in September 1774 to deal with the threat posed by the Coercive Acts.

The gravity of the situation for both Massachusetts and the American colonies as a whole deepened with the battles of Lexington and Concord in April 1775. "The butcheries and devastations of their implacable enemies," as patriots chose to call the actions of the British on that occasion, led the Massachusetts Provincial Congress on May 5, 1775, to depose General Gage as governor, since it was he who had ordered British troops into the countryside to seek powder stored at Concord and to seize patriot leaders Samuel Adams and John Hancock, rumored to be in Lexington.

Without a governor, Massachusetts now turned to the Second Continental Congress, requesting advice on the establishment of "Civil Government, which we think absolutely necessary for the salvation of our country," and agreeing to submit to such "a general plan as congress might direct for the colonies." Massachusetts made it clear that the question related to all the colonies and promised "to establish such a form of government here, as shall not only promote our advantage but the union and interest of all America."[1]

The formal declaration of separation from Great Britain lay a whole year in the future, and the great majority of Americans in 1775 still thought in terms of reconciliation on an honorable basis. Thus although Massachusetts mentioned a general scheme which Congress might devise for the assuming of civil government in all the colonies, most members of the Congress were not yet ready for so drastic a step. Even in the case of Massachusetts, where armed conflict had already broken out and where the old forms of government had dissolved, the members of Congress hesitated to suggest more than a temporary expedient; to advocate thorough remodeling of colonial governments seemed too irrevocable a measure in 1775.

Despite the urging of John Adams, one of the delegates from Massachusetts, the most that Congress was ready to recommend for Massachusetts was that elections be held to choose a House of Representatives, which in turn would elect a Council, "which assembly and Council should exercise the powers of Government, until a Governor, of his Majesty's appointment, will consent to govern the colony according to its charter."[2] In his autobiography (No. 1), John Adams recalls the action by Congress and summarizes the background for state constitution-making in the months preceding the Declaration of Independence.

QUESTIONS

1. What method of proceeding to institute state government does Adams recommend?

1. *Journals of the Continental Congress,* II, 77.
2. *Ibid.,* p. 84.

2. How closely was his advice followed in the case of Massachusetts? Why? In the case of New Hampshire and South Carolina? Why? In answering, consider both method of proceeding and the permanency of the government to be formed.

3. In his narrative, Adams lays stress upon what aspect of the debates and maneuverings in Congress?

4. What specific suggestions for the content of state constitutions does Adams make?

5. Why did not Congress draft a model plan for state constitutions?

1. John Adams Gives the Background for State Constitution-Making, 1775

["Autobiography," Charles Francis Adams, ed., *The Works of John Adams* (Boston, 1851), III, 12-23]

It is necessary that I should be a little more particular, in relating the rise and progress of the new government of the States.

On Friday, June 2d, 1775, "The President laid before Congress a letter from the Provincial Convention of Massachusetts Bay, dated May 16th, which was read, setting forth the difficulties they labor under for want of a regular form of government, and as they and the other Colonies are now compelled to raise an army to defend themselves from the butcheries and devastations of their implacable enemies, which renders it still more necessary to have a regular established government, requesting the Congress to favor them with explicit advice respecting the taking up and exercising the powers of civil government, and declaring their readiness to submit to such a general plan as the Congress may direct for the Colonies, or make it their great study to establish such a form of government there as shall not only promote their advantage, but the union and interest of all America."

This subject had engaged much of my attention before I left Massachusetts, and had been frequently the subject of conversation between me and many of my friends, —Dr. Winthrop, Dr. Cooper, Colonel Otis, the two Warrens, Major Hawley, and others, besides my colleagues in Congress,—and lay with great weight upon my mind, as the most difficult and dangerous business that we had to do; (for from the beginning, I always expected we should have more difficulty and danger, in our attempts to govern ourselves, and in our negotiations and connections with foreign powers, than from all the fleets and armies of Great Britain.) It lay, therefore, with great weight upon my mind, and when this letter was read, I embraced the opportunity to open myself in Congress, and most ernestly to entreat the serious attention of all the members, and of all the continent, to the measures which the times demanded. For my part, I thought there was great wisdom in the adage, "when the sword is drawn, throw away the scabbard." Whether we threw it away voluntarily or not, it was useless now, and would be useless forever. The pride of Britain, flushed with late triumphs and conquests, their infinite contempt of all the power of America, with an insolent, arbitrary Scotch faction, with a Bute and Mansfield at their head for a ministry, we might depend upon it, would force us to call forth every energy and resource of the country, to seek the friendship of England's enemies, and we had no rational hope, but from the *Ratio ultima regum et rerumpublicarum.* These efforts could not be made without government, and as I supposed no man would think of consolidating this vast continent under one national government, we should probably, after the example of the Greeks, the Dutch, and the Swiss, form a confederacy of States, each of which must have a separate government. That the case of Massachusetts was the most urgent, but that it could not be long before every other Colony must follow her example. That with a view to this subject, I had looked into the ancient and modern confederacies for examples, but they all appeared to me to have been huddled up in a hurry, by a few chiefs. But we had a people of more intelligence, curiosity, and enterprise, who must be all consulted, and we must realize the theories of the wisest writers, and invite the people to erect the whole building with their own hands, upon the broadest foundation. That this could be done only by conventions of representatives chosen by the people in the several colonies, in the most exact proportions. That it was my opinion that Congress ought now to recommend to the people of every Colony to call such conventions immediately, and set up governments of their own, under their own authority; for the people were the source of all authority and original of all power. These were new, strange, and terrible doctrines to the greatest part of the members, but not a very small number heard them with apparent pleasure, and none more than Mr. John Rutledge, of South Carolina, and Mr. John Sullivan, of New Hampshire.

Congress, however, ordered the letter to lie on the table for further consideration.

On Saturday, June 3d, the letter from the convention of the Massachusetts Bay, dated the 16th of May, being again read, the subject was again discussed, and then, "*Resolved,* That a committee of five persons be chosen, to consider the same, and report what in their opinion is the proper advice to be given to that Convention."

The following persons were chosen by ballot, to compose that committee, namely, Mr. J. Rutledge, Mr. Johnson, Mr. Jay, Mr. Wilson, and Mr. Lee. These gentlemen had several conferences with the delegates from our State, in the course of which, I suppose, the hint was suggested, that they adopted in their report.

On Wednesday, June 7th, "On motion, *Resolved,* That Thursday, the 20th of July next, be observed throughout the twelve United Colonies as a day of humiliation, fasting, and prayer; and that Mr. Hooper, Mr. J. Adams, and Mr. Paine, be a committee to bring in a resolve for that purpose.

"The committee appointed to prepare advice, in answer to the letter from the Convention of Massachusetts Bay, brought in their report, which was read and ordered to lie on the table for consideration.

"On Friday, June 9th, the report of the committee on the letter from the Convention of Massachusetts Bay being again read, the Congress came into the following resolution.

"*Resolved,* That no obedience being due to the Act of Parliament for altering the charter of the Colony of Massachusetts Bay, nor to a Governor or Lieutenant-Governor who will not observe the directions of, but endeavor to subvert, that charter, the Governor and Lieutenant-Governor of that Colony are to be considered as absent, and their offices vacant; and as there is no Council there, and the inconveniences arising from the suspension of the powers of government are intolerable, especially at a time when General Gage hath actually levied war, and is carrying on hostilities against his Majesty's peaceable and loyal subjects of that Colony; That, in order to conform as near as may be to the spirit and substance of the charter, it be recommended to the Provincial Convention to write letters to the inhabitants of the several places, which are entitled to representation in Assembly, requesting them to choose such representatives, and that the Assembly when chosen to elect Counsellors; and that such assembly or Council exercise the powers of government, until a Governor of His Majesty's appointment will consent to govern the Colony according to its charter.

"Ordered, That the President transmit a copy of the above to the Convention of Massachusetts Bay."

Although this advice was in a great degree conformable to the New York and Pennsylvania system, or in other words, to the system of Mr. Dickinson and Mr. Duane, I thought it an acquisition, for it was a precedent of advice to the separate States to institute governments, and I doubted not we should soon have more occasions to follow this example. Mr. John Rutledge and Mr. Sullivan had frequent conversations with me upon this subject. Mr. Rutledge asked me my opinion of a proper form of government for a State, I answered him that any form that our people would consent to institute, would be better than none, even if they placed all power in a house of representatives, and they should appoint governors and judges; but I hoped they would be wiser, and preserve the English Constitution in its spirit and substance, as far as the circumstances of this country required or would admit. That no hereditary powers ever had existed in America, nor would they, or ought they to be introduced or proposed; but that I hoped the three branches of a legislature would be preserved, an executive, independent of the senate or council, and the house, and above all things, the independence of the judges. Mr. Sullivan was fully agreed with me in the necessity of instituting governments, and he seconded me very handsomely in supporting the argument in Congress. Mr. Samuel Adams was with us in the opinion of the necessity, and was industrious in conversation with the members out of doors, but he very rarely spoke much in Congress, and he was perfectly unsettled in any plan to be recommended to a State, always inclining to the most democratical forms, and even to a single sovereign assembly, until his constituents afterwards in Boston compelled him to vote for three branches. Mr. Cushing was also for one sovereign assembly, and Mr. Paine was silent and reserved upon the subject, at least to me.

Not long after this, Mr. John Rutledge returned to South Carolina, and Mr. Sullivan went with General Washington to Cambridge, so that I lost two of my able coadjutors. But we soon found the benefit of their cooperation at a distance.

On Wednesday, October 18th, the delegates from New Hampshire laid before the Congress a part of the instructions delivered to them by their Colony, in these words:—"We would have you immediately use your utmost endeavors to obtain the advice and direction of the Congress, with respect to a method for our administering justice, and regulating our civil police. We press you not to delay this matter, as its being done speedily will probably prevent the greatest confusion among us."

This instruction might have been obtained by Mr. Langdon, or Mr. Whipple, but I always supposed it was General Sullivan who suggested the measure, because he left Congress with a stronger impression upon his mind of the importance of it, than I ever observed in either of the others. Be this, however, as it may have been, I embraced with joy the opportunity of haranguing on the subject at large, and of urging Congress to resolve on a general recommendation to all the States to call conventions and institute regular governments. I reasoned from various topics, many of which, perhaps, I could not now recollect. Some I remember; as,

1. The danger to the morals of the people from the present loose state of things, and general relaxation of laws and government through the Union.

2. The danger of insurrections in some

of the most disaffected parts of the Colonies, in favor of the enemy, or as they called them, the mother country, an expression that I thought it high time to erase out of our language.

3. Communications and intercourse with the enemy, from various parts of the continent could not be wholly prevented, while any of the powers of government remained in the hands of the King's servants.

4. It could not well be considered as a crime to communicate intelligence, or to act as spies or guides to the enemy, without assuming all the powers of government.

5. The people of America would never consider our Union as complete, but our friends would always suspect divisions among us, and our enemies who were scattered in larger or smaller numbers, not only in every State and city, but in every village through the whole Union, would forever represent Congress as divided and ready to break to pieces, and in this way would intimidate and discourage multitudes of our people who wished us well.

6. The absurdity of carrying on war against a king, when so many persons were daily taking oaths and affirmations of allegiance to him.

7. We could not expect that our friends in Great Britain would believe us united and in earnest, or exert themselves very strenuously in our favor, while we acted such a wavering, hesitating part.

8. Foreign nations, particularly France and Spain, would not think us worthy of their attention while we appeared to be deceived by such fallacious hopes of redress of grievances, of pardon for our offences, and of reconciliation with our enemies.

9. We could not command the natural resources of our own country. We could not establish manufactories of arms, cannon, saltpetre, powder, ships, &c., without the powers of government; and all these and many other preparations ought to be going on in every State or Colony, if you will, in the country.

Although the opposition was still inveterate, many members of Congress began to hear me with more patience, and some began to ask me civil questions. "How can the people institute governments?" My answer was, "By conventions of representatives, freely, fairly, and proportionably chosen." "When the convention has fabricated a government, or a constitution rather, how do we know the people will submit to it?" "If there is any doubt of that, the convention may send out their project of a constitution, to the people in their several towns, counties, or districts, and the people may make the acceptance of it their own act." "But the people know nothing about constitutions." "I believe you are much mistaken in that supposition; if you are not, they will not oppose a plan prepared by their own chosen friends; but I believe that in every considerable portion of the people, there will be found some men, who will understand the subject as well as their representatives, and these will assist in enlightening the rest." "But what plan of a government would you advise?" "A plan as nearly resembling the government under which we were born, and have lived, as the circumstances of the country will admit. Kings we never had among us. Nobles we never had. Nothing hereditary ever existed in the country; nor will the country require or admit of any such thing. But governors and councils we have always had, as well as representatives. A legislature in three branches ought to be preserved, and independent judges." "Where and how will you get your governors and councils?" "By elections." "How,—who shall elect?" "The representatives of the people in a convention will be the best qualified to contrive a mode."

After all these discussions and interrogatories, Congress was not prepared nor disposed to do any thing as yet. They must consider farther.

"*Resolved,* That the consideration of this matter be referred to Monday next.

Monday arrived, and Tuesday and Wednesday passed over, and Congress not yet willing to do any thing.

On Thursday, October 26th, the subject was again brought on the carpet, and the same discussions repeated; for very little new was produced. After a long discussion, in which Mr. John Rutledge, Mr. Ward, Mr. Lee, Mr. Gadsden, Mr. Sherman, Mr. Dyer, and some others had spoken on the same side with me, Congress resolved, that a committee of five members be appointed to take into consideration the instructions given to the delegates of New Hampshire, and report their opinion thereon. The members chosen,—Mr. John Rutledge, Mr. J. Adams, Mr. Ward, Mr. Lee, and Mr. Sherman.

Although this committee was entirely composed of members as well disposed to encourage the enterprise as could have been found in Congress, yet they could not be brought to agree upon a report and to bring it forward in Congress, till Friday, November 3d, when Congress, taking into consideration the report of the committee on the New Hampshire instructions, after another long deliberation and debate,— "*Resolved,* That it be recommended to the Provincial Convention of New Hampshire, to call a full and free representation of the people, and that the representatives, if they think it necessary, establish such a form of government, as in their judgment will best produce the happiness of the people, and most effectually secure peace and good order in the Province, during the continuance of the present dispute between Great Britain and the Colonies."

By this time I mortally hated the words, "Province," "Colonies," and "Mother Country," and strove to get them out of the report. The last was indeed left out, but the other two were retained even by this committee, who were all as high Americans as any in the house, unless Mr. Gadsden should be excepted. Nevertheless, I thought this resolution a triumph, and a most important point gained.

Mr. John Rutledge was now completely with us in our desire of revolutionizing all the governments, and he brought forward immediately some representations from his own State, when "Congress, then taking into consideration of the State of South Carolina, and sundry papers relative thereto being read and considered,

"*Resolved,* That a committee of five be appointed to take the same into consideration, and report what in their opinion is necessary to be done. The members chosen, Mr. Harrison, Mr. Bullock, Mr. Hooper, Mr. Chase, and Mr. S. Adams."

On November 4th, "The committee appointed to take into consideration the State of South Carolina, brought in their report, which being read," a number of resolutions passed, the last of which will be found in page 235 of the Journals, at the bottom.

"*Resolved,* That if the Convention of South Carolina shall find it necessary to establish a form of government in that Colony, it be recommended to that Convention to call a full and free representation of the people, and that the said representatives, if they think it necessary, shall establish such a form of government as in their judgment will produce the happiness of the people, and most effectually secure peace and good order in the Colony, during the continuance of the present dispute between Great Britain and the Colonies."

Although Mr. John Rutledge united with me and others, in persuading the committee to report this resolution, and the distance of Carolina made it convenient to furnish them with this discretionary recommendation, I doubt whether Mr. Harrison or Mr. Hooper were, as yet, sufficiently advanced to agree to it. Mr. Bullock, Mr. Chase, and Mr. Samuel Adams, were very ready for it. When it was under consideration, I labored afresh to expunge the words "Colony," and "Colonies," and insert the words "State," and "States," and the word "dispute," to make way for that of "war," and the word "Colonies," for the word "America," or "States," but the child was not yet weaned. I labored, also, to get the resolution enlarged, and extended into a recommendation to the people of all the States, to institute governments, and this occasioned more interrogatories from one part and another of the House. "What plan of government would you recommend?" &c. Here it would have been the most natural to have made a motion that Congress should appoint a committee to prepare a plan of government, to be reported to Congress and there discussed, paragraph by paragraph, and that which should be adopted should be recommended to all the States. But I dared not make such a motion, because I knew that if such a plan was adopted it would be, if not permanent, yet of long duration, and it would be extremely difficult to get rid of it. And I knew that every one of my friends, and all those who were the most zealous for assuming governments, had at that time no idea of any other government but a contemptible legislature in one assembly, with committees for executive magistrates and judges. These questions, therefore, I answered by sporting off hand a variety of short sketches of plans, which might be adopted by the conventions; and as this subject was brought into view in some way or other almost every day, and these interrogatories were frequently repeated, I had in my head and at my tongue's end as many projects of government as Mr. Burke says the Abbé Sieyes had in his pigeon-holes, not however, constructed at such length, nor labored with his metaphysical refinements. I took care, however, always to bear my testimony against every plan of an unbalanced government.

I had read Harrington, Sidney, Hobbes, Nedham, and Locke, but with very little application to any particular views, till these debates in Congress, and the interrogatories in public and private, turned my thoughts to these researches, which produced the "Thoughts on Government," the Constitution of Massachusetts, and at length the "Defence of the Constitutions of the United States," and the "Discourses on Davila," writings which have never done any good to me, though some of them undoubtedly contributed to produce the Constitution of New York, the Constitution of the United States, and the last Constitutions of Pennsylvania and Georgia. They undoubtedly, also, contributed to the writings of Publius, called the Federalist, which were all written after the publication of my work in Philadelphia, New York, and Boston. Whether the people will permit any of these Constitutions to stand upon their pedestals, or whether they will throw them all down, I know not. Appearances at present are unfavorable and threatening. I have done all in my power according to what I thought my duty. I can do no more.

CHAPTER II

THE PROVISIONAL GOVERNMENT CHALLENGED

THE RECOMMENDATION of the Continental Congress that Massachusetts establish a modified charter government as a temporary expedient pending reconciliation with Great Britain pleased the moderates in the province and in the country at large. The Congressional proposal left the door open for peaceful negotiation, and at the same time gave substance to the charge that the British were the aggressors who had violated the charter. But the action of Congress did not please everyone in Massachusetts. In Berkshire, the westernmost county of the province, a vocal minority known as the Constitutionalists declared that the government of Massachusetts had no proper basis because the people had not been consulted about the kind of government Massachusetts should have.

Although the government's failure to consult the people was a persistent theme in Constitutionalist thought, their full argument matured only over the space of several months. At first their complaints were directed against the naming of judges and justices for Berkshire County by the newly established provisional government. Massachusetts had responded promptly to the advice of the Continental Congress. In June 1775, the Provincial Congress ordered an election for members to a General Court, and when that body met the next month, it duly elected twenty-eight councilors in accordance with the charter of 1691. Since the offices of royal governor and lieutenant-governor were regarded as vacant, the Council assumed executive powers in addition to its other functions. Among the Council's early executive acts was the appointment of judges and other officers for the fourteen counties of the province, thus reopening the courts which Patriots had closed because the Government Act had made the tenure of judges dependent upon the royal governor. With the government of the province now safely in the hands of the Patriots, the courts could resume their functions. The Council, following the practice of royal governors, had not thought it necessary to seek the advice of county residents in naming county officials. And at first, only Berkshire people seemed to mind.

In December 1775, the Berkshire Constitutionalists called a county convention of the committees of correspondence to meet at Stockbridge. The convention vigorously protested the action of the Council in naming officials and suggested that judges of common pleas should be nominated by the people of the county and commissioned by the Council. However, not all county leaders were agreed on the Berkshire protest. Selection No. 2 recapitulates the votes of the Constitutionalists and presents the arguments of the dissenters, who represented eight towns in the southern part of the county.

Five of the men who objected to the convention's votes had recently received commissions from the Council: John Ashley, Theodore Sedgwick, Mark Hopkins, Elijah Brown, and Jahleel Woodbridge. Ashley, who had long played a leading part in the political life of Sheffield, had been one of the unpopular seventeen who voted to rescind the Massachusetts Circular Letter of 1768, a document that protested taxation without representation and that sought to unite the colonies against the Townshend Acts. Ashley's acquiesence in Lord Hillsborough's demand that the House of Representatives repudiate the Letter had branded him an enemy to his country in 1768. Although he subsequently embraced the Whig cause, many in the west remembered him as a rescinder. Theodore Sedgwick was just beginning a political career destined to make him a leader on the conservative side in Massachusetts. Mark Hopkins and Jahleel Woodbridge had been justices of the peace before the Revolution and as beneficiaries of the patronage of the royal governor were suspect in the eyes of the Constitutionalists.

The dissent of the eight Berkshire towns from the resolutions of the Stockbridge convention was soon answered by a petition from Pittsfield (No. 3), written by the Reverend Thomas Allen, Congregational minister and leader of the Constitutionalists. This petition makes it clear why the Constitutionalists wanted the people to have the right of nominating county officials. The Constitutionalists also called for the popular election of a governor and lieutenant-governor, an important step in the evolution of their political thinking. Six months before the Declaration of Independence, this Berkshire faction was ready to drop the pretense that charter government was operating with the office of governor temporarily vacant, a pretense designed to keep open the possibility of reconciliation with Great Britain. To enforce their point of view, the Constitutionalists kept the courts closed in Berkshire County.

Oblivious of the unrest brewing in Berkshire, the General Court issued a formal proclamation calling for loyal support of the government (No. 4). But dissatisfaction with the provincial government spread to Hampshire County, Berkshire's eastern neighbor, where a technicality was seized upon to justify keeping the courts closed (Nos. 5 and 6); elsewhere the courts began to open. Opponents of the Constitutionalists, alarmed by the activities of the

Reverend Mr. Allen, made reply to his slurs on their character (Nos. 7A and B).

In May 1776, the legislature reduced the table of fees for the courts and ordered all commissions to run in the name of the "Government and People of the Massachusetts Bay," thus seeking to mollify opponents of the courts in the western counties. The altered style of commissions, incidentally, implied, whether intentionally or not, that charter government under king and royal governor would not be resumed. In the same month, Pittsfield again expressed its constitutional theory (No. 8). More sophisticated and elaborate than its earlier statement, this petition drew heavily upon the natural rights philosophy in its analysis of conditions in Massachusetts. Since the hope of reconciliation with Great Britain was clearly a forlorn one, no shred of reasoning could justify continuance of the provisional government; to the Pittsfield petitioners complete reconstitution of government was plainly a necessity. But most of the colonists held that it was premature to undertake reorganization of the government (No. 9).

QUESTIONS

1. Why did some Berkshire people object to the appointment of civil officers by the Council?

2. Why did some dissent from the resolutions adopted at Stockbridge in December 1775?

3. What was essentially defective about the charter of 1691 according to Pittsfield?

4. What is meant by "a secret poison . . . spread thro' out all our Towns"? By a "suspension of government"? (No. 3)

5. How does Pittsfield answer the arguments of the eight objecting towns? Which has the sounder argument respecting the advice of the Continental Congress?

6. In its first petition, what constitutional provisions does Pittsfield ask for, and how does it propose to establish a constitution?

7. What dangers does Pittsfield see if the present course is continued?

8. What statements suggest that the Constitutionalists might have had a debtor viewpoint?

9. On what principle did the Hampshire towns base their opposition to operation of the courts?

10. What view of Allen's character and motives is expressed by his opponents?

11. In what sense does the second Pittsfield petition turn the arguments of the proclamation of the General Court back against that body?

12. How does the General Court justify the government that has been instituted for Massachusetts? Why did this argument fail to satisfy Pittsfield?

13. How does Pittsfield's second petition add to its argument respecting the advice of the Continental Congress?

14. What development in thought regarding constitution making is discernible in Pittsfield's second petition as compared with the first?

15. Compare and contrast the eastern views of "O.P.Q." (No. 9) on constitutional and commercial questions with those of the western Constitutionalists.

The Constitutionalists Object to the Provisional Government

2. Resolves of the Stockbridge Convention, December 15, 1775

[Peter Force, ed., *American Archives* . . . (Washington, 1837-53), 4th ser., V, 807]

Whereas a majority of the gentlemen belonging to the Committee of Correspondence of this County, at their Convention, holden at *Stockbridge,* on the 14th and 15th days of *December,* current, did vote and resolve that they would come into some method whereby the inhabitants of this County shall recommend and nominate to the Council suitable persons to be appointed Judges of the Inferior Court in this County:

2d. That they would not recommend it to the inhabitants of said County to support the Government formed and established within this Colony, agreeable to the recommendation of the Continental Congress, and to assist and support the several Executive Officers in the execution of their offices:

3d. That this Convention recommend it to the Freeholders, and other inhabitants qualified, of the several Towns within this County, that they meet in their respective Towns, Districts, and Plantations, some time before the 1st day of *January* next; in which meeting they bring in to the Moderator thereof their votes, or ballots, for four persons who, in their esteem, should be commissionated to sustain the offices of Judges of the Pleas for the County; which ballots, or votes, so brought in, shall, in the presence of the Selectmen and Clerk of each respective Town, be enclosed and sealed and subscribed to a Committee appointed by the several Towns and Districts and Plantations in the County, to sort and count the same; which Committee shall meet on the 2d *Tuesday* of *January* next, at the house of *Samuel Goodrich,* Innholder, in *Lenox,* and then and there shall sort, count, and discover the persons thus nominated by the people; which persons thus chosen by the greatest number of votes shall be, by said Committee, represented to the honourable Council Board, praying that the same may be commissioned to exercise the office of Judges of the County: provided that, if it should so happen that a greater number than four persons should have an equal number of votes, then, and in that case, it is submitted to the honourable Council, that they exercise their pleasure in appointing, out of said number nominated, which four shall officiate:

4th. *Voted,* That this body do not approve of any civil officer not nominated by the Representatives of the County.

Which Votes and Resolutions we, the subscribers, (being likewise of the Committee of Correspondence,) dissented from and disapproved of—*First,* Because we imagine that they are directly opposed to the present civil Constitution of this Colony, which has been taken up by the people in consequence of, and agreeable to, the advice of the Continental Congress; *Secondly,* They tend to dissolve all Government, and introduce dissension, anarchy, and confusion, among the people; for when we deviate from the established rules, we are lost in the boundless field of uncertainty and disorder. Therefore, that we may evidence to the people of the several Towns from whence we came, and to all other good people, our great desire for order and good government, our firm adherence to the Resolves of the Continental Congress and the present Constitution of this Colony, agreeable to said Resolves, and an abhorrence of all anarchy and disorder, we hereby manifest our disapprobation of the Votes and Resolves of said Committee of Correspondence aforesaid.

Stockbridge, December 15, 1775.
John Ashley,
Theodore Sedgwick,
Committee of Sheffield.
Mark Hopkins,
Benedict Dearey,
Committee of Great Barrington.
William Brown,
John Hurleat,
Committee of Alford.
Eleazer Barritt,
Giles Jackson,
Committee of Tyringham.
Benjamin Warren,
Jabez Ward,
Committee of New Marlborough.
Elijah Brown,
Joseph Raymond,
Committee of Richmond.
Samuel Brown, Jun.,
Jah. Woodbridge,
Committee of Stockbridge.
Erastus Sergeant,
Elisha Hooper,
Committee of West Stockbridge

3. Petition of Pittsfield, December 26, 1775

[Massachusetts Archives, CLXXX, 150]

The Petition Remonstrance & Address of the Town of Pittsfield to the Honourable Board of Councellors & House of Representatives of the Province of the Massachusetts Bay in General Assembly now sitting in Watertown———

May it please your Honors,

The Inhabitants of the Town of Pittsfield unalterably attached to the Liberties of their Country & in the fullest Approbation of Congressional Measures, with all humility Deference & Candor beg leave to manifest the painful Anxieties & Distresses of our minds in this definitive Crisis not only in behalf of ourselves but this great & powerful Province, & declare our abhorrence of that Constitution now adopting in this province. Nothing but an invincible Love of Civil & religious Liberty for ourselves & future posterity has induced us to add to your accumulated Burdens at this Great Period.———

Our forefathers left the delightful Abodes of their native Country, passed a raging Sea that in these then solitary Climes they might enjoy Civil & religious Liberty, & never more feel the hand of Tyranny & Persecution; but that despotic persecuting power from which they fled reached them on these far distant shores the weight of which has been felt from their first Emigration to the present Day. After the Loss of the Charter of this province in the reign of Charles the second a popish Tyrant, a new one was obtained after the Revolution of King William of glorious Memory which was lame & essentially defective & yet was of great value for the support of tolerable order till we had grown up to our present strength to seek that by force of Arms which was then unjustly denied us.

The Nomination & appointment of our Governors by the King has been the Source of all the Evils & Calamities that have befallen this province & the united Colonies. By this means a secret poison has been spread thro' out all our Towns & great Multitudes have been secured for the corrupt Designs of an abandoned Administration. Many of those Men who had drank of this baneful poison could not be confided in to aid & assist their Country in the present Contest, which [was] one Reason of the necessity of a Suppression of Government. At this Door all Manner of Disorders have been introduced into our Constitution till it has become an Engine of Oppression & deep Corruption & would finally, had it been continued, have brought upon us an eternal Destruction. The want of that one previlege of confessing Judgment in Cases of Debt has overwhelmed great Multitudes in Destruction & affoarded Encouragement to mercenary Lawyers to riot upon the spoils of the people. ———

We have been ruled in this Country for many years past with a rod of Iron. The Tyranny, Despotism & oppression of our fellow Subjects in this Country have been beyond belief. Since the Suspension of Government we have lived in peace, Love, safety, Liberty & Happiness except the Disorders & Dissentions occasioned by the Tories. We find ourselves in Danger of [returning] to our former state & of undergoing a Yoke of Op[pression] which we are no longer able to bear.

We have calmly viewed the nature of our antient Mode of Government—its various sluices of Corruption & oppression—the dangerous Effects of nominating to office by those in power, & must pronounce it the most defective discordant & ruinous System of Government of any that has come under our Observation. We can discern no present necessity of adopting that mode of Government so generally reprobated by the good people of this province; or which will inevitably be so as soon as the great rational Majority of the people have had Time for proper Reflection. The adopting this Mode of Government to the length we have gone has in our view been hasty & precipitate. It was surprising to this Town & directly contrary to the Instructions given to their Representatives. By this Means a considerable Number of incurable Enemies to a better Constitution has been made & if once adopted by the people we shall perhaps never be able to rid ourselves of it again.

We have seen nothing done by the Continental Congress which leads us to conclude that they would limit us to this mode of Government. We do not know of their having given us any Advice that must necessarily be construed in Opposition to what they gave [the Gov]ernments of New Hampshire & South Carolina. ["]Who if they think it necessary are to chuse such form of Government as they in their Judgment shall think will best promote the happiness of the people & preserve peace & good order during the present dispute with Great Britain." Certainly the Continental Congress could have no Intention of forcing upon us a Constitution so detested by the people & so abhorrent to common Sense, & thus to reward us for our unparalleled Sufferings. We have been led to wish for new previleges which we still hope to obtain, or remain so far as we have done for some Time past in a State of Nature. ———

We have with Decency & Moderation attended to the various Arguments of those Gentlemen lately created our Rulers, particularly we have heard it urged as the Advice of the [vene]rable Continental Congress, we have sufficiently attended to that & various other Arguments in favor of reassuming our antient Constitution, & are of opinion there is no such advice, the qualifying Expressions leaving ample room to new model our Constitution; but if there is, we are of opinion that unlimited passive obedience & Non-Resistance to any human power whatever is what we are now contending with Great Britain & to transfer that power to any other Body of Men is equally dangerous to our Security & happiness. ———

We chuse to be known to future posterity as being of the Number of those who have timely protested against the Reassumption of this discordant Constitution, & shall be restless in our endeavours that we may obtain the previlege of electing our Civil & military officers. We assure your Honors that some of those who have been appointed to rule us are greatly obnoxious to people in General, especially those who have protested against the Just proceedings of a Congress lately held at Stockbridge. We beg leave further to assure your Honors that a Court has been held in this Town in a Clandestine Manner & great Dishonour hereby done to the Dignity of Magistracy. ———

We therefore pray your Honors to issue out your orders to the good people of this province that their Votes may be collected in the Election of a Governor & Lieut Governor to act in Concert with the Honourable Board & house of Representatives. After which we pray that every Town may retain the previlege of nominating their Justice of the peace & every County their Judges as well as the Soldiers of every Company of the Militia their officers. If the right of nominating to office is not invested in the people we are indifferent who assumes it whether any particular persons on this or the other side of the [w]ater. When such a Constitution is assumed you'll [fi]nd us the most meek & inoffensive Subjects of any in this province, though we would hope in such a case that the wisdom of our Rulers would not admit of collecting private Debts for the present as we imagine that Measure would be of great Detriment to our common cause as it would put much Money into the hands of our Enemies & create Divisions among ourselvts. But if this Just & reasonable request is denied us, we pray that as we have lived in great love peace & good order in this County for more than 16 Months past in the most vigorous unintermitted Exertions in our Countrys cause, that you would dispense with a longer Suspension of this antient Mode of Government among us which we so much detest & abhor. The Government of our respective Committees is lenient & efficacious. But if it is necessary for the carrying into more effectual Execution the means of our Common safety that some Mode of government should be adopted we pray it may be one De novo agreeable to that formentioned Advice of the Continental Congress & no more of our antient form be retained than what is Just & reasonable. We hope in the Establishment of such a new Constitution regard will be had for such a broad Basis of Civil & religious Liberty as no Length of Time will corrupt & which will endure as long as the Sun & Moon shall endure. And as in Duty bound will ever pray.

[Per] Order of the Town Israel Dickinson Town Clerk. N. B. Upon the foregoing premise & on accoun[t] of obnoxious persons being appointed to rule us The Court of this County of Quarter Sessions is ordered to desist from any future Sessions.———

Our Resolves may be seen at Mr. Thomas's which were entered into at the same Time this petition was accepted by this Town ———

Drafted by John Adams

The General Court Calls for Loyal Support

4. Proclamation of the General Court, January 23, 1776

[Force, ed., *American Archives*, 4th ser., IV, 833-35]

By the Great and General Court of the Colony of Massachusetts-Bay

A Proclamation

The frailty of human nature, the wants of individuals, and the numerous dangers which surround them, through the course of life, have, in all ages and in every country, impelled them to form societies and establish governments.

As the happiness of the people is the sole end of Government, so the consent of the people is the only foundation of it, in reason, morality, and the natural fitness of things; and, therefore, every act of Government, every exercise of sovereignty against, or without the consent of the people, is injustice, usurpation, and tyranny.

It is a maxim, that, in every Government there must exist, some where, a supreme, sovereign, absolute, and uncontrollable power; but this power resides, always, in the body of the people, and it never was, or can be delegated to one man or a few; the great Creator having never given to men a right to vest others with authority over them unlimited, either in duration or degree.

When Kings, Ministers, Governours, or Legislators, therefore, instead of exercising the powers intrusted with them according to the principles, forms, and proportions, stated by the Constitution, and established by the original compact, prostitute those powers to the purposes of oppression, to subvert, instead of supporting a free Constitution, to destroy, instead of preserving the lives, liberties, and properties of the people, they are no longer to be deemed magistrates vested with a sacred character, but become publick enemies, and ought to be resisted.

The Administration of *Great Britain*, despising equally the justice, humanity, and magnanimity, of their ancestors, and the rights, liberties, and courage of *Americans*, have, for a course of years, laboured to establish a sovereignty in *America*, not founded in the consent of the people, but in the mere will of persons a thousand leagues from us, whom we know not, and have endeavoured to establish this sovereignty over us against our consent, in all cases whatsoever.

The Colonies, during this period, have recurred to every peaceable resource in a free Constitution, by petitions and remonstrances, to obtain justice, which has been not only denied to them, but they have been treated with unexampled indignity and contempt, and, at length, open war, of the most atrocious, cruel, and sanguinary kind, has been commenced against them. To this, an open, manly, and successful resistance has, hitherto, been made. Thirteen Colonies are now firmly united in the conduct of this most just and necessary war, under the wise councils of their Congress.

It is the will of Providence, for wise, righteous, and gracious ends, that this Colony should have been singled out, by the enemies of *America*, as the first object both of their envy and their revenge, and, after having been made the subject of several merciless and vindictive statutes, (one of which was intended to subvert our Constitution by charter,) is made the seat of war.

No effectual resistance to the system of tyranny prepared for us could be made, without either instant recourse to arms, or a temporary suspension of the ordinary powers of Government and tribunals of justice. To the last of which evils, in hopes of a speedy reconciliation with *Great Britain* upon equitable terms, the Congress advised us to submit; and mankind has seen a phenomenon without example in the political world: a large and populous Colony subsisting, in great decency and order, for more than a year, under such a suspension of Government.

But, as our enemies have proceeded to such barbarous extremities, commencing hostilities upon the good people of this Colony, and, with unprecedented malice, exerting their power to spread the calamities of fire, sword, and famine through the land, and no reasonable prospect remains of a speedy reconciliation with *Great Britain,* the Congress have

"*Resolved,* That no obedience being due to the Act of Parliament for altering the Charter of the Colony of *Massachusetts-Bay,* nor to a Governour or Lieutenant-Governour, who will not observe the directions of, but endeavour to subvert that Charter, the Governour and Lieutenant-Governour of that Colony are to be considered as absent, and their offices vacant; and, as there is no Council there, and inconveniences arising from the suspension of the powers of Government are intolerable, especially, at a time when General *Gage* hath actually levied war, and is carrying on hostilities against His Majesty's peaceable and loyal subjects of that Colony, that, in order to conform, as near as may be, to the spirit and substance of the Charter, it be recommended to the Provincial Convention, to write letters to the inhabitants of the several places which are entitled to representation in Assembly, requesting them to choose such Representatives; and, that the Assembly, when chosen, do elect Counsellors, and that such Assembly and Council exercise the powers of Government, until a Governour of His Majesty's appointment will consent to govern the Colony according to its Charter."

In pursuance of which advice, the good people of this Colony have chosen a full and free representation of themselves, who, being convened in Assembly, have elected a Council, who, as the Executive branch of Government, have constituted necessary officers through the Colony. The present generation, therefore, may be congratulated on the acquisition of a form of Government more immediately, in all its branches, under the influence and control of the people, and, therefore, more free and happy than was enjoyed by their ancestors.

But, as a Government so popular can be supported only by universal knowledge and virtue in the body of the people, it is the duty of all ranks to promote the means of education for the rising generation, as well as true religion, purity of manners, and integrity of life, among all orders and degrees.

As an army has become necessary for our defence, and, in all free States the civil must provide for and control the military power, the major part of the Council have appointed magistrates and courts of justice in every County, whose happiness is so connected with that of the people, that it is difficult to suppose they can abuse their trust. The business of it is, to see those laws enforced, which are necessary for the preservation of peace, virtue, and good order. And the Great and General Court expects, and requires, that all necessary support and assistance be given, and all proper obedience yielded to them, and will deem every person who shall fail of his duty in this respect towards them, a disturber of the peace of this Colony, and deserving of examplary punishment.

That piety and virtue, which, alone, can secure the freedom of any people, may be encouraged, and vice and immorality suppressed, the Great and General Court have thought fit to issue this Proclamation, commanding and enjoining it upon the good people of this Colony, that they lead sober, religious, and peaceable lives, avoiding all blasphemies, contempt of the holy Scriptures, and of the *Lord's* day, and all other crimes and misdemeanours, all debauchery, profaneness, corruption, venality, all riotous and tumultuous proceedings, and all immoralities whatsoever; and that they decently and reverently attend the publick worship of *God,* at all times acknowledging, with gratitude, his merciful interposition in their behalf, devoutly confiding in him, as the *God* of armies, by whose favour and protection, alone, they may hope for success in their present conflict.

And all Judges, Justices, Sheriffs, Grand-Jurors, Tything-Men, and all other civil officers within this Colony, are hereby strictly enjoined and commanded, that they contribute all in their power, by their advice, exertions, and examples, towards a general reformation of manners, and, that they bring to condign punishment every person who shall commit any of the crimes or misdemeanours aforesaid, or that shall be guilty of any immoralities whatsoever; and that they use their utmost endeavours to have the resolves of the Congress, and the good and wholesome laws of this Colony, duly carried into execution.

And as the Ministers of the Gospel within this Colony have, during the late relaxation of the powers of civil Government, exerted themselves for our safety, it is hereby recommended to them, still to continue their virtuous labours, for the good of the people, inculcating, by their publick ministry and private example, the necessity of religion, morality, and good order.

In Council, January 19, 1776

Ordered, That the foregoing Proclamation be read at the opening of every Superior Court of Judicature, &c., and Inferior Common Pleas, and Court of General Sessions for the Peace within this Colony, by their respective Clerks; and at the annual town meetings in *March,* in each town. And it is hereby recommended to the several Ministers of the Gospel throughout this Colony, to read the same in their respective assemblies on the *Lord's* day next after receiving it, immediately after Divine service.

Sent down for concurrence.

Perez Morton, *Deputy Secretary.*

In the House of Representatives, January 23, 1776.

Read and concurred.

William Cooper, *Speaker, Pro Tem.*

Consented to. . . . By order of the General Court:

Perez Morton, *Deputy Secretary*

God *Save the King.*

Constitutional Arguments in Western Massachusetts

5. A Letter from the Chesterfield Committee of Correspondence, March 4, 1776

[Hawley Papers, Box I, N.Y. Public Lib.]

To the Chairman of the Committee of correspondence in Northampton———

At a Meeting of the Committee of Correspondence, inspection & Safety for the Town of Chesterfield, upon mature Deliberation, in consequence of the advice of our constituents, do desire of the Chairman of the Committee of Northampton that they immediately write Letters to the Committees of the Several Towns in the County that they be notifyed to meet on Monday next at three o'clock in the afternoon not exceeding the Time to consult on the following particulars and others that may be proposed to said convention—

I Whether it be not proper at present that the Court of Quarter Sessessions be suspended or adjourned to some future Season—

II Whether the Justices of the County Shall in any Case act under their present Commissions—

Gentlemen the Reason of these Inquiries & of our urgent desire for this convention is, least, the People should be so inraged against the Setting of the Courts at present that it will be detrimental to the Common Cause, and if we do not suspend them, (without the advice of the Convention be to the contrary) we fear the Consequences will be very fatal

Chesterfield March 4. 1776

By order of the Committee of Chesterfield

6. From the Proceedings of a Convention in Hampshire, March 11, 1776

[James R. Trumbull, *History of Northampton* (Northampton, 1902), II, 389-90]

Voted that it is inexpedient and improper that the Court of general Sessions of the Peace for the County of Hampshire should set at the Time of their Adjournment on the second Tuesday of March instant. [Adopted by a vote of 43 to 39.]

And that the reason why this Congress are of opinion that the Court aforesaid should not sit at the time & place aforementioned Is on account of their holding their commissions in the name of George the Third King of Britain, &c., and by the authority of the same. [On the second question raised by Chesterfield, the convention voted to let it "subside."]

7. Opponents of the Constitutionalists Counterattack

A. Petition of John Ashley *et al.* to the General Court, April 12, 1776

[Force, ed., *American Archives,* 4th ser., V, 1275-76]

Petition of *John Ashley* and others, in the County of *Berkshire,* setting forth: That from our known attachment to that order and subordination which is necessary for the existence and well-being of society, we are set up by a few unthinking, rash, and designing men, as the butts of popular resentment, and are (as well as your Honours) by them represented as seeking our own private emolument only at the expense of the interest of the people. And although every step by us taken to lay open and manifest the conduct of these incendiaries is, by them, blazed abroad as an evidence of our guilt and rapacity, yet we should hold ourselves inexcusable if, at the present alarming crisis, we should neglect to inform your Honours of some late transactions which have taken place in this country.

The Reverend *Thomas Allen,* of *Pittsfield,* for a long time past seems to have been restless in his endeavours to raise the prejudice of the people against the present Constitution of this Colony, and the Legislative and Executive authority of the same; in order to effect which, and prevent the Court of Sessions sitting at *Pittsfield,* on the last *Tuesday* of *February* last, he, with his associates, procured a meeting of divers people of this country, by the appellation of Committee of Inspection, to be called at *Pittsfield,* on the last *Monday* of said *February;* previous to which meeting, and in order properly to prepare the minds of the people of *Richmont* (who of late had almost unanimously voted to adhere to and support the present Constitution of Government) to fall in with the schemes of said *Allen,* he, on a *Sabbath* evening, in said *Richmont,* delivered a discourse, in the form of a Sermon, to a large number of the inhabitants of said *Richmont,* and, among other things, informed his auditory that the present Constitution of this Colony, as established in consequence of the advice and recommendation of the Continental Congress, is oppressive, defective, and rotten to the very core; that it ought not, by any means, to be submitted to; that your Honours and the honourable House of Representative were a number of designing men, who sought after emolument for yourselves, your children, and friends, without any regard to the good of the people, and that you ought to be opposed; and many such like things, which will appear by the depositions herewith sent to your Honours. The people, being accustomed to pay great regard to the sacred character of a priest, and to receive for truth and sound doctrine everything delivered by a clergyman, the aforementioned harangue, together with Mr. *Allen's* private exhortations and advice, had the desired effect, and the people were inflamed to the degree the preacher designed. The time of the meeting of the aforementioned Committees being come, Mr. *Allen* (though not a member of the same) appeared as the chief agitator and spokesman, and, after having read a pamphlet called *Common Sense,* as his text, and made great reflections upon the General Assembly of this Colony, as his doctrine and improvement, he produced a large number of resolves by himself previously compiled, which were put and voted by a majority of the people present; a copy of which resolves, together with the protests of the dissentients, we herewith send to your Honours. The people being inflamed, no Court was suffered to sit, and they immediately took away such commissions from the civil officers of the County on which they could lay their hands, and we are reduced to a state of anarchy and confusion. We would hope the people may soon see the folly of their proceedings, and return to a sense of their duty; but as longs as such incendiaries are tolerated, it is hardly to be expected. We hope your Honours will take some wise steps for our relief.

Read, and committed, with the Papers accompanying it, to the Committee on the state of the Colony.

B. Affidavit on Thomas Allen, March 2, 1776

[Massachusetts Archives, CXXXVII, 77-78]

County of Berkshire ss. March 1^{s}-2^{d} A^{d} 1776

Elijah Brown & David Rosseter Esq^{rs} Mes^{rs} Elisha Blin. Benjamin Peirson Joseph Raymond William Lush, each of Lawfull age deposeth and Saith, That they attended a lecture at the Dwelling house of Doctor Thomas Tarbell in Richmont on the Evening next after the Eighteenth Day of February Current, preached by the Rev. Thomas Allen, of Pittsfield, from those words in the 10th Chapter of Matthew 17th verse, beware of men; After a Short Explanitory Introduction, in which he attempted to Demonstrate what was the Reason of this Caution of our Saviour to his Disciples which was to the following Purpose viz: That men when compared with beasts of prey, were most to be feared and guarded against, he observed that our Saviour did not Caution his Disciples against those, but against men, That men would Use all manner of Deceit & Craft to Circumvent and entangle them,—That men would haul them before Councils, and Magistrates and to Prison, and that they should Suffer many ways and on many accounts, by the hands of wicked and Deceitfull men. When he proceeded to the Improvement of his Sermon, which was altogether Political,—he gave it as his Opinion that the words of the Text might with Propriety be applied to the present Circumstances of this Province. He attempted to Shew the badness of the Constitution of this Colony—He Said it was rotten to the Core gave it as his Opinion that it was by no means best to Suffer it to take place But that it was the Duty of the People to oppose it, and that he had rather be without any Form of Government than to Submit to this Constitution He Said it was very Oppressive—That he had often Seen the Tears of those who were oppressed by it, and that they had no Comforter, that on the side of the Oppressors was Power but they had no Comforter—he Said the People of this Province had lived in peace and good order for more than a year, without Government, as the General Assembly themselves had Confessed—That although the Continental Congress had advised to the assumption of this form of Government, yet they were to be considered as failable Creatures: that they had failed in one Instance already as they themselves had confessed,—That no Power ought to be given to any man or Body of men so far as to Deprive any man of Judging for himself and that if the People upon Strict Examination Judged that they (the Congress) had abused their power they were to be opposed in the Same manner, as the King and Parliment ought to be opposed—In speaking of the Congress and General Court, the said Mr. Allen frequently repeated the words, beware of men—and Said it concerned the People to See to it that whilst we are fighting against oppression from the King and Parliment, That we did Did not Suffer it to rise up in our own Bowels, That he was not so much concerned about Carrying our Point against Great Brittain, as he was of having Usurpers rising up amongst ourselves, he further Endeavoured to Insinuate into the minds of the People that our Provincial Congress and General Court had been, and were Composed of designing men—he Said the Provincial Congress had deceived the Continental Congress, that they had petitioned to them for our former mode of Government, and induced them to believe the people were attached to it. That if we Suffered it to take place we Should find it very Difficult to rid ourselves of it—That the General Court had taken up the old Constitution contrary to the minds of the People. He further Said that by the old Constitution the King appointed the Governer that the Governer put in the Officers and in Consequence they were all Dependant on the King. It therefore Mattered not whether they were appointed by North, our Council[,] Hutchinson, Gage, our General Court, or any other man or Body of men: for they (the officers) were not put in by the great Majority of the People. That all those who have taken Commisions ought to Deliver them into the hands of the People: Mr. Allen often during his Sermon refered to Something he Should read by and by, for Evidence that the members of the General Court were Designing men, and inconsistant with themselves.—In the Close of his Sermon he Said here is a Proclimation which I Shall read to you, which is Directly Contrary to what I have now Delivered. I will read it to you and you must hear for yourselves and Judge for yourselves. He then read the late Proclimation of the General Court and Said he had received it but the Day before. Nevertheless he had made a few remarks which he would read to us among other things he Said the Proclimation was Inconsistant, for that theirin it was Set forth that the Suspension of Government was intolerable and at the Same Time Said that the People had behaved in great

Decency and order for more than Twelve Months, and further the Said Mr. Allen in Shewing the Necessity of Opposing the present Government of this Colony Urged that the General Court is Composed of men who are Seeking places for themselves and Sons

Sworn the 2nd Day of March
Above written—
Before Timothy Edwards Jus. Pac.

Elijah Brown
David Rosseter
Elisha Blin
Benjamin Peirson
Joseph Raymond
William Lush

8. The Constitutionalists Reaffirm Their Dissatisfaction, Pittsfield, May 1776

[Petition of Pittsfield, May 1776, Massachusetts Archives, CLXXXI, 42-45]

To the Honourable Council, & the Honourable House of Representatives of the Colony of Massachusetts Bay in General Assembly met at Watertown May 29th. 1776——

The Petition & Memorial of the Inhabitants of the Town of Pittsfield in said Colony,

Humbly Showeth,

That they have the highest sense of the Importance of Civil & religious Liberty.—The destructive nature of Tyranny & lawless power, & the absolute necessity of legal Government to prevent Anarchy & Confusion.

That they, with their Brethren in other Towns in this County, were early & vigorous in opposing the destructive Measures of British Administration against the Colonies.—That they early signed the Non-Importation League & Covenant, raised Minute Men, agreed to pay them, ordered their public Monies to be paid to Henry Gardiner Esqr receiver General, cast in their mite for the Relief of Boston, & conformed in all things to the Doings of the Honourable Continental & Provincial Congresses.

That they met with the most violent opposition from an unfriendly party in this Town in every step in every Measure they pursued agreeable to the Common Councils of this Continent, which nothing but the most obstinate persevereance has enabled them to overcome & surmount; Which, together with the Inconveniences we have laboured under, affoard the true Reason why we have been so behind in the payment of our public Taxes. ——

That they with the other Towns in this County, have come behind none in their Duty & attachment to their Countrys Cause & have exerted themselves much beyound their strength on all occasions. A fresh Instance of their Zeal was conspicuous on our late Defeat at Quebec, when a considerable Number of Men were raised & sent off in the Dead of Winter & lay dying with sickness before the walls of Quebec before any one Man from this Colony had so much as left his own habitation for the Relief of our Distressed Friends in Canada. ——

That from the purest & most disinterested Principles, & ardent Love for their Country, without selfish Considerations & in conformity to the Advice of the wisest Man in the Colony, they aided & assisted in suspending the executive Courts in this County in August 1774.

That on no Occasion have they spared either cost or Trouble, without hope of pecuniary reward, vigorously & unweariedly exerting ourselves for the support & in the Defence of our Countrys cause not withstanding the most violent Discouragements we have met with by open or secret Enemies in this Town & County & in a Neighbouring province.

That 'till last fall your Memorialists had little or no Expectation of obtaining any new previleges beyound what our defective Charter secured to us. ——

That when they came more maturely to

refect upon the nature of the present Contest, & the Spirit & obstinacy of Administration—What an amazing Expence the united Colonies had incured? How many Towns had been burnt or otherwise damaged? what Multitudes had turned out to beg & how many of our valiant Heroes had been slain in the Defence of their Country & the Impossibility of our being ever again dependant on Great Britain or in any Measure subject to her Authority—When they further considered that the Revolution in England affoarded the Nation but a very imperfect Redress of Grievances the Nation being transported with extravagant Joy in getting rid of one Tyrant forgot to provide against another—& how every Man by Nature has the seeds of Tyranny deeply implanted within him so that nothing short of Ommipotence can eradicate them—That when they attended to the Advice given this Colony by the Continental Congress respecting the Assumption of our antient Constitution, how early that Advice was given, the Reasons of it & the principles upon which it was given which no longer exist, what a great Change of Circumstances there has been in the Views & Designs of this whole Continent since the giving said Advice—That when they considered, now is the only Time we have reason ever to expect for securing our Liberty & the Liberties of future posterity upon a permanent Foundation that no length of Time can undermine—Tho' they were filled with pain & Anxiety at so much as seeming to oppose public Councils yet with all these Considerations in our View, Love of Virtue freedom & posterity prevailed upon us to suspend a second Time the Courts of Justice in this County after the Judges of the Quarter Sessions had in a pricipitate & clandestine Manner held one Court & granted out a Number of Licences to Innholders at the rate of six shillings or more each & divided the Money amongst themselves with this boast that now it was a going to be like former Times & had discovered a Spirit of Independance of the People & a Disposition triumphantly to ride over their heads & worse than renew all our former Oppressions. We further beg leave to represent that we were deeply affected at the Misrepresentations that have been made of us & the County in general, as Men deeply in Debt, dishonest, ungovernable, heady untractable, without principle & good Conduct & ever ready to oppose lawful Authority, as Mobbes disturbers of peace order & Union, unwilling to submit to any Government, or ever to pay our Debts, so that we have been told a former House of Representatives had it in actual Contemplation to send an armed force to effect that by violence which reason only ought to effect at the present Day. We beg leave to lay before your Honors our Principles real Views & Designs in what we have hitherto done & what Object we are reaching after, with this Assurance if we have erred it is thro' Ignorance & not bad Intention. ——

We beg leave therefore to represent that we have always been persuaded that the people are the fountain of power. That since the Dissolution of the power of Great Britain over these Colonies they have fallen into a state of Nature. That the first step to be taken by a people in such a state for the Enjoyment or Restoration of Civil Government amongst them, is the formation of a fundamental Constitution as the Basis & ground work of Legislation.

That the Approbation of the Majority of the people of this fundamental Constitution is absolutely necessary to give Life & being to it. That then & not 'till then is the foundation laid for Legislation. We often hear of the fundamental Constitution of Great Britain, which all political Writers (except ministerial ones) set above the King Lords, & Commons, which they cannot change, nothing short of the great rational Majority of the people being sufficient for this.

That a Representative Body may form,

but cannot impose said fundamental Constitution upon a people. They being but servants of the people cannot be greater than their Masters, & must be responsible to them. If this fundamental Constitution is above the whole Legislature, the Legislature cannot certainly make it, it must be the Approbation of the Majority which gives Life & being to it. ——

That said fundamental Constitution has not been formed for this Province the Corner stone is not yet laid & whatever Building is reared without a foundation must fall into Ruins. That this can be instantly effected with the Approbation of the Continental Congress & Law subordination & good government flow in better than their antient Channels in a few Months Time.—That till this is done we are but beating the air & doing what will & must be undone afterwards, & all our labour is lost & on divers Accounts much worse than lost.

That a Doctrine lately broached in this County by several of the Justices newly created without the Voice of the People, that the Representatives of the People may form Just what fundamental Constitution they please & impose it upon the people & however obnoxious to them they can obtain no relief from it but by a New Election, & if our Representatives should never see fit to give the people one that pleases them there is no help for it appears to us to be the rankest kind of Toryism, the self same Monster we are now fighting against.

These are some of the Truths we firmly believe & are countenanced in believing them by the most respectable political Writers of the last & present Century, especially by Mr. Burgh in his political Disquisitions for the publication of which one half of the Continental Congress were subscribers.

We beg leave further to represent that we by no Means object to the most speedy Institution of Legal Government thro' this province & that we are as earnestly desirous as any others of this great Blessing.

That knowing the strong Byass of human Nature to Tyranny & Despotism we have Nothing else in View but to provide for Posterity against the wanton Exercise of power which cannot otherwise be done than by the formation of a fundamental Constitution. What is the fundamental Constitution of this province, what are the unalienable Rights of the people the power of the Rulers, how often to be elected by the people &c have any of these things been as yet ascertained. Let it not be said by future posterity that in this great this noble this glorious Contest we made no provision against Tyranny amongst ourselves

We beg leave to assure your Honors that the purest & most disinterested Love of posterity & a fervent desire of transmitting to them a fundamental Constitution securing their sacred Rights & Immunities against all Tyrants that may spring up after us has moved us in what we have done. We have not been influenced by hope of Gain or Expectation of Preferment & Honor. We are no discontented faction we have no fellowship with Tories, we are the staunch friends of the Union of these Colonies & will support & maintain your Honors in opposing Great Britain with our Lives & Treasure.

But if Commissions should be recalled & the Kings Name struck out of them, if the Fee Table be reduced never so low, & multitudes of other things be done to still the people all is to us as Nothing whilst the foundation is unfixed the Corner stone of Government unlaid. We have heared much of Governments being founded in Compact. What Compact has been formed as the foundation of Government in this province?—We beg leave further to represent that we have undergone many grievous oppressions in this County & that now we wish a Barrier might be set up against such oppressions, against which we can have no security long till the foundation of Government be well established. ——

We beg leave further to represent these

as the Sentiments of by far the Majority of the people in this County as far as we can Judge & being so agreeable to Reason Scripture & Common Sense, as soon as the Attention of people in this province is awakened we doubt not but the Majority will be with us.

We beg leave further to observe that if this Honourable Body shall find that we have embraced Errors dangerous to the safety of these Colonies it is our Petition that our Errors may be detected & you shall be put to no further Trouble from us but without an Alteration in our Judgment the Terrors of this World will not daunt us we are determined to resist Great Britain to the last Extremity & all others who may claim a similar Power over us. Yet we hold not to an Imperium in Imperio we will be determined by the Majority. ——

Your Petitioners beg leave therefore to Request that this Honourable Body would form a fundamental Constitution for this province after leave is asked & obtained from the Honourable Continental Congress & that said Constitution be sent abroad for the Approbation of the Majority of the people in this Colony that in this way we may emerge from a state of Nature & enjoy again the Blessing of Civil Government in this way the Rights & Liberties of future Generations will be secured & the Glory of the present Revolution remain untarnished & future Posterity rise up & call this Honourable Council & House of Representatives blessed.

Defense of the Provisional Government

9. "To the Electors of Representatives for the Colony of Massachusetts," May 18, 1776

[*Massachusetts Spy*, May 18, 1776]

Number I.

MY FRIENDS AND FELLOW COUNTRYMEN,

The subject upon which I am now to address you, is so important in itself and in its remotest consequences, as to require that unreserved freedom and simplicity which, while it may seem to need, will apologize for an apology—for when every thing which is valuable in life is at stake, to sacrifice to the graces would be criminal.

The government to be formed, and the administration of that government, are of vast importance; the men, therefore, who are to constitute and to have the appointment of those who are to execute it, ought to be chosen with the utmost care and caution.—They should be men of the best understanding, the strictest integrity and the purest patriotism.

We have by melancholy experience found the misfortune of placing our confidence in men of weak and contracted minds, in men of sordid and selfish spirits, in cursing and designing men and in pretended patriots,—let us, now we have the opportunity, resume our misplaced confidence, and delegate the powers of government to those, and to those only, who will act upon the genuine, the unadulterated principles of the constitution, and conscientiously endeavour, in the execution of the trust reposed in them, to promote the greatest happiness of the greatest numbers —who will not devote their time, their abilities and the powers with which they are vested, in advancing their personal profits and honors, and those of their respective families and friends.—Who will not do every thing in their power to destroy the commercial part of the community, without considering that the value of our lands is enhanced in proportion to the demand, which an extensive commerce, the opulence of the merchant, and the number of mechanics necessarily occasion, and that excessive burdens [al]ways operate as prohibitions, and that therefore, the end in view will be frustrated by the very means taken to accomplish it.

We have had in some former houses, men who under the banners of the constitution, have, either through ignorance or design, been undermining its foundations; and in some late ones, those who have been so exceedingly prudent of the public monies, or *so much more advantageously employed,* as to leave the capital of the province, *committed to their care and guardianship,* to be fortified and secured by the improverished and distressed inhabitants, at their own expence and that of a few patriotic neighbours,—but for whose spirited exertions, we might have had a melancholy experimental comment, in the military operations of the ensuing season, upon that trite, but very emphatical characteristick of the wisdom of the late legislature, expressed in the proverb by *saving at the spiket and letting out at the bung.*

From such statesmen, such politicians, good Lord deliver us!

Our situation, my friends, is exceedingly critical—it is no time to contend for the preservation and use of a charter, which in its most perfect and peaceful operation gave us scarcely the shadow of right—it is no time to debate about the prerogatives, which that charter might have given to the upper or the lower house—it is no time to scramble for posts and places—it is no time to contrive expedients for depressing one part of the community, to exalt another; which is at all times contrary to the spirit of patriotism and to the equitable maxims of our holy religion: It is, in fine, no time to deliberate upon the internal police of the colony, but to exert all the powers of our minds and bodies, to devote all our estates and influence, to secure the colony from invasion, and to prepare for the instant defence of our lives, our liberties, and properties, against the tyranny of the British government, and the force of the British arms.

Wherefore, my friends, let no man have your suffrages, whose conduct in any former house, on whose known or even suspected principles, not only in politics, but in private life, may lead you to think he could in any instance postpone the public to his private interests—who possesses any place in the executive department, other or higher than that of a justice of the peace—who has ever manifested a disposition to oppress or distress the trading part of the colony—or whose inattention or avarice had like to have exposed the capital to destruction, by leaving it in the most unguarded state, and by it have sacrificed the colony.

Such men are always dangerous in the legislature, but incomparably more so at this time—and though they may pay their addresses to you, by an apparent design to advance your interest, believe me, they would eventually destroy it.

The uniting the legislative and executive powers in the same person, the unjust and oppressive taxation of the trading and monied interests, the proposed method of representation and pay of representatives, the state of the militia and the fortifications, shall be the subject of a future speculation; in which, by a minute deduction of facts, and reasons drawn from first principles, I shall endeavour to convince you of the necessity of placing your confidence in such men, and such only, as I have recommended, and at the same time justify my intruding my advice upon you.

If there is wisdom in the measures at which I have hinted and which shall be more particularly considered, I confess it is beyond my penetration, and I should thank any person who would instruct me in it—and if the men who have originated or prosecuted them are patriots, I confess myself a stranger to patriotism.

I revere a government in which regal power has no part, and which I hope will be universally established in these colonies —but would most sacredly guard the fountains of that government, least any thing should gain admittance, which might contaminate its purity, obstruct its due course, or destroy its salutary influences.

There is something in genuine patriotism, I had almost said, adorably amiable; it is the fairest transcript, *but one,* within the compass of the human mind, of that *good will to men,* which brought the son of God from Heaven, and Angels to celebrate his incarnation. I doubt not that the soverign of the universe approves of every struggle for the rights of humanity; however he may see fit to punish, in that very struggle, the vices of the community by which it is supported. Happy, beyond expression happy, must I therefore esteem these colonies, in a cause, which they can with conscious integrity commit to him that judgeth and avengeth in the earth. May the God of armies and the wonderful counsellor be our guide and guardian; that by the wisdom and unanimity of our councils, and by the vigor and success of our arms, America may become, and ever continue, the dread of tyrants and the asylum of the oppressed; while her virtue, freedom and happiness shall be her unrivaled glory, the admiration and joy of successive generations. O. P. Q.

Number II.

MY FRIENDS AND FELLOW COUNTRYMEN,

OBSTA PRINCIPIIS, is a maxim of such importance both in religion and politics that it cannot be too frequently or too earnestly inculcated.

At the first establishment of a civil constitution, so important as ours is like to be to ourselves, and by its connections to the whole continent, we should strenuously oppose, in its first appearance, every thing which is contracted, and which has a tendency to bring the colony into disrepute. These colonies to form an invincible union should be severally modeled upon the most generous principles of the constitution, and every Assembly composed of such men, and such only, as are incapable of postponing the public to their private interests.

In my last, I contented myself with general advice founded on general though forcible reasons.

I shall now in confirmation of the same, and the more seriously to engage the public attention and a correspondent conduct, proceed to the minute consideration of the several particulars, which I then proposed to resume. . . .

In the first place, I shall attempt to convince you, that *the placing the legislative and executive powers in the same hands,* is unconstitutional, impolitic, oppressive and absurd.

Among the first fruits of the fair seeds of opposition to the tyranny of the British administration, from whence we may justly expect a glorious harvest of freedom and happiness, is a clear understanding of the constitution of civil government amongst all orders and ranks of people:—It will be therefore, too much like proving a self-evident proposition, to labour the unconstitutionality of an investiture of such inconsistent powers in the same person.

I shall only point out the wisdom of the early provision made to guard against it, which will shew that the reasons of that provision existed in the nature and necessity of government, before any express constitution took place, and consequently are fundamental to that constitution: This will at the same time evince its absurdity, impolicy and mischievous tendency.

The first reason might arise from experience and observation, that the highest improvements in every art and science, as well as in every kind of business in life, is made by attending to but one thing at a time; and from the evident confusion which the interference of a multiplicity of concerns militant with each other necessarily occasions.

Another motive for making the executive and legislative separate departments was, doubtless, the undue weight and influence which those who were in both might have in the legislature;—an influence to which the British Parliament has ever been subject (and these colonies have but too sensibly felt its ill effects) though they have apparently censured and disclaimed it, by the disqualifying bill; by which a precept must issue for a new choice upon an executive appointment, giving the people an opportunity, if they see cause, to restore to the crown-officer his legislative capacity.—An influence by which we of this colony have formerly suffered, but which by the seasonable exertions of some patriotic members in both houses, we have, till of late, been happily freed from, and if we were as consistent as we ought to be in all our public conduct to the spirit of the constitution, should ever remain so.

The last reason which I shall mention to shew the absurdity of making laws for the same person to execute, is that appeals from executive courts lay to the legislative, at least, to the upper house: And for a judge to determine upon appeals from his own judgment, is so repugnant to the common law, yea to the first principle of justice and equity, that it need only be mentioned as incident to the investiture of the legislative and executive powers in the same person, to shew its absurdity, its impolicy, its unconstitutionality and oppressive tendency.

To shew that the inhabitants of this colony are now suffering, and if by a change of men in the next choice of representatives and counsellors, they do not prevent it, will continue to suffer, all the inconvenience which arise from blending the executive and legislative powers, I shall just observe,

That since, by the approbation of the honourable the Continental Congress, the General Assembly was formed in May last, the members of that assembly have divided among themselves, and their particular friends, all the civil and military offices in the colony. That the public business has been exceedingly impeded, by the attention necessary to executive offices perpetually changing the acting members, and but seldom leaving enough to make a majority or a governor; at a time when the constant attendance of the best members (and such are those *principally* among whom the executive offices are distributed) was of the highest importance to the colony, and to individuals.

And, That as soon as the executive courts return to their accustomed business, every inconvenience, before mentioned, will be encreased and confirmed,—unless the elections of this month shall happily relieve us.

I shall close this subject with observing the surprizing difference between the assembly which left all the executive officers out of the council, and that which has devoted all their ingenuity and great part of their time in distributing their respective offices among them—when the principles which actuated the former at the early periods of the opposition, might reasonably be expected much more forcibly to actuate the latter in the present stages of it; and while the conduct of the former was perfectly consonant to the spirit of the opposition, the proceedings of the latter bear too near a resemblance to those of the administration we so justly oppose.—But,

"Tempora mutantur et nos mutamur in illis."

[I had prepared, agreably to my engagement, some serious strictures upon the military conduct of our late legislature, but the fortifications of the town and harbour of Boston being undertaken and almost compleated by and at the expence of the inhabitants, through their neglect, being both in a moral and political view censure sufficient, and fully evidential of the confidence proper to be placed in such men, at such a time as this, I shall wave all I had to say of the prudence and care of the province in this important respect; and after apologizing for one more omission arising from the unexpected alteration which has taken place in the proposed representation bill; and by which an enormous landed influence, a vast clog upon the wheels of government, the introduction of a large majority of people into public business, unacquainted with it and incapable of it, an immense and disproportionate burden on the trading part of the community;—and what would have compleated our misery the immortality of such a mischievous body, are happily removed, shall proceed to]

The last thing upon which I engaged to remark at this time, which is *the oppressive taxation of the trading and monied interests,* which obtained in the last assembly: Than which I know of nothing which could have been devised more unjust, or of a more baneful tendency.

This measure will drive all trade out of the colony, to such places as have the wisdom and foresight to give it every possible encouragement—and this colony will be proportionally impoverished; having no vent for their surplus produce, either for exportation or consumption—For no person who has a trading stock, or who has money to let out on interest will tarry in the colony where he is obliged to pay not only three times the tax for that profit or interest, which he ever paid before (which, were it his proportion and arose wholly from the encreasing charges of government by reason of the war, he would chearfully pay, were it much more) but three times his proportion—as the court have ordered, for the relief of the landed interest on a prospect of great war charges, directing the assessors, in what is usually called the state bill, to assess stock in trade and money at interest at the rate of 1801. [180£] on the 10001. [1000£] whereas it usually was assessed in the proportion of only 601. [60£].

Shall I repeat it, that while real estate stands just as it has done for many years, only with an exception in favor of necessary repairs, "All monies at interest either within or without the colony, are by the last tax bill ordered to be set at three times the yearly lawful interest thereof," and "incomes by trade at three times the sum of such incomes." Money and incomes used to be set, "the former at six per cent, the real interest, the latter at what the assessors in their consciences thought the real income"; now both are trebled; and the consciences of the Assessors thro' the colony are to be stretched by this act in due proportion;—this is the most extraordinary exertion of power over the consciences of men I ever heard of.

The evident intent of this iniquitous bill is to lay the burden of the encreasing charges of government, on account of the war, on the trading and monied interests. The consequences of which will be, that the monied men, whose expences, and whose accommodating the farmer with money on loan, are exceedingly beneficial, and who instead of reaping an advantage, as the farmer does by the war in the enhanced price of his produce, of his labour and transportation, and by the rise of his lands, really suffers in his necessary charges in proportion to the other's gain, will quit the colony and repair to that which lays no tax on money at interest. And the trader whose commerce is so very beneficial to the community, and would be so much more beneficial in proportion to its extent as that they would gain much by not taxing him at all, will also seek a settlement where he will not be obliged to pay out of his profits the taxes of all his neighbours in addition to his own.

Will the end in view be answered?—Will not the enormous and now encreasing influence of the landed interest at court, ruin the colony—will not the very persons who are intended to be relieved have ail [all?] his charge to pay, when by straining to over burden the merchants and monied men, they generally withdraw, and leave them to the just effects of their iniquitous policy.

Formerly it was sufficient reason against high taxes of monies at interest, that it would be unjust to the lender or injurious to the borrower—for the former was limited, to prevent extortion, to six per cent—and the latter would be disappointed of his purpose if an excessive tax obliged the former to transfer his money into the public funds in England (which could then be done) or to remove himself out of the province.

Another reason, which ought to have some weight, is, that money lent is, in effect, twice taxed if not oftner. The lender parts with it to the husbandman, he purchases lands or stock, which are again taxed; or if he lets it to a trader, he purchases goods which are taxed in their place.

The last reason I shall mention is that most governments do not tax monies at interest at all.

A gentleman of great abilities in Massachusetts Assembly once said "no wise government ever did tax money at interest."

Were the men who could press such a bill capable of moral sense, I could make them blush at the view of those arguments which arise from natural conscience, and from the divine principles and equitable precepts of the religion they possess; but as the presumption is, that the conviction resulting from them is to operate to their utter exclusion from any future share in the administration of government, I shall address them, as the preceeding, to the electors of the ensuing assembly.

Wherefore, my friends, let me beg your patience a little longer, while I ask you a few plain, but serious questions.

In the first place, had the fortune of war placed the inhabitants of the frontier towns in the same situation as those of the sea ports, what would have been their sentiments respecting this matter?

Had the destructive policy of our unnatural enemies succeeded to their wish, and the Canadians and Indians driven them from their peaceful recesses into the heart of the country, or to the sea ports, obliging them to leave all their interests to the mercy of those lawless ravagers, and to support their families among strangers, and at an enhanced price, with the small pittance which they were able to save, at the risque of their lives and liberties, out of the flames, would they have thought it reasonable or just, instead of being relieved of their accustomed proportion of the public charge, to have had it trebled upon them?—Even though some late houses of assembly, from a conviction that they had always paid a disproportionate part of the taxes, had reduced them near one half? Would the prospect of an increase of public charge justify it? Would it not rather plead in their favour?

Should is [it] be said, that they were not injured, because they were taxed by their own representatives in a constitutional way,—they would readily and very justly reply, that the force of that representation was in a great measure abated, if not wholly destroyed, should the sea ports have taken the advantage of their situation and encreased the number and influence of their members; hereby rendering their boasted representation of much the same value with that proposed to the colonies by some minions of power, in the British Parliament in order to secure unlimited taxation, and but little more than virtual.

Secondly, Whether there is any essential difference in the moral qualities of oppression, or any other iniquity, arising merely from the different situation of its subject? Or whether my being an inhabitant of one part of the colony, makes it more equitable to oppress me than if my residence was in another? If not,

Thirdly, Whether the late tax bill, is reconcileable to that grand maxim of commutative justice, "Whatsoever ye would that men should do unto you, do ye even so unto them." And if not,

Lastly, Whether you can consistently and conscientiously give your votes for returning the same members to court, as have past so unrighteous and oppressive acts: And whether you would not shew yourselves more truly and justly tenacious of the reputation, the virtue, and the interests of the colony by electing, in their place, men of honest minds, enlarged views and inflexible patriotism; who, setting aside all selfish and party considerations, will devote their time, abilities and influence, to the promoting those things, and those only, by which the public security, interest and happiness may be advanced.

Happy is it for us, my friends, that our constitution of civil government (though not so pure and perfect as it might be, and I hope soon will be) is free from the curse of triennial and septennial parliaments; that the revolution of a single year puts it in our power to correct some errors, and to prevent worse. And that it must be our own fault, if in a government so often reverting to first principles, and revolving upon the electors, any capital deviation from those principles, and consequent acts of oppression or iniquity are suffered to continue. O. P. Q.

CHAPTER III

THE GENERAL COURT REQUESTS PERMISSION TO DRAFT A CONSTITUTION

ALTHOUGH PEOPLE in other parts of the province did not join the residents of Berkshire in their clamor for a constitution in the spring of 1776, they did desire some changes in the provisional government of Massachusetts. The Essex convention (No. 10) complained of the government's failure to take into account the growth of population and property. Boston (No. 11) made the same complaint and also pointed out the dangers of pluralism in office-holding, emphasizing the need for a separation of powers.

But patchwork changes in the provisional government were difficult to justify after July 4, 1776. Formal declaration of independence from Great Britain removed the only possible excuse for the modified charter—the now futile hope of reconciliation with Great Britain. It was obvious to nearly everyone now, as it had been to the Berkshire Constitutionalists earlier, that a fresh beginning in government was essential. The returns of several towns clearly implied that after the Declaration of Independence Massachusetts had no government worthy of the name.

In the fall of 1776 the General Court made its first offer to draft a constitution (No. 12). The resolution of the House was sent to approximately 260 towns, but the responses of only 98 have been preserved in the Archives. If one ignores five towns that gave no reasons for their rejection of the proposal, it can be said that not a single town was opposed to having a constitution as such. In fact, nearly three-fourths of the towns responding favored giving the General Court power to proceed at once. These towns are not represented in the selection of documents because they simply recorded their favorable vote without much comment.

Those towns that voted down the proposal did so for a variety of reasons: some, like Wareham (No. 13), thought wartime inappropriate for constitution-making; some, like Topsfield (No. 14) and Ashfield (No. 15), wanted relatively minor changes in the proposed method of drafting a constitution;

and some, like Boston (No. 16) and Attleborough (No. 17), wanted to involve more people than just the members of the General Court in the drafting process. In the effort to get a constitution, new issues came to the fore, and attention shifted slowly to the method of drafting a constitution and to the right of the people to ratify one. To Concord (No. 18) must go the honor of being the first town clearly to recognize the difference between constitution-making and legislative powers and the need to keep them separate.[1] Hers was the earliest call for the "fully developed convention" praised by McLaughlin (see Introduction), although other towns, including those in Worcester County (No. 19), called for a special state convention to frame a constitution. But numerous towns must be credited with demanding assent by the people to any constitution drawn up; even many of those towns that approved the House resolve insisted upon the right of the people to accept or reject. The urgent need for action, so long stressed by the Berkshire Constitutionalists, was by this time self-evident.

"The Late Act of Tolleration" mentioned by Topsfield refers to a law passed in May 1776, which permitted towns with 120 *voters* to send two delegates and allowed another representative for each additional 100 *voters.* Compare this with the earlier provision described in Chapter I, p. 2.

QUESTIONS

1. What did towns in Essex County find most unsatisfactory about the existing government?

2. What additional suggestions were made by Boston?

3. What does a comparison of the views of these eastern towns with those of Pittsfield reveal?

4. In responding to the Resolution of the House, do the towns seem to agree or disagree with the position Pittsfield took earlier on the compliance of Massachusetts with the recommendation of the Continental Congress regarding the establishment of government?

5. For what various reasons do the several towns reject the General Court as the appropriate body to draft a constitution? Which view is reminiscent of the position of Thomas Paine on written constitutions?

6. How would you sum up the governmental ideas of the Town of Ashfield?

1. Professor S. E. Morison has pointed out that Middleborough anticipated by two weeks the position Concord took. See his *The Formation of the Massachusetts Constitution,* 1955.

The Demand for Reforms in the Provisional Government

10. Resolutions of an Essex County Convention, April 25, 1776

[Massachusetts Archives, CLVI, 192-96]

To the Honourable the Council & the Honourable the House of Representatives for the Colony of the Massachusetts-Bay in General Court assembled April 1776.—

The Subscribers delegated, by the several Towns in the County of Essex to our Names affixed, to represent them in County Convention, to be held at Ipswich in said County on the twenty-fifth of this Instant April, for the Purposes appearing in this Memorial, beg Leave to Represent—

That, in the present Important Crisis, when every member of the community must be anxiously solicitous for the public Weal, and when a new, and we trust a glorious Empire is forming on the Basis of Liberty, the present State of Representation in this Colony has gained the Attention of the Towns from whence we are delegated, & we are chosen to meet in a County Convention for the Purpose of endeavoring to procure one more equal, than is at present enjoyed—

When the natural Rights which men possess are given up to Society, they ever expect to receive an equivalent, from the Benefits derived from a social State; Freemen submitting themselves to the Controul of others, and giving up the entire Right of Legislation and Taxation without reserving any Share to themselves, can receive no possible equivalent for the Concession; for they become absolute Slaves; But if they delegate a Number from themselves to conduct these important Articles of State, over whom they retain a suitable Controul, they enjoy a qualified Liberty, in many Respects preferable to what they relinquish—

If this Representation is equal, it is perfect; as far as it deviates from this Equality, so far it is imperfect and approaches to that State of Slavery; & the want of a just Weight in Representation is an Evil nearly akin to being totally destitute of it——An Inequality of Representation has been justly esteem'd the Cause which has in a great Degree sapped the foundation of the once admired, but now tottering Fabric of the British Empire; and we fear that if a different Mode of Representation from the present, is not adopted in this Colony, our Constitution will not continue, to that late Period of Time, which the glowing Heart of every true American now anticipates——

In the early Period of our Settlement, when thirty or forty Families were first permitted to send each a Representative to the general Assembly, there can be no Doubt, but the proportionate Equality was duly adjusted; nor is there much more Doubt, but that, as just an equality took Place in the Representation of the several Corporations of the British Empire, when the Rule was first established there——That striking, that unjust Disproportion, which fills us with Disgust & Detestation, has arisen in Britain, chiefly from the great Increase of Numbers and Wealth in some Places of that Empire and a Decrease in others, & continued from a blind Attachment to the Forms of Antiquity in some, and a wicked Disposition in others, who found an effectual Way to turn this Inequality to their own Advantage, tho' to the Destruction of the State——

We cannot realize that, your Honours, our wise political Fathers have adverted to the present Inequality of Representation in this Colony, to the Growth of the Evil or to the fatal Consequences which will probably ensue from the Continuance of it——Each Town & District in the Colony is by some late Regulation permitted to send one Representative to the general Court, if such Town or District consists of thirty Freeholders & other Inhabitants qualified to elect, if one hundred & twenty to send two——No town is permitted to send more than two except the Town of Boston, which may send four——There are some Towns and Districts in the Colony in which there are between thirty and forty Freeholders & other Inhabitants qualified to elect only; there are others besides Boston, in which there are more than five hundred,—The first of these may send one Representative;—The latter can send only two, if these Towns as to Property are to each other in the same respective Proportion, is it not clear to a mathematical Demonstration, that the same Number of Inhabitants of Equal Property, in the one Town, have but an Eighth Part of the Weight in Representation with the other, & with what colourable Pretext we would decently enquire——

If we regard Property as the Rule of Representation, it will be found that there are certain thirty Towns & Districts in the Colony, which altogether pay to the publick Expence, a sum not equal to what is paid by one other single Town in this County; yet the former may have a Weight in the Legislative Body, fifteen Times as large as the latter; nay it will be found by Examination, that a Majority of Voices in the Assembly may be obtained from the Members of Towns, which pay not more than one fourth Part of the publick Tax ——The County of Essex, which we represent in Convention, pays more than one sixth part of the publick Tax; & they have not a Right to send one tenth Part of the Number of Representatives which may be by Law returned to the general Assembly; This County contains one or two thousand Polls more than any other County in the Colony——The Town of Ipswich is in Property (and we suppose in Numbers) nearly equal to the several Towns & Districts of Hadley, South Hadley, Amherst, Granby, Deerfield, Greenfield, Shelburne & Conway (and more than equal to the like Number of other Places in the Colony) who are or may be represented in the general Court; Ipswich can send only two Members; the other Towns and Districts above mentioned may send ten Members at the least; can the Division of two Towns into eight, Towns and Districts furnish an Argument for the disproportionate Representation which of Consequence has taken Place; if the Property and Numbers remain the same, the Reason is to us Paradoxical.[1]——

If a new System of Government, or any material alteration in the old is to be in the Contemplation of the next general Assembly; Is it not fitting that the whole Community should be equally concerned in adjusting this System——

The many evil Consequences that will naturally & must inevitably arise from this Inequality of Representation, we trust, we need not attempt to mark out to a wise and free House of Americans; the Delineation would be disagreeable as well as indecent—Nor would we arrogantly suggest, to your Honours, the Mode of Redress, we confide in your Wisdom and Justice, and if an Equality of Representation takes Place in the Colony, we shall be satisfied whether it has Respect to Numbers, to Property or to a Combination of both.

1. South Hadley and Amherst were districts created from Hadley; Granby was an incorporated town created from Hadley. Greenfield, Shelburne, and Conway were all districts created from Deerfield. All were in Hampshire County.

11. From the Instructions to the Representatives of the Town of Boston, May 30, 1776

[*Boston Town Records, 1770 through 1777,* in *A Report of the Record Commissioners of the City of Boston, 1887,* 237-38]

Touching the internal Police of this Colony, it is essentially necessary, in Order to preserve Harmony among ourselves, that the constituent Body be satisfied, that they are fully & fairly represented—The Right to legislate is originally in every Member of the Community; which Right is always exercised of a State: But when the Inhabitants are become numerous, 'tis not only inconvenient, but impracticable *for all* to meet in One Assembly; & hence arose the Necessity & Practice of legislating by a few freely chosen by the many. —When this Choice is free, & the Representation, equal, 'tis the People's Fault if they are not happy: We therefore entreat you to devise some Means to obtain an *equal Representation* of the People of this Colony in the Legislature. But care should be taken, that the Assembly be not unweildy; for this would be an Approach to the Evil meant to be cured by Representation. The largest Bodies of Men do not always dispatch Business with the greatest Expedition, nor conduct it in the wisest manner——

It is essential to Liberty that the legislative, judicial & executive Powers of Government be, as nearly as possible, independent of & separate from each other; for where they are united in the same Persons, there will be wanting that natural Check, which is the principal Security against the enacting of arbitrary Laws, and a wanton Exercise of Power in the Execution of them.—It is also of the highest Importance that every Person in a Judiciary Department, employ the greatest Part of his Time & Attention in the Duties of his Office.—We therefore farther instruct you, to procure the making such Law or Laws, as shall make it incompatible for the same Person to hold a Seat in the legislative & executive Departments of Government, at one & the same time: —That shall render the Judges in every Judicatory thro' the Colony, dependent, not on the uncertain Tenure of Caprice or Pleasure, but on an unimpeachable Deportment in the important Duties of their Station, for their Continuance in Office: And to prevent the Multiplicity of Offices in the same Person, that such Salaries be settled upon them, as Will place them above the Necessity of stooping to any indirect or collateral Means for Subsistence.——

We wish to avoid a Profusion of the public Monies on the one hand, & the *Danger of sacrificing our Liberties to a Spirit of Parsimony on the other*:—Not doubting of your Zeal & Abilities in the common Cause of our Country, we leave your Discretion to prompt such Exertions, in promoting any military Operations, as the Exigency of our public Affairs may require: And in the same Confidence in your Fervor & Attachment to the public Weal, we readily submit all other Matters of public Moment, that may require your Consideration to your own Wisdom & Discretion.——

The foregoing Draught of Instructions to our Representatives, having been read & considered, the Question was put—"Whether the same shall be accepted, & given to our Representatives, as their Instructions"—Passed in the Affirmative unanimously.——

The General Court's Proposal

12. The House of Representatives Offers to Draft a Constitution, September 17, 1776

[Massachusetts Archives, CLVI, 133]

In the House of REPRESENTATIVES,
September 17, 1776

RESOLVED, That it be recommended to the Male Inhabitants of each Town in this State, being Free and Twenty One Years of Age, or upwards, that they assemble as soon as they can in Town-Meeting, upon reasonable previous Warning to be therefor given, according to Law, and that in such Meeting, they consider and determine whether they will give their Consent, that the present House of Representatives of this State of the *Massachusetts-Bay* in *New England,* together with the Council if they consent, in One Body with the House, and by equal Voice, should consult, agree on, and enact such a Constitution and Form of Government for this State, as the said House of Representatives & Council aforesaid, on the fullest and most mature Deliberation shall judge will most conduce to the Safety, Peace, and Happiness of this State, in all after Successions and Generations; and if they would direct that the same be made Public for the Inspection and Perusal of the Inhabitants, before the Ratification thereof by the Assembly. And that each Town as soon as may be after they have passed on the Question aforesaid, cause their Votes or Resolutions thereon to be certified into the Office of the Secretary of this State. And all Towns having a Right according to Law to a Representation in the General Assembly, and not having chose a Representative in Pursuance of the Precepts issued in *April* last, are at the Meeting aforementioned, impowered if they see Cause upon this Occasion, to return a Member or Members in the same Manner as they were by the Laws of this State impowered to do in Consequence of the Precepts aforesaid.

Also, Ordered, That *David Cheever,* Esq; procure the foregoing Resolve to be Published in Hand-Bills, and sent to the Selectmen of each Town.

J. Warren, Speaker

The Reaction of the Towns

13. The Return of Wareham (Plymouth County), October 14, 1776

[Massachusetts Archives, CLVI, 167]

At a Town Meeting in Wareham October 14th 1776

To Consider of the within Request of the Honorable General Assembly——Resolved as follows——

1 That we Judge it best; that the Plan of Government by the late Charter (viz) by the House of Representatives and Council be Still Continued & Strictly adheared to and that no Alteration be made

therein Respecting a form of Government at least During the present war——

2[dly] that Should the Major Part of the Towns in this State vote for A New Form of Government to be Erected we desire that No Form of Goverment be Erected on any account untill the Plan of Goverment Be Made Publick & that the Inhabitants May have the Perusall Thereof & to give their approbation before any ratifycation of the Same be Made——

14. The Return of Topsfield (Essex County), October 22, 1776

[Massachusetts Archives, CLVI, 183]

Att a Legal Town meeting in Topsfield held by adjournment 22nd. of October AD 1776——

The Committee that was Chosen to Consider and report to the Town what they Should Judge proper for the town to do respecting giveing their Consent that the present House of Representatives with the Council, Should anact a forme of Constitution and forme of Government for the future, made report as followeth——

It Being a time (as we apprehend) that the perplexing affairs of this State are Sufficient to take up the whole attention of the General Court, properly to Conduct the Same and altho' the members of the present House of Representatives are numerus, many of them are new, and we are not aquainted with them. And we Cannot but hope that before the next Choice of Representatives, the Late Act of Tolleration for townes to Send to Court, Such numbers of persons, which Act we fear was Obtained only to Serve the Interest of perticuler parties under a pretence of Equal representation, will be repealed & the Court will return to or near to the antient rule of representation in the General Court, and we hope members will be then Chosen that will Look upon it their duty not only to represent perticuler parties, nor their owne town only but the whole State in general, and then, and not till then we Shall have and Equal representation in the General Court—Therefore this Town are not willing that the present House of Representatives and Council Should an act [*sic*] and pass a Constitution and forme of Government for this State of Massachusetts Bay for the future, But we are willing that if present house of Representatives and the Council Should Draw Such a Draft of Constitution and forme of Government as they Shall Judge will most Conduce to the Safty peace and happiness of this State, and also Cause a Printed Copy thereof to be Sent to Every town and destrict in this State, for the Inspection and perusal of the Inhabitants, till after the next may Session of the General Court, That the Several Towns if they see Cause may then Instruct their Representatives to Cause the whole or Such part thereof, or with Such allterations as they may think proper to make, to be anacted, and pass into a Law for this State

Which was accepted after being Sundry times read over and also voted that the Town Clerke draw the Same into a faire draft and attest the Same, and forward it to the Secretary of this State by the first opertunity

15. Return of Ashfield (Hampshire County), October 4, 1776

[Massachusetts Archives, CLVI, 131]

To the Honorabel House of Representatives of the State of the Massachusets Bay in New England Assembled for the Good of this State Having Reseved your Resolve of September the 17 1776 Directing the Several Towns to Call a Meting for the Spesal Pirpos of Causing thair Vots or Resolves to be Returned to the Secertarys Office of this State, the Town After having Ben Previously Warned, Met on thusda 26 of September instant and After Debating the Matur [Measure?] Ajurned to October the 4 1776 Then Met and in the Fullest and Most Mature Dilibrate Maner Came into the folowing Resolves

Viz 1 Voted that it is our mind that we would have the forme of Sivil goverment Set up for the Good of this State

2 Voted that the Presant Representatives of the Peopel Shall forme the Constitution Exclusive of the Counsel for the Good of this State and Returne it to the Sevarale Towns for their Exceptanc Before the Ratifycation thairof

3 Voted that we will take the Law of God for the foundation of the forme of our Goverment for as the Old Laws we have Ben Ruled by under the British Constitution have Proved Inefectual to Secuer us from the more than Savige Crualty of tinanical Opressars Sense the God of Nature hath Enabeled us to Brake that Yoke of Bondage we think our Selves Bound in Duty to God and our Country to Opose the Least Apearanc of them Old Tinanical Laws taking Place again

4 Voted that it is our Opinnion that we Do not want any Goviner but the Goviner of the univarse, and under him a States Ginaral to Consult with the wrest of the united Stats for the Good of the whole

5 Voted that it is our opinian that Each Town is Invested with a Native Athority to Chuse a Comitte or Number of Juges Consisting of a Number of wise understanding and Prudent Men that Sall Jug and Detarmin all Cases betwixt Man and Man, Setel Intesttate Estates and Colect all Debts that have Ben Contracted, or may be Contracted within their Limits and all Contravarsies what Soever Exept in the Case of Murdor and then it will be Nesesary to Call in Eleven men from Eleven Nabouring Towns that Shall be Cose for that Porpos Anuly to Joge and Condem Such Moderrers

6 Voted that it is our Opinion that the Town Clark Shal Regester all Deads within the Liminits of Said Town

7 Voted that it our Opinan that the Asembelly of this Stat Consist of one Colective body the Members of which body Shall Anually be Alected

8 Voted that we Do Not Want any Laws made to Govern in Eclaiasties Afairs fairmly Believing the Divine Law to be Safficiant and that by which we and all Our Religious affairs ought to be Governed by

9 Voted that it is our opinion tha the Reprisentitive of this State Be Payed out of the Publick Treshuour of this State which monies Shall be Colected of the whole State

10 Voted that it is ower Opinion that all acts Pased by the Ginaral Court of this State Respecting the Several Towns Be Sent to the Sevarals Towns for thair acceptants Before thay Shall be in force

Ashfield October 4th 1776

16. From the Return of Boston (Suffolk County), 1776

[*Boston Town Records, 1770-1777,* 248]

1t. To form Government & establish a Constituion for the present & succeeding Generations, is a Task or Consideration the most important, it extends as much to our *Religious* as *Civil Liberties,* & includes our *All*—It effects every Individual; every Individual therefore ought to be consulting, acting & assisting.

2d. A Subject of such General, & indeed Infinite Concernment ought to be proceeded in with the greatest Caution & maturest Deliberation.—The Means or Channels of Information should all lay open to the People, & not restricted or confined to any particular Assembly however respectable.——

3d. Precipitancy is to be guarded against time & Opportunity should be taken by the people whose right it is to form Government, to collect the wisest Sentiments on this Subject; not of the present House only, but also of the Council, & every other Society, or Member of the State, that would favor the Public with their Sentiments, In Order that they may possess themselves of such Principles, & wise Maxims sounded on the best Precedents, & thereby be enabled to form a judicious & happy Constitution of Government. . . .

[This report was unanimously accepted by the town.]

17. The Return of Attleborough (Bristol County), October 28, 1776

[Massachusetts Archives, CLVI, 171]

At a Town-meeting legally assembled at Attleborough, October the 14th 1776. In consequence of a Resolve of September 17th 1776 passed by the Honorable House of Representatives for the State of Massachusetts-Bay,

—The following Resolves were passed—

1st Resolved that good Government is the Basis of Liberty, and absolutely necessary for the Safty & Welfare of a People——

2dly Resolved, that as the End of Government is the Happiness of the People; so the Sole Power & right of forming a Plan thereof is essentially in the People——

3dly Resolved, that as this State is at present destitute of a fixed & established form of Government, it is expedient & necessary that one be formed and established as soon as conveniently may be; agreeable to the Recommendation of the Continental Congress——

4thly Resolved, that wheres the present honorable House of Representatives have passed a Resolve of September 17th 1776, referring to the Consideration & Determination of the male Inhabitants &c. of this State; whether they will impower the Said Honorable House with the Council &c, to agree on, and enact a Constitution & Form of Government for this State, we can by no means consent to give them such a Power, for two Reasons especially (viz) because we apprehend the present honorable House is not a fair Representation of the Inhabitants of this State,—many Towns (not having this important matter in view) having chosen and sent fewer than their just Proportion of Members to that Honorable Boddy,—and also because the right of the Inhabitants of the Said State by their Votes in Town-meeting to negative the Said form, or any Article in it when drawn is not expressly acknowledged in the Said Resolve. For——

5thly it is resolved that it appears absolutely necessary for the Safty & Liberty of this State, that the Plan of Government when formed & published should be thoroughly examined & actually approved & consented unto by the good People of this State & convenient time for that Purpose be allowd before the establishment thereof—the establishment itself to be by a State Convention by them appointed for that Purpose

6thly Resolved that the Honorable House be requested, to call upon the Several Towns in this State to chose one, or more Members for the purpose of draughting & publishing a Form of Government for this State, to be approved by the Several Towns,—in order to which Draught we would humbly purpose the following method (viz) that the Members so chosen for the Several Towns in each County, meet together in County Conventions & therein draught Said Forms—, which done, that they by themselves, or their Committee meet in a State Convention or Congress & compare their Several Forms together, whereby the Wisdom of the whole State may be collected & a Form extracted, to be published for the Inspection & approbation of the Several Towns, also that the time for the meeting of the Said County & State Conventions for carrying into execution the Said Prosess, be appointed by the Court; & finally that after the Said form Shall have been published, examined & consented to by the Several Towns in this State, or the major part of them—the Said State Convention to be impowered by their Constituents to establish the Same.

Dated at Attleborough October the 28—1776 } test Jonathan Stanley { Town Clerk

18. The Return of Concord (Middlesex County), October 22, 1776

[Massachusetts Archives, CLVI, 182]

At a meeting of the Inhabitents of the Town of Concord being free & twenty one years of age and upwards met by adjournment on the twenty first Day of October 1776 to take into Consideration a Resolve of the Honorable House of Representatives of this State on the 17th of September last the Town Resolved as followes——

Resolve 1st That this State being at Present Destitute of a Properly established form of Government, it is absolutly necessary that one should be immediatly formed and established——

Resolved 2 That the Supreme Legislative, either in their Proper Capacity, or in Joint Committee, are by no means a Body proper to form & Establish a Constitution, or form of Government; for Reasons following. first Because we Conceive that a Constitution in its Proper Idea intends a System of Principles Established to Secure the Subject in the Possession & enjoyment of their Rights and Priviliges, against any Encroachments of the Governing Part——2d Because the Same Body that forms a Constitution have of Consequence a power to alter it. 3d Because a Constitution alterable by the Supreme Legislative is no Security at all to the Subject against any Encroachment of the Governing part on any or on all of their Rights & priviliges.

Resolve 3d That it appears to this Town highly necesary & Expedient that a Convention, or Congress be immediatly Chosen, to form & establish a Constitution, by the Inhabitents of the Respective

Towns in this State, being free & of twenty one years of age, and upwards, in Proportion as the Representatives of this State formerly were Chosen; the Convention or Congress not to Consist of a greater number then the house of assembly of this State heretofore might Consist of, Except that each Town & District Shall have Liberty to Send one Representative, or otherwise as Shall appear meet to the Inhabitents of this State in General

Resolve 4th that when the Convention, or Congress have formed a Constitution they adjourn for a Short time, and Publish their Proposed Constitution for the Inspection & Remarks of the Inhabitents of this State

Resolved 5ly that the Honorable house of assembly of this State be Desired to Recommend it to the Inhabitents of the State to Proceed to Chuse a Convention or Congress for the Purpas abovesaid as soon as Possable——

A True Copy of the Proceeding of the Town of Concord at the General Town meeting above mentioned—attest Ephraim Wood Jr, Town Clerk

Concord October the 22 1776

19. Resolutions of Towns in Worcester County, November 26, 1776

[*Massachusetts Spy,* Dec. 4, 1776]

At a meeting of the Committees of [S]afety &c. From a majority of the Towns in the County of Worcester, held by adjournment, at the Court House in said Worcester. November 26, 1776.

Voted,

THAT the Members inform the Convention what were the general sentiments of the inhabitants of their respective Towns, concerning a Resolve of the House of Representatives, on the 17th of September last, respecting the formation of a system of Government.

Lancaster, Rutland, Harvard, Princeton. Paxton, Southborough, Hardwick, Uxbridge, New-Brantree, Oakham, Shrewsbury, Winchendon, Consented, subject to the approbation or rejection of the people,

Oxford, Dissented by reason of unequal representation and brethen absent. *Sutton, Bolton Sturbridtge, Holden, Northbridge,* Dissented for unequal representation.

Worcester, Postponed acting on said resolve, till the third Monday in December next, to have the voice of their brethren in the Army.

Leicester, Dissented, presuming the people were excluded the right of approbation or rejection.

Dudley, Charlton, Objected to the present House.

Petersham, The same and against any Council.

Brookfield, Consented with right of approbation or rejection, and Government to be established by a future House.

Mendon, Not to comply with said resolve.

Spencer, The same, the Court not being in a proper situation,

Templeton, Fitchburg, Douglas, Objected to the present Court.

Northborough, Upton, Westborough, Ashburnham, Had no resolve, nor acted thereon.

Grafton, Did not act thereon.

Westminster, Had no resolve or acted thereon.

Voted,

That a system of Government is necessary to be established in this State so soon as it may be done with safety.

Whereas the Honorable the Continental Congress have thought fit, with the consent, and for the safety, peace and happiness of the American States to declare them free & independent on the Crown of Great-Britain &c. And have recommended to said States the forming such systems of Government as may be most agreeable to their respective situations and circumstances;

And whereas the present House of Representatives, to bring forward this important business have asked the consent of the people to impower that body with the Council, to form such a system of Government for this State;—The Committees of Safty &c. from a great majority of the Towns in the County of Worcester, convened at the Court House in said Worcester, on Tuesday the 26 of November 1776, for the purpose of reconciling the various sentiments of the inhabitants respecting said request, and preserving unanimity in the County; and also considering the loose and disjointed State, the people of the Massachusetts-Bay, have been in for divers years past, in which time, many errors have crept in and been supported with the remains of the late constitutions; that the evils are daily increasing and in all probability will continue till a fixed and permanent form of Government be established. Therefore to prevent, (as much as in themselves) anarchy and confusion, and the undue influence or power of individuals in monopolizing incompatible offices in the hands of particular persons, on the one hand and on the other to strengthen the hands of Government, against an unatural enemy, and lay a permanent foundation for safety, peace and happiness for this and succeeding generations; said Convention have come into the following votes, &c. with intention to lay the same before their respective Towns for their consideration.

Whereas an act passed in the late General Court. making the representation of the State very unequal and unsafe, this Convention is of opinion that the present General Court is not the most suitable body to form a system of Government for this State, moreover the business being of the greatest importance, will require more time and closeer attention than can be spared, by a house of representatives, from the ordinary and daily concerns of the State, Therefore voted, That a State Congress chosen for the sole purpose of forming a Constitution of Government is (in the opinion of this Convention) more eligible than an House of Representatives.
Voted, That it be recommended to our respective Towns, that they instruct their Representatives, to exert their influence, that writs be issued from the General Court impowering and directing the Towns to chuse members, to form a State Congress, by a mode of representation agreeable to the last charter and as practised in the year 1775, for the purpose of forming a plan of Government, which, when formed, to be laid before the people for their inpection, approbation, rejection, or amendment, (if any they have to propose) and when approved by the people, that said Congress solemnly establish the same, issue out writs for convening a legislative body agreeable to said Constitution and dissolve.
Voted, That the proceedings of this Convention be submitted to the consideration of the other counties in this State, and request the favour of their sentiments on the subject.
Voted, To publish the foregoing in the Boston, Worcester and Hartford News-Papers, also in Hand Bills.

By order of the Convention
JOSEPH HENSHAW, Chairman

CHAPTER IV

THE CONSTITUTION OF 1778 REJECTED

EARLY IN 1777 the House of Representatives appointed a committee to examine town returns on the House offer (made in September) to draft a constitution and to report what measures should be taken to establish "a new and good constitution and form of government." Although the great majority of towns responding favored the House offer, the committee reported on January 28, 1777, that the people favored a new constitution "framed by themselves so soon as conveniently may be." The committee also drafted a resolve recommending that the people be requested to elect delegates to a general convention, but this report was rejected on March 27, 1777, by a vote of 85 to 25. After rejecting the idea of a specially called convention, the House on April 4 suggested to the Council that the towns authorize their representatives to draft a constitution to be referred back to the towns for ratification (No. 20). The Council, which was generally opposed to a new constitution, finally agreed with the House on May 5 to a joint resolution recommending this action.

Although the returns on this question have not been preserved, the newly elected House did appoint a committee on June 5, 1777, which polled the representatives to find out what instructions had been received from the towns respecting a constitution. On June 12, this committee reported to the House, voting "to proceed in one body with the Council to form a constitution . . . agreeable to the resolve . . . of the 5th of May." The House and Council then resolved themselves on June 15 into Massachusetts' first constitutional convention.

The actual work of drafting was done by a committee made up of one member from each county, chosen by the county delegation, plus five members elected at large by the convention through written ballot. On December 11, 1777, the drafting committee submitted its report, which was accepted finally on February 28, 1778 (No. 21). Most troublesome for the convention were provisions covering apportionment of the House, particularly whether every incorporated town should be entitled to a representative regardless of size.

Two efforts were made to expunge from Article V the phrase "Negroes, Indians, and molattoes," but such efforts lost by a large majority. Also a failure was an attempt to protect taxpayers from having to pay for the support of ministers whose services they would not attend. The constitution was submitted to universal suffrage on March 4.

During the spring of 1778 the towns debated the Constitution of 1778 and then rejected it by a majority of about 5 to1. The convention did not ask the towns to submit a clause by clause vote nor to suggest amendments, but a number of towns did these things anyway. The Archives contain 173 returns. Fifteen towns made specific objections to Article V, nine of them rejecting the color clause and eight rejecting property qualification to vote for senators. Twenty-three towns found fault with the appointive power granted to the governor and senate. Various objections were raised also against Article VI, which provided for payment of representatives and apportionment of the House.

The returns selected here illustrate the variety of objections and the thinking of the people about governmental problems. They range from very detailed returns like that of Lenox (No. 22), with its heavy emphasis on natural rights and its desire for as much direct control by the people over their officers as possible, to Wheelersborough (No. 31), with its rather casual acceptance of a document unread by many in the town. Mendon (No. 23) strikes out against an established church and Sutton (No. 24), against slavery. Lexington (No. 25), Westminster (No. 26), and Brookline (No. 27), like a number of other towns, call for a bill of rights. The liberal attitudes of these towns contrast with the narrowness of Belchertown (No. 28). Greenwich (No. 29) represents an extreme desire for direct democracy free of checks and balances. Pittsfield (No. 30) is included to show what action was taken by the town that led the Constitutionalists. Probably the reaction to the Constitution of 1778 most cited by historians is that called the "Essex Result" (No. 33), the views of twelve towns (out of twenty-one) in Essex County. The emphasis which it placed upon separation of powers and upon the nature and mode of election of the executive anticipate in many respects the later debates of the Federal Convention.

It will be recalled that the House rejected its own committee report advocating the electing of a special convention to frame a constitution, preferring instead to sit with the Council as a convention. Three towns, among them Lexington (No. 25) and Beverly (No. 32), persisted in demanding a true constitutional convention. Concord, which had made the same demand earlier (see Chapter III), unanimously rejected the Constitution of 1778, "for Reasons heretofore given by the town on that important affair."[1] This issue was finally resolved when such a convention was elected to draft the Constitution of 1780.

1. Massachusetts Archives, CLX, 24.

QUESTIONS

1. In what ways did the Constitution of 1778 violate proper separation of powers?

2. What parts of the returns of the towns suggest a basic suspicion of government?

3. How would you sum up the views expressed by the several towns on the right to vote?

4. How does the Essex Result stand on this right?

5. How would you compare the views of the several towns and those of the Essex Result on executive power?

6. What difference in emphasis on or approach to the principle of separation of powers is found in the returns of the towns and in the Essex Result?

7. How justified would one be in calling the Essex Result a conservative reaction to the Constitution of 1778 as compared with the reaction of other towns here illustrated?

8. What objections to this constitution seem to be aimed at actual past abuses which it is feared may continue?

20. Resolution of the House to Empower the General Court to Frame a Constitution, April 4, 1777

[Massachusetts Archives, CLVI, 200-2]

State of Massachusetts Bay
In the House of Representatives
April 4, 1777

That the happiness of Mankind depends very much on the Form of Constitution of Government they live under. that the only object and design of Government should be the good of the people are truths well understood at this day & truths taught by reason & Experience very clearly at all times and yet by far the greater part of Mankind are governed only for the advantage of their masters & are the miserable slaves of a single or a few despots whose Ideas or humanity never extend beyond the limits of their own [Grandeur?] or Interest and indeed among the Multitude of Mankind who have lived and the variety of people who have succeeded each other in the several ages of the world very few have ever had an oppertunity of choosing and forming a Constitution of Government for themselves. this is a great privilege & such an one the good People of this state by the distinguished favours of a kind Providence now En joy and which the Interst & happiness of themselves & posterity loudly call upon them to improve with wisdom & prudence. the Infatuated Policy of Britain instead of destroying has in all probability (by the Goodness of God) promoted & accelerated the happiness of the people of the United States of America. the Cruelty and Injustice of Britain has driven u[s] to a declaration of Independence & a dissolution of our former Connections with them and made it necessary for each of the United States to form & constitute a mode of Goverment for themselves—and whereas by the suffrages of the good People of this State it has become more especially our duty to Consult & promote the happiness of our Constituents & haveing duly Considered the Advantages & necessity of immediately forming a fixed and permanent Constitution of Goverment & Conceiving it to be the Expectation of our Constituents that we should originate and recommend to them the most suitable method for Effecting this valuable and Important purpose. do Resolve—That it be & hereby is recommended to the several Towns & places in this State—Impowered by the Laws thereof to send members to the General Assembly that at their next Election of a Member or Members to represent them they make choice of men in whose Intigrity & Ability they can place the greatest Confidence & in addition to the Common & ordinary powers of Representation vest them with full powers to form such a Constitution of Goverment as they shall Judge best Calculated to promote the happiness of this State & when Compleated to Cause the same to be printed in all the Boston Newspapers & also in hand Bills one of which to be transmitted to the Selectmen of each town or the Committe of each plantation to be by them laid before their respective Towns or plantations at a regular meeting for that purpose to be called. to be by each Town & Plantation Considered. and a return of their approbation or disapprobation to be made to the Clerk of the House of Representatives specifiing the Numbers present in Such meeting voteing for & those voteing against the same at a reasonable time to be fixed on by said House and if upon a fair Examination of said returns it shall appear that said form of Goverment be approved of by at least two thirds of those who are Free & twenty one years of age within this State and present in the several meetings then the same shall be deemed and Established as the Constitution & form of Goverment of the state of Massachusetts Bay according to which the Inhabitants thereof shall be Governed in all succeeding Generations unless altered by their own Express direction or that of a fair Majority of them. and it is further recommended to the Selectmen of the several Towns in the return of their Precepts for the Choice of Representatives to signify their having Considered this resolve & their doings thereon

and it is also Resolved that Mr Storey, Mr Freeman & Capt. Page—be a committee to get these Resolves printed in hand Bills & sent to the several Towns & Plantations in this State as soon as may be & also to cause the same to be published in all the Boston Newspapers three weeks successively——

Sent up for Concurrence

21. The Constitution of 1778

[Chester A. McLain, ed., *Old South Leaflets, No. 209* (Boston, n.d.), 3-15]

A CONSTITUTION AND FORM OF GOVERNMENT

For the State of Massachusetts Bay, agreed upon by the Convention of said State, February 28, 1778—to be laid before the several towns and plantations in said State, for their aprobation or disaprobation.

State of Massachusetts Bay.

In Convention, February 28, 1778

Whereas, upon the Declaration of Independence, made by the Representatives of the United States, in Congress assembled, by which all connections between the said States and Great Britain, were dissolved, the General Assembly of this State thought it expedient that a new constitution of Government for this State, should be formed; and, apprehending that they were not invested with sufficient authority to deliberate and determine upon so interest-

ing a subject, did, on the fifth day of May 1777, for the effecting this valuable purpose, pass the following Resolve:

"*Resolved,* That it be, and hereby is recommended to the several towns and places in this State, impowered by the laws thereof to send members to the General Assembly, that, at their next election of a member or members to represent them, they make choice of men, in whose integrity and abilities they can place the greatest confidence; and, in addition to the common and ordinary powers of representation, instruct them with full powers, in one body with the Council, to form such a constitution of government as they shall judge best calculated to promote the happiness of this State, and when compleated to cause the same to be printed in all the Boston news-papers, and also in hand-bills, one of which to be transmitted to the selectmen of each town, or the committee of each plantation, to be by them laid before their respective towns or plantations, at a regular meeting of the inhabitants thereof, to be called for that purpose, in order to its being by each town and plantation duly considered, and a return of their approbation or disapprobation to be made into the Secretary's office of this State, at a reasonable time to be fixed on by the General Court, specifying the numbers present in such meeting, voting for, and those voting against the same; and if upon a fair examination of the said returns, by the General Court or such a committee as they shall appoint for that purpose, it shall appear that the said form of government is approved of by at least two thirds of those who are free and twenty-one years of age, belonging to this State, and present in the several meetings, then the General Court shall be impowered to establish the same as the constitution and form of government of the State of Massachusetts-Bay; according to which the inhabitants thereof shall be governed in all succeeding generations, unless the same shall be altered by their own express direction, or that of at least two thirds of them. And it is further recommended to the selectmen of the several towns in the return of their precepts for the choice of Representatives to signify their having considered this resolve, and their doings thereon."

And whereas the good people of this State, in pursuance of the said resolution, and reposing special trust and confidence in the Council and in their Representatives, have appointed, authorized and instructed their Representatives in one body with the Council, to form such a constitution of government as they shall judge best calculated to promote the happiness of this State, and when compleated, to cause the same to be published for their inspection and consideration.

We therefore the Council and Representatives of the people of the State of Massachusetts-Bay, in Convention assembled, by virtue of the power delegated to us, and acknowledging our dependence upon the all-wise Governor of the Universe for direction, do agree upon the following form of a constitution of government for this State, to be sent out to the people, that they may act thereon, agreeably to the afore-recited resolve.

I.—There shall be convened, held and kept a General Court, upon the last Wednesday in the month of *May* every year, and at all other times as the said General Court shall order and appoint; which General Court shall consist of a Senate and House of Representatives to be elected as this Constitution hereafter directs.

II.—There shall be elected annually a Governor and Lieutenant-Governor, who shall each have, by virtue of such election, a seat and voice in the Senate; and the stile and title of the Governor shall be *His Excellency;* and the stile and title of the Lieutenant-Governor shall be *His Honor.*

III.—No person shall be considered as qualified to serve as Governor, Lieutenant-Governor, Senator or Representative, unless qualified respectively at the time of their several elections as follows, viz: The Governor and Lieutenant-Governor shall have been inhabitants of this State five years immediately preceeding the time of their respective election; the Governor shall be possessed, in his own right, of an estate of the value of *one thousand pounds, whereof five hundred pounds* value, at the least, shall be in real estate, within this State; the Lieutenant-Governor shall be possessed, in his own right, of an estate of the value of *five hundred pounds, two hundred and fifty pounds* thereof, at the least, to be in real estate, within this State: A Senator shall be possessed, in his own right, of an estate to the value of *four hundred pounds, two hundred pounds* thereof, at least, to be in real estate, lying in the district for which he shall be elected: A Representative shall be possessed, in his own right, of an estate of the value of *two hundred pounds, one hundred pounds* thereof, at the least, to be in real estate, lying in the town for which he shall be elected. Senators and Representatives shall have been inhabitants of districts and towns for which they shall be respectively elected one full year immediately preceeding such election; provided that when two or more towns join in the choice of a Representative, they may choose an inhabitant of either of said towns, he being otherwise qualified as this article directs.

IV.—The Judges of the Superior Court, Secretary, Treasurer-General, Commissary-General, and settled Ministers of the Gospel, while in office; also all military officers while in the pay of this or of the United States, shall be considered as disqualified for holding a seat in the General Court; and the Judges and Registers of Probate for holding a seat in the Senate.

V.—Every male inhabitant of any town in this State, being free, and twenty-one years of age, excepting Negroes, Indians and molattoes, shall be intitled to vote for a Representative or Representatives, as the case may be, in the town where he is resident, provided he has paid taxes in said town (unless by law excused from taxes) and been resident therein one full year immediately preceeding such voting, or that such town has been his known and usual place of abode for that time, or that he is considered as an inhabitant thereof; and every such inhabitant qualified as above, and worth *sixty pounds* clear of all charges thereon, shall be intitled to put in his vote for Governor, Lieutenant-Governor and Senators; and all such voting for Governor, Lieutenant-Governor, Senators or Representatives, shall be by ballot and not otherwise.

VI.—Every incorporated town within this State shall be intitled to send one Representative to the General Court; any town having three hundred voters, may send three; having seven hundred and sixty, may send four, and so on; making the increasing number necessary for another member, twenty more than the last immediately preceeding increasing number, 'till the whole number of voters in any town are reckoned. And each town shall pay the expense of its own representative or representatives; and the inhabitants of any two or more towns, who do not incline to send a Representative for each town, may join in the choice of one, if they shall so agree.

VII.—The Selectmen of each town shall some time in the month of *April* annually, issue their warrant or warrants under their hands and seals, directed to some Constable or Constables within their towns respectively, requiring him or them to notify the inhabitants qualified to vote for a representative, to assemble in some convenient place in such town, for the choice of some person or persons, as the case may be, to represent them in the General Court the ensuing year: the time and place of meeting to be mentioned in the warrant or warrants for calling such meeting: And the selectmen of each town respectively, or the major part of them, shall make return of the name or names of the person or persons elected by the major part of the voters present, and voting in such meeting, to represent said town in the General Court the ensuing year, into the Secretary's office, on or before the last Wednesday of *May,* then next ensuing: And when two or more towns shall agree to join for such choice, the major part of the Selectmen of those towns, shall in the manner above directed, warn a meeting to be held in either of the said towns, as they shall judge most convenient, for that purpose, and shall make return as aforesaid, of the person chosen at such meeting.

VIII.—The number of Senators shall be twenty eight; (exclusive of the Governor and Lieutenant-Governor) Their election shall be annual, and from certain districts, into which the State shall be divided as follows, viz: The middle district to contain the counties of *Suffolk, Essex,* and *Middlesex,* within which ten Senators shall be elected: the southern district to contain the counties of *Plymouth, Barnstable, Bristol, Dukes' County* and *Nantucket,* within which six Senators shall be elected; the western district to contain the counties of *Hampshire, Worcester* and *Berkshire,* within which eight Senators shall be elected; the northern district to contain the counties of *York,* and *Cumberland,* within which three shall be elected; the eastern district to contain the county of *Lincoln,* within which one shall be elected: And as the numbers of the inhabitants in the several districts may vary from time to time, the General Court shall in the way they shall judge best, sometime in the year one thousand seven hundred and ninety, and once in twenty years ever after, order the number of the inhabitants in the several districts to be taken, that the Senators may be apportioned a new to the several districts, according to the numbers of the inhabitants therein. And the General Court may at such new apportionment increase the number of Senators to be chosen as they may see fit; provided that the whole number shall never exceed thirty six, exclusive of the Governor and Lieutenant-Governor.

IX.—The inhabitants of the several towns in this State qualified as this Constitution directs, shall on the first Wednesday in the Month of *November* annually, give in their votes in their respective towns, at a meeting which the Selectmen shall call for that purpose, for Senators for the year ensuing the last Wednesday in *May* then next. The votes shall be given in for the members of each district separately according to the foregoing apportionment, or such as shall be hereafter ordered; and the Selectmen and Town Clerk of each town, shall sort and count the votes, and by the third Wednesday in *December* then next, transmit to the Secretary's office, a list certified by the town-clerk, of all the persons who had votes as Senators for each district at such meeting, and the number each person had affixed to his name. The lists so sent in shall be examined by the General Court at their then next sitting, and a list for each district of those voted for, to the amount of double the number assigned such district (if so many shall have votes) taking those who had the highest numbers, shall be made out and sent by the first of *March,* the next after, to the several towns in this State, as a nomination list, from which said towns shall, at their meetings for the choice of Governor in the month of *May,* vote for the Senators assigned the respective districts; which votes shall be counted and sorted, and lists certified as before directed, made out and sent in to the Secretary's office, by ten o'clock in the forenoon of the last Wednesday in said *May,* and not afterwards; which lists shall be examined by the House of Representatives for the first time of the election of Senators, and ever afterwards by the Senate and House of Representatives on said last Wednesday of *May,* or as soon after as may be; and those persons in each district, equal to the number assigned such district, who have the greatest number of votes, shall be

Senators for the ensuing year, unless it shall appear to the Senate that any member or members thereof were unduly elected, or not legally qualified; of which the Senate shall be the judges. And the Senate when so constituted shall continue in being 'till another Senate is chosen, and the members thereof gone through all the steps necessary to qualify them to enter on the business assigned them by this Constitution.

X.—There shall forever hereafter, on the first Wednesday in the month of *May* annually, to be held, in each town in this State, a meeting of the inhabitants of such towns respectively, to give or put in their votes for Governor, Lieutenant-Governor and Senators; which meeting the Selectmen shall cause to be notified in the manner before directed, for the meeting for the choice of Representatives: and the town-clerk shall return into the Secretary's office by ten o'clock in the morning of the last Wednesday of said *May,* and not afterwards, an attested list of all the persons who had votes for Governor and Lieutenant-Governor respectively, certifying the number of votes each person so voted for had, which lists shall be, on said last Wednesday of *May,* or as soon after as may be, examined by the Senate and House of Representatives; and the persons who on such examination, shall appear to have the greatest number of votes for those offices respectively, provided it be a majority of the whole number, shall be by the two Houses declared Governor and Lieutenant-Governor, and intitled to act as such the ensuing year: and if no person shall have such majority for Governor or for Lieutenant-Governor, the Senate and House of Representatives shall as soon as may be, after examining said lists, proceed by joint ballot to elect a Governor or Lieutenant-Governor, or both, as the case may require, confining themselves to one of those three who had the greatest number of votes collected in the several towns for the office to be filled.

XI.—If any person chosen Governor, Lieutenant-Governor, Senator or Representative, whose qualification shall be questioned by any one member of the Senate or House of Representatives, within twenty-four days after his appearing to enter upon the execution of his office, shall not make oath before a Senator, the Speaker of the House of Representatives, or some Justice of the Peace, that he is qualified as required by this Constitution, and lodge a certificate thereof in the Secretary's office, within ten days after notice given him of such questioning by the Secretary, whose duty it shall be to give such notice, his election shall be void; and any person claiming privilege of voting for Governor, Lieutenant-Governor, Senators, or Representatives, and whose qualifications shall be questioned in town-meeting, shall by the Selectmen be prevented from voting, unless he shall make oath that he is qualified as this Constitution requires; said oath to be administered by a Justice of the Peace, or the Town-Clerk, who is hereby impowered to administer the same when no Justice is present.

XII.—Whenever any person who may be chosen a member of the Senate, shall decline the office to which he is elected, or shall resign his place, or die, or remove out of the State, or be any way disqualified, the House of Representatives may, if they see fit, by ballot, fill up any vacancy occasioned thereby, confining themselves in the choice to the nomination list for the district to which such member belonged, whose place is to be supplied, if a sufficient number is thereon for the purpose; otherwise the choice may be made at large in such district.

XIII.—The General Court shall be the supreme legislative authority of this State, and shall accordingly have full power and authority to erect and constitute judicatories and Courts of record, or other Courts; and from time to time to make and establish all manner of wholesome and reasonable orders, laws, and statutes; and also, for the necessary support and defence of this government, they shall have full power and authority to levy proportionable and reasonable assessments, rates and taxes, and to do all and every thing they shall judge to be for the good and welfare of the State, and for the Government and ordering thereof; provided nevertheless, they shall not have any power to add to, alter, abolish, or infringe any part of this constitution. And the enacting stile in making laws shall be "by the Senate and House of Representatives in General Court assembled, and by the authority of the same."

XIV.—The Senate and House of Representatives shall be two separate and distinct bodies, each to appoint its own officers, and settle its own rules of proceedings; and each shall have an equal right to originate or reject any bill, resolve or order, or to propose amendments in the same, excepting bills and resolves, levying and granting money or other property of the State, which shall originate in the House of Representatives only, and be concurred or non-concurred in whole by the Senate.

XV.—Not less than sixty members shall constitute or make a quorum of the House of Representatives; and not less than nine shall make a quorum of the Senate.

XVI.—The Senate and House of Representatives shall have power to adjourn themselves respectively; provided such adjournment shall not exceed two days at any one time.

XVII.—The Governor shall be President of the Senate. He shall be General and Commander in Chief of the Militia, and Admiral of the Navy of this State; and impowered to embody the militia, and cause them to be marched to any part of the State, for the public safety, when he shall think necessary; and in the recess of the General Court, to march the militia, by advice of the Senate, out of the State, for the defence of this, or any other of the United States; provided always that the Governor shall exercise the power given by this constitution, over the militia and navy of the State, according to the laws thereof, or the resolves of the General Court. He shall, with the advice of the Senate, in the recess of the General Court, have power to prorogue the same from time to time, not exceeding forty days in any one recess of said Court; and in the sitting of said Court, to adjourn or prorogue the said Court to any time they shall desire, or to dissolve the same at their request, or to call said Court together sooner than the time to which it may be adjourned or prorogued, if the welfare of the State shall require the same. He shall have power at his discretion to grant reprieves to condemned criminals for a term or terms of time, not exceeding six months. It shall be the duty of the Governor to inform the legislature at every session of the General Court, of the condition of the State, and from time to time to recommend such matters to their consideration, as shall appear to him to concern its good government, welfare and prosperity.

XVIII.—Whenever the person, who may be chosen Governor shall decline the trust to which he is thereby elected, or shall resign, or die, or remove out of the State, or be otherwise disqualified, the Lieutenant-Governor shall have the like power during the vacancy in the office of Governor, as the Governor is by this Constitution vested with; and in case of a vacancy in the office of Governor and Lieutenant-Governor, the major part of the Senate shall have authority to exercise all the powers of a Governor during such vacancy; and in case the Governor and the Lieutenant-Governor are both absent from the Senate, the Senior or first Senator then present shall preside therein.

XIX.—All Civil officers annually chosen, with salaries annually granted for their services, shall be appointed by the General Court, by ballot; each branch to have a right to originate or negative the choice: All other Civil officers, and also all General, Field and Staff officers, both of the militia and of the troops, which may be raised by and be in the pay of this State, shall be appointed by the Governor and the Senate; Captains and Subalterns of troops raised by and in the pay of this State, to be also appointed by the Governor and Senate.

XX.—The Governor and Senate shall be a Court for the trial of all impeachments of any officers of this State, provided that if any impeachment shall be prosecuted against the Governor, Lieutenant-Governor, or any one of the Senate; in such case the person impeached shall not continue one of the Court for such trial. Previous to the trial of any impeachment, the members of the Court shall be respectively sworn, truly and impartially to try and determine the charge in question, according to evidence, which oath shall be administered to the members by the President, and to him by any one of the Senate; and no judgment of said Court shall be valid, unless it be assented to by two thirds of the members of said Court present at such trial; nor shall judgment extend further than to removal of the person tried from office, and disqualification to hold or enjoy any place of honor, trust or profit, under the State; the party so convicted shall nevertheless be liable and subject to indictment, trial, judgment and punishment, according to the laws of the State; and the power of impeaching all officers for malconduct in their respective offices, shall be vested in the House of Representatives.

XXI.—The Governor may, with the advice of the Senate, in the recess of the General Court, lay an embargo, or prohibit the exportation of any commodity for any term of time, not exceeding forty days in any one recess of said Court.

XXII.—The Governor shall have no negative as Governor, in any matter pointed out by this Constitution to be done by the Governor and the Senate, but shall have an equal voice with any Senator, on any question before them; provided that the Governor (or, in his absence out of the State, the Lieutenant-Governor) shall be present in Senate to enable them to proceed on the business assigned them by this Constitution, as Governor and Senate.

XXIII.—The power of granting pardons shall be vested in the Governor, Lieutenant-Governor and Speaker of the House of Representatives, for the time being, or in either two of them.

XXIV.—The Justices of the Superior Court, the Justices of the Inferior Courts of Common Pleas, Judges of Probate of Wills, Judges of the Maritime Courts, and Justices of the Peace, shall hold their respective places during good behavior.

XXV.—The Secretary, Treasurer-General, and Commissary-General, shall be appointed annually.

XXVI.—The Attorney-General, Sheriffs, Registers of the Courts of Probate, Coroners, Notaries-Public, and Naval-Officers, shall be appointed and hold their places during pleasure.

XXVII.—The Justices of the Superior Court, Justices of the Inferior Courts, Courts of General Sessions of the Peace, and Judges of the Maritime Courts, shall appoint their respective Clerks.

XXVIII.—The Delegates for this State to the Continental Congress shall be chosen annually by joint ballot of the Senate and House of Representatives, and may be superseded in the mean time in the same manner. If any person holding the office of Governor, Lieutenant-Governor, Senator, Judge of the Superior Court, Secretary, Attorney-General, Treasurer-General, or Commissary-General, shall be chosen a member of Congress, and accept the trust, the place which he so held as aforesaid shall be considered as vacated thereby, and some other person chosen to succeed him therein: And if any person serving for this State at said Congress, shall be appointed to either of the aforesaid offices, and accept thereof, he shall be considered as resigning his seat in Congress, and some other person shall be chosen in his stead.

XXIX.—No person unless of the Protestant religion shall be Governor, Lieutenant-Governor, a member of the Senate or of the House of Representatives, or hold any judiciary employment within this State.

XXX.—All Commissions shall run in the name of the "State of *Massachusetts-Bay*," bear test, and be signed by the Governor or Commander in Chief of the State, for the time being, and have the seal of the State thereunto affixed, and be attested by the Secretary or his deputy.

XXXI.—All writs issuing out of the Clerk's office of any of the Courts of law within this State, shall be in the name of the "State of *Masachusetts-Bay*," under the seal of the Court from whence they issue, bear test of the Chief Justice, or senior or first Justice of the Court, where such writ is returnable, and be signed by the Clerk of such Court. Indictments shall conclude "against the peace and dignity of the State."

XXXII.—All the statute laws of this State, the common law, and all such parts of the English and British statute laws, as have been adopted and usually practised in the Courts of law in this State, shall still remain and be in full force until altered or repealed by a future law or laws of the legislature; and shall be accordingly observed and obeyed by the people of this State, such parts only excepted as are repugnant to the rights and privileges contained in this Constitution: and all parts of such laws as refer to and mention the Council shall be construed to extend to the Senate; and the inestimable right of trial by jury shall remain confirmed as part of this Constitution forever.

XXXIII.—All monies shall be issued out of the Treasury of this State, and disposed of by warrants under the hand of the Governor for the time being, with the advice and consent of the Senate, for the necessary defence and support of the Government, and the protection and preservation of the inhabitants thereof agreeable to the acts and resolves of the General Court.

XXXIV.—The free exercise and enjoyment of Religious profession and worship shall forever be allowed to every denomination of protestants within this State.

XXXV.—The following oath shall be taken by every person appointed to any office in this State, before his entering on the execution of the office; viz. *I, A. B. do swear* (or *affirm,* as the case may be) *that I will bear faith and true allegiance to the State of Massachusetts Bay, and that I will faithfully execute the business of the office of agreeably to the laws of this State, according to my best skill and judgment, without fear, favor, affection or partiality.*

XXXVI.—*And whereas it may not be practicable to conform to this Constitution in the election of Governor, Lieutenant Governor, Senators and Representatives for the first year:*

Therefore the present Convention, if in being, or the next General Assembly, which shall be chosen upon the present Constitution, shall determine the time and manner, in which the people shall choose said officers for the first year, and upon said choice, the General Assembly, then in being, shall be dissolved, and give place to the free execution of this Constitution.

By Order of the Convention,

JEREMIAH POWELL, President.

Attest. SAMUEL FREEMAN, Clerk

Objections to the Constitution of 1778

22. From the Return of Lenox (Berkshire County), May 20, 1778

[Massachusetts Archives, CLVI, 375-81]

And whereas the People of this County have been stigmatized as being a Lawless & disobedient part of this State and averse to all Righteous Government; which is as false as it is Scandalous, for we hearty wish to have a Basis of Government firmly established upon the pure Principles of Liberty, by which the Rights & Priviledges of the People may be secured & handed down unsull'd to Posterity; But when we take into our serious Consideration the said Form of a Constitution, we humbly conceive it is not calculated to answer the valuable Purposes above mentioned, but Contrawise, for the following Reasons—

Objections against Article 1st will be found in the sequel

Objections against Article the 3d, Money ought not to be made a necessary Qualification of a Senator or Representative; which countenances averice & rejects Merit.

There appears a Contradictory Sense in the Words General Court in the first Article & the same words in the fourth, by the fourth Article it appears, that Judges of the Superior Court, Secretary, Treasurer General, Commissary General & Settled Ministers of the Gospel while in Office, are not disqualified for a Seat in the Senate, tho, they are for a Seat in the General Court, & that the Judges & Registers of Probate are disqualified for a Seat in the Senate, tho, they are not for a Seat in the General Court, when the first Article declares that the Senate and House of Representatives shall constitute the General Court. In the fourth Article the Senate & General Court appears two distinct Bodies, but in the first the Senate is comprehended in the General Court. All Fundamental Rules or Laws ought to be plain & explicit & intirely free from ambiguties & not give the Attornies a propriety in drinking their former Toast, 'The Glorious uncertainty of Law or Constitution.

Objections against Article the 5th All Men were born equally free and independent, having certain natural & inherent, & unalienable Rights, among which are the enjoying & defending Life and Liberty & acquiring, possessing & protecting Property, of which Rights they cannot be deprived but by injustice, except they first forfit them by commiting Crimes against the Public. We conceive this Article declares Honest Poverty a Crime for which a large Number of the true & faithfull Subjects of the State, who perhaps have fought & bled in their Countrys Cause are deprived of the above mentioned Rights (which is Tyranny) for how can a Man be said to [be] free & independent enjoying & defending Life and Liberty & protecting Property, when he has not a voice allowed him in the choice of the most important officers in the Legislature, which can make laws to bind him and appoint Judges to try him in all cases as well of Life & Liberty as of Property—No Person ought to be allowed to vote for any offices of the Community except he has taken an Oath of Allegiance to the said Community—An Oath is the bond of Society & if ever necessary it is necessary in the present case.——

Reasons against Article the 6th. The charges of Representation ought to be equal as well as representation, no part of the State can justly be put to an unequal or disproportionable Cost to defray the necessary expences of Government mearly because they are remote from the Seat of Government, it has a tendency to induce the Remote parts of the State (if not necessitate them) to neglect keeping a Representative at the General Court In a word it is making Representation unequal, All the Necessary Charges of Government ought to equally assessed upon & paid by the Community——

Reasons against Article the 8th Each County ought to have its just proportion of Senators as well as Representatives otherwise Representation will still remain unequal, for according to this Article the largest County in each district containing the Majority of Voters in said District (which may be the case if it is not now) will have it in its Power to represent the whole District—it is not to be supposed that representation can be exactly equal, but it ought to be as equal as possible——

Reasons against Article the 9th According to this Article the Senate are to be the Sole Judge of the legality or illegality of the choice of Senators for an ensuing year likewise of the Qualifications or disqualifications for said office. If they judge the Person or Persons not duly elected or not legally qualified, they still hold the Power in their own hands, and if impeached by the House of Representatives for their Conduct in so doing, there is no Court to try them agreeable to this Form of a Constitution except their own Body, for which reason it will be in the Power of the Senate to perpetuate themselves in that Office to the end of Life, if they can only agree among themselves, which perhaps they may, as all may be equally anxious to continue their Political existance; in which case there can no legal redress be had, except the People fired with a just Resentment, rise like a Whirlwind & spurn them from the Earth and take the Power again into their own hands, which they may neglect to do, by being lulled asleep by the influence & popolarity of the many Court Tools which this Form of a Constitution enables the Senate to make both in the Civil & Military Department. In which case we may bid farewell to Liberty and expect nothing but the Roman Triumviri, with their bloody proscriptions. But the General Court or the whole Legislative body ought to be the judges, the danger is not so great when Power is lodged in a large Number of Mens hands as it is when lodged in a few.

Reasons against Article 11th The Selectmen & Assessors of a Town are sufficient to determine by their Lists whether a Person be a legal Voter or not, without puting a Person under a Temptation to take a false Oath—Oaths ought not to be administred except where they are absolutly necessary, because by their frequency they loose their Sacredness.

Reasons against Article 15th Not less than a majority of the Senate or House of Representatives ought to make a Quorum for the business of the State cannot be safe in the hands of any Number inferior to that; especially as those nigh the Seat of Government will always have the advantage in their hands and by watching their opportunities be enabled to carry into execution their own private views, any Number short of a Majority is not the State assembled in General Court, consequently have no just right to act for the State.

Reasons against Article 19th By this article the Senate have the sole Right of appointing all Civil Officers (except those annually chosen, with Salaries annually granted) likewise all General, Field & Staff Officers both of the Militia and Troops, likewise Captains & Subalterns of Troops which we humbly conceive is more power than can be safe in the hands of one Branch of the Legislature, it give them too great an opportunity to provide for their Connections to the injury of the Public, & which puts the Military Power in a State of dependency upon them, which power we conceive cannot be safe but immediately in the hands of the People or in the hands of the General Court according to the sense of those words in the first Article.

Reasons against Article 20th Every officer of the State ought to be liable to impeachment by any Member of the House of Representatives for male-Conduct in his office otherwise it may prove very difficult if not impossible many times to bring such offenders to justice. The People ought not to be put under such embarrisments in bringing to justice those who may wantonly abuse the Power they have intrusted them with, an Trial of Senators ought to be before the General Court, Trial by their own Body appears very pertial.

Reasons against Article 23d The Power of Granting Pardons ought not to be vested in the Governor, Lt Governor and Speaker of the House, such a small Number may be bribed by money or connections, by which the Criminal may escape with impunity to the prejudice of the State and Contempt of the Laws, but that Power ought to be vested in the Legislative Body——

Reasons against Article 24th According to which the officers therin enumerated are rendered independent both of the People & Legislature, which is making the delegated Power greater than the Constituent & independent of it, or in other words, the Creature greater than the Creator. The People have an undoubted right to be pleased with those officers who are to be their judge in all cases both of Life & property, if they are not pleased with them, the wheels of Government must move very heavily & the laudable ends of the Legislature rendered abortive.

Reasons against Article 26th The Officers therein mentioned are rendered very obnoxious to Court influence & it is to be supposed they will act accordingly & always be ready to executed & defend the Measures which may be persued by the Senate be they ever so bad. The Senate ought not to have the Power of appointing Civil or Military Officers as that will create too great a Dependency upon one Branch of the Legislature. No Officer ought to be dependent but upon the People or the Legislature, not a part, but the whole.

Reasons against Article 28th Members of Congress ought to be chosen annually by the People as the Governor is directed to be in the Form of a Constitution, admiting the emendations implied in the Objections against Article 5th—we conceive that if they are appointed agreeable to this Article, it is puting the delegated Power one degree further out of the hands of the Constituent, which is one step towards Tyranny and ought not to be done but where it would be inconvenient or impossible to be otherwise, especially in cases of such Importance to the State, Members of Congress as well as all other Officers of the State ought not to hold a plurality of Offices, the execution of which requires them to be at different Places at the same time and different requisite Talents in which case one or the other of their Duties must unavoidably be neglected, which supposes the State must be injured or that there was no need of such Offices——

Addition proposed to Article 29th we suppose no person ought to be a Member of Congress unless he is of the Protestant Religion.

Reasons against Article 32d, It is very reasonable to suppose that many of those Laws which were fraimed and enacted under the direct influence of the Crown of Great Britain (in the Governor) laboring to suppress the groth of this State and fix us for the Chain tho not repugnant to this Form of a Constitution, are very improper to be adopted in a Free State and would prove oppressive to the People, Witness the Law which obliged a poor Debtor to go through a course of Law and pay the extravigant Costs, when he was willing to confess Judgement and submit to justice, which is an oppression and Tyrannical Law and beneficial to none but attornies Pettifoggers and those connected with them. And notwithstanding the repeated efforts of every free & unbiased Representative, heretofore, to have that Law repealed & another passed in its stead, enabling the Poor Debtor to confess Judgement and save the costs, it never could be efected; because the Majority found their account in it; And what has been may be again, especially when those whoes interest it is to have it continued, are not disqualified for being Representatives. This Article declares those Streems sweet which issued from a Bitter Fountain, which is contrary to reason as well as Scripture— But the last Clause with regard to trial by Jury, appears unexceptionable, if it may be construed to be by the Peers of the Vicinage.

We furthermore suppose there ought to be a Bill of Rights, annexed to a Constitution and declared part of it, which might serve as a Clue to lead the Legislature through the otherwise intricate parts of the Constitution, Likewise we suppose that all entailments of Estates ought to be provided against in a Constitution, which is a distructive thing in a free State & like swelled Legs & an emaciated Body Symtoms of a Disolution. We further suppose that by a Constitution the printing presses ought to be declared free for any Person who might undertake to examin the proceedings of the Legislature or any part of Government.

We likewise suppose the fifth Article of this Form of a Constitution where it prohibits a Person from having a voice in the choice of Governor, Lieut. Governor & Senators if not worth sixty Pounds, is a violation of that clause of fourth Article of the Confederation of the United States of America, which declares that the free Inhabitants of each of the States, paupers, vagabonds, and fugatives from Justice excepted, shall be intitled to all priviledges and immunities of Free Citizens.

In offering the aforesaid Objections & reasons we supp[ose] we have exercised the undoubted Right of Freemen, an[d] most humbly submit them, with all their inaccuracies to your perusal——

Attest Saml Wright T Cl

Lenox May 20th 1778

23. Return of Mendon (Worcester County), May 21, 1778

[Massachusetts Archives, CLVI, 393]

To the Inhabitants of the Town of Mendon in Town meeting assembled May 21 : 1778

Gentlemen

We Your Committee Chosen and Appointed for the purpose of considering the plan or form of Government offered to the people of the State of Massachusetts Bay for their Approbation or disapprobation have mett [?] and considered the Same and Are of Oppinion that the Said plan (in Some Articles) is not So well fraimed and made as it might and ought to have been for the good, well being, and Safety, of the Natural Rights of the people Article 5th we find by Said plan that no persons Shall have the priviledges of Giving their votes for the Choice of Governor, Lieutenant Governor, nor Senators unless they are worth £60—it appears to us Unreasonable that Men Should be Governed by Laws made by a Legislature and they debased from Giving their votes in the Choice of such Legislature

article 11 it appears to us that it is very unreasonable that no person Shall be allowed to give his vote for Governor Lt. Governor or Senators (if his Qualifications is Quistioned) unless he makes oath that he is Qualified viz that he is worth £60 = Should 1-2-3 or more be Question in that Respect is it Not Likely that Every Member of the Meeting would be Qestioned and so of Conseiquence Every Member must be put upon Oath before the Election or votes Can be given in and So Great Confusion may arise Article 15th we find that 9 Senators will Make a Corum and that 5 will be a Major part, and that they will have power to Negative the house, in all Cases and so business of the Utmost Importance may be detarded untill a Greater Number of Senators be present article 17th we find that the Governor is Invested with power to Imbody the Militia of this State and Cause them to be Marched to Any part of the State for the publick Safety when he Shall think Necessary: Should it be the Misfortune of this State to Chuse a Governor that was Enemical to the people; Could not he Imbody the Militia and Cause them to be marched to one End of the State when a most vigorous Asault was planed to Attack the other end by a powerful Enemy and So the State fall a pray to an Enemy—was not our Publick Stoars Seized in the Year 1774 and the people Alarmed and Marched for Securing the Remainder but before the people Arived at the Metropilus where they were Marching the posts were Sent out to Stop them because it was Law that the Governor Should have the Care of the Military Stores and Remove them at his pleasure—

would it not be much Safer that the Governors power Should be Limited; that he Should not have power to Imbody the Militia and Cause them to marched unless upon Some Sudden Danger of an Invasion and that then they Should not be held no longer than untill the Senat Could be assembled and their Concurance——

article 32 we find that all the Statute Laws of this State, the Common Laws and all Such part of the English & British Statute Laws as have been Adopted and usually practised in the Courts of Law in this State, Shall Still Remain and be in full force untill altred or Repealed by a future Law or Laws of the Legislature it appears to us that Notwithstanding the 34 article which is (the free Exercise and Enjoyment of Religeous profession and worship Shall forever be allowed to Every Denomination of Protestants within this State)—that the Same Laws Are Still in force as formaly, and that people who are not of the Congregation perswasion are as Liable to be Taxed for the Support and maintenance of Congregational Ministers as formaly they were and that the Assessors Cannot but Tax them unless they bring in their Certificates as in Times past and it Appears to us that there is no man in this World would think that he is Used with Christian Wage if Compelled by Laws made by man To Support a Worship that is not agreeable to the Dictates of his own Conscience and way of thinking in matters of Religeon; and that the Said plan ought Not to be Approved

James Sumner Clerk of the Sd Comtee
Mendon May 7 & 21 1778

Mendon May 21st. 1778. The foregoing Report of the Towns Committee upon the Constitution, being made, and read in the Meeting,—it was thereupon

Voted, That the same should be attested by the Town Clerk, and that the same be transmitted by the Representative to the General Assembly, to the End that it might be known, for what particular Reasons the Town did not approve of the Constitution and Form of Government for the State of Massachusetts Bay, agreed upon by the Convention of said State,

24. From the Return of Sutton (Worcester County), May 18, 1778

[Massachusetts Archives, CLVI, 347-51]

We the Subscribers the committee appointed by the Inhabitants of the Town of Sutton at their Meeting, on the 13th day of April last; to draw up the Sense of the Town, as it appeared on Said Day, respecting the new form of Government, presented to the Town for their Approbation, or disapprobation; to Shew the Objections the Town have against Said Form of Government, and what the Town think would be proper, in Liew of the Things Objected against; and to make Report to the May Meeting; in order for the Town to give it as Instructions to their Representatives; at the next General Court. We the Said Committee having taken Said Matter into serious and deliberate consideration report as follows.

That there is a general Objection, against Said *Constitution and Form of Government;* because of its haveing no Article or clause against corruption or Bribery; purchasing of Seats in the Legislature; or executive Offices, places or Posts of Profit; or buying Pardons &c. But in all those Articles, which respect things of that nature; they appear to us to be wholly adapted to Such Corruption & Bribery, as will more fully appear in the discussion of the Several Articles

We are therefore of the Opinion, that there ought to be an Article of the following purport viz. that no Person be admitted, to vote for any Member of the Legislature; without first taking an Oath, that he will not vote for any person, in any measure, upon consideration of having received, or in hopes of receiving any Reward therefor, by way of Treat, loan or Gratuity; directly or indirectly; from Such person to be voted for or from any other Person, to procure Votes for him. But in all his votes or Suffrages for any Person to any Place or Office to vote for Such as he in his Conscience Judges best qualified for the Place and will best Serve the publick.

And every Member of the Legislature, Shall likewise previous to his entering upon the Business, he is elected to; make Oath that he has not by any Ways or means, directly or indirectly, made Interest for his Place, either by flattery, Threats, reward or promise of Reward.

And if it can ever be made to appear that any Person in either case, has gone contrary to Such Oath, being thereof, Presented by a Grand Jury, & convicted before the Superior Court, Such Person Shall forever be be held disqualified from holding any Seats or Offices.

The four first Articles we don't object against. But the V Art. appears to us to wear a very gross complexion of Slavery; and is diametrically repugnant to the grand and Fundamental Maxims of Humane Rights, viz. *"That Law to boind all must be assented to by all."* which this Article by no means admits of, when it excludes free men, and men of Property from a voice in the Election of Representatives; Negroes &c. are excluded even tho they are free and are men of Property. This is manifestly ading to the already accumulated Load of guilt lying upon the Land in Supporting the Slave Trade, when the poor innocent Affricans who never hurt or offered any Injury or Insult to this country have been so unjustly assaulted inhumanely Murdered many of them; to make way for [s]tealing others, and then cruelly brought from their native Land, and Sold here like Beasts. and yet now by this Constitution, if by any good Providence they or any of their Posterity, obtain their Freedom and a handsome Estate yet they must excluded the Privileges of Men! This must be the *bringing or incurring more Wrath upon us.* And it must be thought more insulting tho not So cruel, to deprive the original Natives of the Land the Privileges of Men. We also cant but observe that by this Article the Convention had in contemplation of having many more Slaves beside the Poor Africans, when they Say of others beside; being *Free* and 21 years old

We therefore think that we ought to have an Article expressive of what the State is to consist of. And to Say in express Terms that every Person within the State 21 years of age Shall have a Sole absolute Property in himself and all his earnings having an exclusive Right to make all manner contracts, and Shall So Remain until they are rendered *non compos Mentis* by lawful Authority, or have forfeited their Freedom by misdemeanour and So adjudged by Authority proper to try the Same; or their Service legally disposed of for the discharge of some Debt Damage or Trespass. And then that every Male Inhabitant free as afforesaid &c provided that Men who lie a Burden upon the publick or have little or no Property ought not to have a full or equal Vote with those that have an Estate, in voting for a Representative, for then a Representative may be chosen without any property, and as the proposed Constitution Stands there is all the chance that could be wished, for designing mischevious Men to purchase themselves Seats in the House; for poor, Shiftless Spenthriftly men & inconsiderate youngsters that have no property are cheap bought (that is) their votes easily procured to Choose a Representative to go to court, to vote away the Money of those that have Estates; and the Representative with all his constituents or Voters not pay So much Taxes as one poor *Negro, Indian or Molatto* that is not allowed to put a Single vote. Perhaps if all under what used to be voters for Representatives, were reconed each Vote equal to half one of the old voters it might be about a just and proper Medium. It is farther to be observed that this Article is grossly inconsistant with the XIV which provides that all Money Bills or Acts for levying & granting Money Shall originate Solely in the House and not be Subject to any amendment, by the Senate; when the Representatives are chosen by Persons of no Property, and there must be sixty Pound clear Estate to vote for a Governor or Senator. If men of no Property might vote for any part of the Legislature and not the whole; it ought to be that part of the Legislature which are under the greatest Restraints as to Money Bills Acts or Resolves.

Art. VI We wholly disapprove as it would make Such an unweildy House if all were to Send; and would by no Means be an equal Representation. But it is well known that all cannot and will not Send, at least to attend Steadily and So there is an unequal Representation, the House constantly Shifting which grossly retards Business, and makes what is done broken incoherent & uninteligible, and for each Town to pay its own Representatives, is a plan essentially to prevent Small Towns or even large ones at a distance from Sending any atall, and is as unjust as it would be for the Massachusetts State to pay all the cost of their Soulders and Stores going so far to the Army over & above what those States pay who are near to it, and is just the same thing; but the Soulders are doing the Service of the continent and ought to be paid out of the publick Chest, and so the Representatives from the remotest part of the State are doing the publick Service of the State and ought to be paid out of the publick Chest of the State; and not fling Such an unequal Burden upon some Towns because they happen to be at a distance from where the court Sits.

And we are confident that we Shall never have a court to the Satisfaction of the People, till this Matter is Remedied about the Representation, and there be a Rational Number concluded upon for the

House & the whole state divided into so many Representative Districts; as near as may be according to the Numbers, Freehold & Invoice at large, and let those district consisting of Sundery Towns and Parishes meet & choose by rotation in the Several Towns or Parishes of which they consist according to their Age and proportion as near as may be always choosing a Representative of the Town or Parish where they meet; and these Representatives Shall be paid for Travel and Tendance out of the publick Chest and Shall constantly attend, or if they or anyone of them leaves the court attall except in case of Sickness or Death of himself or Family, his district Shall have right immediately to Superceed him by Sending another Man or if a Representative dies or moves out of his district or is Sick for the Space of one month, so that he cant attend his District Shall have Right to Send another, these Districts to be new modled once every Seven years or as oft as a general Invoice is Taken. . . .

May 18th 1778 [The town voted unanimous approval of this report.]

25. Return of Lexington (Middlesex County), June 15, 1778

[Massachusetts Archives, CLX, 24-27]

At a legal Meeting of the Freemen of the Town of Lexington, by adjournment, on June 15, 1778. The Committee appointed by the Town to assign Reasons, why the Constitution and Form of Government, draughted & sent out by the State Honorable Convention to the Inhabitants of this State, for their Approbation or Disapprobation, is not approved and accepted by them, as also to prepare Instructions for the Representative of said Town, upon that Subject, Agreeable to a Resolve of the General Court, of said State, dated March 4 1778. reported the following Draught. Viz.——

The Freemen of the Town of Lexington, having, upon mature Consideration voted, that they do not approve of the Constitution and Form of Government, sent out by the State Honorable Convention, to the Inhabitants of this State, for their Approbation, or Disapprobation, cannot look upon it improper to Suggest some Reasons, why they could not cheerfully accept of said Constitution and Form of Government, as calculated to answer the important Ends proposed.

Accordingly, it may be observed, that it appears to Us, 'That, in emerging from a State of Nature, into a State of well regulated Society, Mankind give up some of their natural Rights, in order that others, of greater Importance, to their Well-being, safety & Happiness, both as societies & Individuals, might be the better enjoyed, secured & defended:——

'That a civil Constitution or Form of Government, is of the Nature of a most sacred Covenant, or Contract, entred into by the Individuals, which form the Society, for which such Constitution, or Form of Government is intended, whereby the[y] mutually and solemnly engage to support & defend each other, in the Enjoyment of those Rights, which they mean to retaine.——

'That the great End of establishing any Constitution or Form of Government, among a People, or in Society, is to maintain, secure and defend those retained Rights inviolate: and Consequently, 'that it is of the highist importance both to the Public Peace & Utility, and to the safety & security of Individuals, that said Rights, intended to be retained (at least those that are fundamental to the Well-being of Society & the Liberty & safety of Individuals) should be, in the most explicit Terms, declared.—And that, not only that Government, and Persons in Authority, might know their stated Limits & Bounds; but also that Subjects, and all Members of Such Societies, might know when their Rights and Liberties are infringed or violated; and have some known and established Standard to which they might, with becoming Confidence, appeal, for the (Redress of Grievances and Oppressions, whether real or supposed. And we must readily acknowledge, That the total Omission of a Declaration of Rights, of this Kind, is no small Objection to the Constitution before Us.

Next to a Declaration of Rights it is humbly conceived, That Equality of Representation, is of the greatest Importance to the Preservation of the Liberties of the Subject, and the Peace & Safety of Society. But we cannot think, that the Provission made, in this Form of Government, is adequate to this Purpose. And we are of Opinion, That it is not without grounds, to be feared, that through the Imperfections of Mankind, in some future Times, small Towns may become an easy Prey to the corrupt Influence of designing Men, to the no small Danger of the public Tranquility, as well as the Liberties of the People. As hath been frequently, and *Notoriously* the fact, in England, and many other States.

A Rotation, in the Members of the supreme Council of a Nation and the Legislative Body of a State (even where such are Elective) hath been frequently suggested, and earnestly recommended, by the best Writers on Policy and Government; and by Practice and Experience found, to be a powerful Check, to the Arts and Schemes of Ambitious and designing Men; and a Means under Providence of prolonging the Liberty, Safety & Tranquility of such States and Commonwealths, as have adopted it. Of This the Commonwealth of Rome was a striking Instance; where no Citizen could be legaly elected to the Consulship, which was the Office of the Supreme Magistrate, but once in Ten Years.—and we could have wished, that the Example of the Honorable Congress, in the Articles of Confederation, had been adopted in this Matter:—and that no Citizen of this State had been Eligible to the Office of Supreme Magistrate, or as a Member of the General Court, more than Two Years in Five, Three Years in Seven, or, at least for some limited Term

We have complained of it, in Times past, under the Charter, and still look upon it of dangerous Tendency, to have the Legislative and Executive Powers blended in the same Persons. And the Wise and judicious in all Ages have spoken of it as a very great Grievance to have, in the Supreme Council, or Legislative Body of a State, Placemen and Pensioners; Or which amounts almost to the same Thing, Persons who hold Lucretive Posts, in the Gift of that Court, or are dependent thereupon for their Offices, and the Salaries or Perquisites annexed thereunto. And we cannot persuade ourselves, that the Provision made, in this Constitution, would be an adequate Remedy.

Canvassing for Elections, corrupt Influence and open Bribery, have had the most baleful Effects, to the Subversion of Liberty and the Destruction of good government in Free States; and that in almost all Ages: and yet we cannot find anything in this Constitution, to give the least Check to Practices of this Kinde.

We could have wished, That "the inestimable Right of Trial by Jury," had been more explicitly defined.

We don't find any sufficient Provision for any Alteration, or Amendment of this Constitution, but by the General Court, or by instructing our Representatives. Whereas, it appears to Us, at least, of the highest Importance, That a Door should be left open for the People to move in this Matter; and a Way explicitly pointed out, wherein they might, Legally and Constitutionally, propose, seek & Effect, any such Alterations or Amendments, in any future Time, as might appear to them

Advantageous or Necessary.—And the rather, as this might give Satisfaction to the People; and be an happy Means, under Providence, of preventing popular Commotions, Mobs, Bloodshed and Civil War; which, too frequently, have been the Consequences of the want of Such an Opening, Which They might have legally and Constitutionally improved.

Those, in General, are a Sketch of the Reasons that have induced Us to Withhold our Approbation of the Constitution & Form of Government transmitted to Us, by the late Honorable Convention.

Wherefore, as the late General Court have explicitly recommended it, to the Several Towns in this State to instruct their Representatives upon this Subject:—The Representative of this Town is accordingly, hereby instructed and directed, to lay the Proceedings of Said Town, hereupon, with these Reasons, why this Constitution and Form of Government was not approved, before the General Court. And in Case the Establishment of this Constitution and Form of Government should be proposed in said General Court, in the Name of his Constituents, to give his Voice in the Negative.

If this Form of Government should not be established (as we have some Grounds to believe it will not) and it should be proposed, in Court, to form another We would Say,—That, Notwithstanding this Town instructed & impowered their Representative for this Purpose last Year; and Notwithstanding we earnestly hope to have a good Constitution, in due Time, established, in this State; Yet for various Reasons, which, to Us, at least, appear of Weight, we could wish to have it waved for the Present.—Not only because the Form of Government, We are now Under, as it hath done, may still answer all the Purposes of Government;—But also because it may interrupt the Deliberations of the Court upon Affairs of more immediate Concernment, to the Well-being, and perhaps to the very Existence of the State, which may demand all their Time, and all their attention;—and especially, because our Brethren, absent in the War and foremost in Toils & Danger, in the Great Contest, in which we are engaged, may think themselves not well treated in being deprived of having a Voice in so interesting an Affair.——The Representative of this Town is, therefore, for these and other obvious Reasons, hereby, further instructed, to Use his Influence to have the Matter waved, at least, for the Present.——But in Case the Court should determine to have the Matter further attempted, at present, The Representative is further instructed to use his Influence, that it may be done by a Convention, freely chosen by the People, for that Purpose, and that only.——

All which is submitted by the Said Committee

Thaddeus Bowman
John Chandler
John Bridge
Joshua Reed } Committee

The above Draught, being repeatedly read, was Voted Nemine Contradicente.

26. From the Return of Westminster (Worcester County), June 9, 1778

[Massachusetts Archives, CLX, 17]

To The Honorable The Greate and General Court Assembled att Boston May ad 15, 1778 Agreeable to the Resolve of the Late General assembly the Town of Westminster; att a Legall meeting Called for the purpose of Takeing into their Consideration, the Constitution formed by their Convention, and approved of by the Whole

Legislative Body: and Sent out for Exceptence or Rejection Haveing appointd a Committee to Consider and Report theiron: Which Committee after Duly Weighing the Contents theirof; Have Reported as follows viz That it is the opinion of the Committee that no Constitution Whatsoever ought to be Established, till previous theirto the bill of Rights be Set forth, and the Constitution formed theirfrom: That To the Lowest Capacity may be able to Determine his Natural Rights, and Judge of the acquateableness of the Constitution theirby——as to the Constitution the following articles appears to us Exceptionable viz———

Article 5th Which Deprives a part of the humane Race of their Natural Rights, mearly on account of their Couler—Which in our opinion no power on Earth has a Just Right to Doe: therefore ought to be Expunged the Constitution——

The 9th article that part Which Respects the method of Chusing the Councile, or Sennet, appears to us to be Justly Exceptionable in as much as the Greatest part of the Sennet must be appointed Without the perticuler Knoledge of the Electers; as to their Qualification or fittness, for their high and Importent office—but as to their being appointed from Seperate Destricts We have no Special objections against it—further We are of opinion that the Sennet may be Elected from and out of the house of Representitives, With much Greater Safty, then from any other body of men W[hatso]ever——. . . .

The above Report being Disstinctly Read, and on the first parrigraft With Regard to Establishing a bill of Rights previous to any Constitution being Established—Voted to Except Said Report forty Nine against Said Constitution being Excepted and not one in favour theirof ——The Remainder part of the Report being Read and Voted to Except theirof——

and The Nineteenth article being Refered by the above Said Committee to the Town for their Consideration and Determination theiron: on a motion made Voted that Said article Was Disagreeable to the Town for Reasons following Because it Deprives the people att Large, of appointing their own Rulers and officers, and places the power Where it may (and no Doubt) Will be greately abused; for once Establish a power in the hands of a Selected Number of men, and authorise them to Establish officers over the people over Whome they have no power is a Daring Step to Despotism; Even an attempt to Doe it is an appugnation of the peoples authority, and those that Doe it, Deserve the Resentment of the people att Large: the oftener power Returnes into the hands of the people the better and When for the good of the whole power is Delegated, it ought to be Done by the whole; and no officer Whatsoever from the highest to the Lowest, ought to be putt in Trust, but by the Sufferages of the people; a Neglect hear Will Enevitably prove fatal to the Liberties of amarica, We find by awefull Experience that a Neglect hearin has proved the almost Intire Loss of the Inglish Constitution: England after all her bosted privelidges (by meanes of their own Supine Neglect) Stand but one Step higher in the Seale of Liberty—then almost any power in Europe—Where Can the power be Layed So Safe as in the hands of the people? and Who Can Delegate it So Well as they? or Who has the Boldness—Without blushing? to Say the people are Not Suiteable to putt in their own officers—if So Why Doe we wast owr blood and Treasure to obtaine that which When obtained We are not fitt to Enjoy—if but a Selected few only are fitt to appoint our Rulers—Why Were We uneasie under George——againe if the General Court must be authorised to Elect all officers Will they not monopolise all places of Honour and prophet to therSelves to the Exclusion of many others perhaps as capeable as themselves—and further When they have made a band of officers perhapps Verry Disagreeable to the people, no power is Left in the people to Disband them; Saveing only a Long Worrey to obtaine an Impeachment, Which When obtained is brought before those Verry beings Who Gave them Existance; Who always may, and We bleave will have to Greate a Degree of mercy on the works of their own hands—and Leave the people to Sweat under their heavie burthens——

Then The Vote being putt Whether the above Reasons Were agreeable and it passed in the afarmetive and Voted that They be Sent to our Representitive
A True Coppy attested pr Abner Holden
Town Clerk
Westminster June 9th 1778
To Deacon Joseph Miller Representitive for The Town of Westminster——
To be Layed in the Secreterrees office &c———

27. Return of Brookline (Suffolk County), May 21, 1778

[Massachusetts Archives, CLVI, 395]

At a legal meeting of the Inhabitants of the Town of Brookline on Thursday May 21. 1778

Upon reading and considering the proposed new Form of Government; Voted, that the same is not calculated and adapted, to promote and secure in the best manner attainable, the true and lasting Happiness and Freedom of the People of this State, that it is essential to a Constitution designed for that most important and desireable End, that a full and express Declaration of the Rights of the People, be made a part thereof, and that the powers of Rulers should be accurately defined and properly limited, that as the Form proposed is almost totally deficient in those Respects and imperfect and intricate in many parts, it ought therefore to be Rejected, and this meeting consisting of forty five persons do unanimously and absolutely reject the same

28. From the Return of Belchertown (Hampshire County), May 13, 1778

[Massachusetts Archives, CLVI, 335]

——With Regard to the 5th Article, tho at present there may be no great Inconvenience in that Plan, yet we fear that in Process of Time, it will make way for Corruption & Venality, & would Query whether there ought not to be something as a Qualification for a Voter for a Representative which will more strongly influence him to Seek the publick good, especially as it is highly Probable that the state will be thronged with Foreigners.

——With Regard to the 6th Article—tho' we wish for a free & fair Representation, yet we fear that this Plan will make the House Bulky & unwieldy—& query whether the former Mode in this Province with only the addition of Liberty to each incorporated Town to send one is not preferable

29. Return of Greenwich (Hampshire County), May 3, 1778

[Massachusetts Archives, CLVI, 327]

To the Honourable the Council and House of Representatives of the State of the Massachusetts Bay Assembled,—Gentlemen

The Select-men of Greenwich, (on Receipt of a Pamphlet Intituled a Constitution and Form of Government for the State of Massachusetts Bay &c) Issued their Warrant for Calling a Town-meeting, for the Purpose of Considering Said Form of Government,

The Inhabitants being Assembled Agreable to Said Warrant, Said Form of Government was then Read and Considered, the Vote being Put whether they approved of Said Form of Government, it Passed in the Negative.

Nº of Voters at Said Meeting———111

Nº of Voters for Said Constitution——

Nº of Voters Against Said Constitution ———111

The Said Town of Greenwich at Said Meeting Voted The following as a Reason for their not Approving of the Said Form of Government (viz) Because Said Constitution and Form of Government (if Established) Intirely Divests the good People of this State of Many of the Priviledges which God and Nature has Given them, and which has been so much Contended for, and Giving away that Power to a few Individuals, which ought forever to Remain with the People inviolate, who Stile themselves free and Independant—Also Resolved——

That they will not approve of a Governor, Lieut. Governor, or Senate——

That they will approve of a General Court Consisting of One Representative Body, with a President Presiding over the Same, Annually Chosen by the People——

That they approve of all Officers both Civil & Military to be Chosen by the People.——

That they approve of One General & Commander in Chief Over the Militia of this State, to be Chosen by the People of this State—also One Admiral of the Navy

That they approve of One Court Only held in and for Each County the Officers of which to be Annually Chosen by the People of Said County,——

That they approve of One or more Justice of the Peace in Each Town annually Chosen by Said Town

That all Officers thus Chosen as above be Commissionated by the General Court afore Said——

That there be a Court of Probate of Wills &c be held in and for Each Town, the Officers of which to be annually Chosen by Said Town——

That there be a Register of Deeds for and in Each Town Annually Chosen by Said Town &c with many Other Articles, which would be Necessary In Order to the Forming a Constitution that might lay a foundation for Peace and harmony thro: this State, and forever Secure the Rights and Priviledges to the People Inviolate, to Latest Posterity, which may be more fully Pointed out to a Representative by way of Instruction that may be Chosen for that Purpose

by order & on behalf of Sd. Town

Isaac Towers
abijah Powers
Simon Stone Jr
} Selectmen of Greenwich

Greenwich May 3 - 1778

30. Return of Pittsfield (Berkshire County), May 14, 1778

[Massachusetts Archives, CLVI, 337]

Pittsfield May 14th 1778

At a meeting of the Freeholders and other inhabitants of the Town Pittsfield held for the purposes of considering of the Constitution sent to said Town for their approbation or disapprobation meet to the Number of forty seven and unanimously Voted to accept of the same except the 19th 24th & 26 Articles thier Reasons for so doing are expressed in our Instructions to our Representatives——

31. Return of Wheelersborough (Lincoln County, Maine), June 8, 1778

[Massachusetts Archives, CLX, 10]

Wheelersborough, 8th June 1778

By Virtue of a warrant Issued from the House of Representatives of the State of the Massachusetts Bay, the 4th Day of March Ultimo, Directing the Selectmen and Committees of the several Towns & Plantations in this State, to take the Votes for and against the Form of a Constitution now abroad. Agreeable to & in compliance of which Warrant, We the Select Men and Committee of this Township (Tho under the great Disadvantage of having no Book of Said Form sent us, by which we were not Able to Act 'till we could Borrow one, which happening very late involv'd us into the extreme Busy Season of Fishing and Planting; whereby a Majority of the Inhabitants were prevented from Meeting at all. Wherefore the Votes obtained were Seventeen for the Said Form of Constitution

Three——against Said Form

one——Neuter

N: B: By inquireing of those who did not meet we find the Inhabitants who did not meet are generally in Favour of the Constitution as far as they could Judge from the Verbal Account given them.

32. From the Return of Beverly (Essex County), 1778

[Massachusetts Archives, CLVI, 432]

These being the sentiments of the town, in conformity thereto, you are hereby instructed to oppose the ratification of the Plan proposed by the State Convention, & should it be voted in, when it appears a considerable part of the People are not in favor of it, to enter your Protest explicitly against it. Should the same be set aside, we expect that some other Body, distinct from the General Court, be delegated from among the People for the sole & entire purpose of forming a Bill of Rights & Constitution of Government; the 1st of which, we conceive, ought to describe the Natural Rights of Man pure as he inherits them from the Great Parent of Nature, distinguishing those, the Controul of which he may part with to Society for Social Benefits, from those He cannot; & the 2d mark out, with perspicuity & plainness, what portion of them, & on what Conditions, they are parted with, clearly defining all the Restrictions & Limitations of Government, so as to admit of no Prevarication: It should also contain a full & fixed assurance of the Equivalent to be secured in return.

33. From the Essex Result, 1778

[Theophilus Parsons, Jr., *Memoir of Theophilus Parsons* (Boston, 1859), 359-402]

Result of the Convention of Delegates holden at Ipswich in the County of Essex, who were Deputed to take into Consideration the Constitution and Form of Government proposed by the Convention of the State of Masachusetts-Bay. Newbury-Port: Printed and Sold by John Mycall. 1778.

In Convention of Delegates from the several towns of Lynn, Salem, Danvers, Wenham, Manchester, Gloucester, Ipswich, Newbury-Port, Salisbury, Methuen, Boxford, & Topsfield, holden by adjournment at Ipswich, on the twenty-ninth day of April, one thousand seven hundred & seventy-eight.

Peter Coffin Esq; in the Chair.

The Constitution and form of Government framed by the Convention of this State, was read paragraph by paragraph, and after debate, the following votes were passed.

1. That the present situation of this State renders it best, that the framing of a Constitution therefor, should be postponed 'till the public affairs are in a more peaceable and settled condition.

2. That a bill of rights, clearly ascertaining and defining the rights of conscience, and that security of person and property, which every member in the State hath a right to expect from the supreme power thereof, ought to be settled and established, previous to the ratification of any constitution for the State.

3. That the executive power in any State, ought not to have any share or voice in the legislative power in framing the laws, and therefore, that the second article of the Constitution is liable to exception.

4. That any man who is chosen Governor, ought to be properly qualified in point of property—that the qualification therefor, mentioned in the third article of the Constitution, is not sufficient—nor is the same qualification directed to be ascertained on fixed principles, as it ought to be, on account of the fluctuation of the nominal value of money, and of property.

5. That in every free Republican Government, where the legislative power is vested in an house or houses of representatives, all the members of the State ought to be equally represented.

6. That the mode of representation proposed in the sixth article of the constitution, is not so equal a representation as can reasonably be devised.

7. That therefore the mode of representation in said sixth article is exceptionable.

8. That the representation proposed in said article is also exceptionable, as it will produce an unwieldy assembly.

9. That the mode of election of Senators pointed out in the Constitution is exceptionable.

10. That the rights of conscience, and the security of person and property each member of the State is entitled to, are not ascertained and defined in the Constitution, with a precision sufficient to limit the legislative power—and therefore, that the thirteenth article of the constitution is exceptionable.

11. That the fifteenth article is exceptionable, because the numbers that constitute a quorum in the House of Representatives and Senate, are too small.

12. That the seventeenth article of the constitution is exceptionable, because the supreme executive officer is not vested with proper authority—and because an independence between the executive and legislative body is not preserved.

13. That the nineteenth article is exceptionable, because a due independence is not kept up between the supreme legislative, judicial, and executive powers, nor between any two of them.

14. That the twentieth article is exceptionable, because the supreme executive officer hath a voice, and must be present in that Court, which alone hath authority to try impeachments.

15. That the twenty second article is exceptionable, because the supreme executive power is not preserved distinct from, and independent of, the supreme legislative power.

16. That the twenty third article is exceptionable, because the power of granting pardons is not solely vested in the supreme executive power of the State.

17. That the twenty eighth article is exceptionable, because the delegates for the Continental Congress may be elected by the House of Representatives, when all the Senators may vote against the election of those who are delegated.

18. That the thirty fourth article is exceptionable, because the rights of conscience are not therein clearly defined and ascertained; and further, because the free exercise and enjoyment of religious worship is there said to be *allowed* to all the protestants in the State, when in fact, that free exercise and enjoyment is the natural and uncontroulable right of every member of the State.

A committee was then appointed to attempt the ascertaining of the true principles of government, applicable to the territory of the Massachusetts-Bay; to state the non-conformity of the constitution proposed by the Convention of this State to those principles, and to delineate the general outlines of a constitution conformable thereto; and to report the same to this Body.

This Convention was then adjourned to the twelfth day of May next, to be holden at Ipswich.

The Convention met pursuant to adjournment, and their committee presented the following report.

The committee appointed by this Convention at their last adjournment, have proceeded upon the service assigned them. With diffidence have they undertaken the several parts of their duty, and the manner in which they have executed them, they submit to the candor of this Body. When they considered of what vast consequence, the forming of a Constitution is to the members of this State, the length of time that is necessary to canvass and digest any proposed plan of government, before the establishment of it, and the consummate coolness, and solemn deliberation which should attend, not only those gentlemen who have, reposed in them, the important trust of delineating the several lines in which the various powers of government are to move, but also all those, who are to form an opinion of the execution of that trust, your committee must be excused when they express a surprise and regret, that so short a time is allowed the freemen inhabiting the territory of the Massachusetts-Bay, to revise and comprehend the form of government proposed to them by the convention of this State, to compare it with those principles on which every free government ought to be founded, and to ascertain it's conformity or non-conformity thereto. All this is necessary to be done, before a true opinion of it's merit or demerit can be formed. This opinion is to be certified within a time which, in our apprehension, is much too short for this purpose, and to be certified by a people who, during that time, have had and will have their minds perplexed and oppressed with a variety of public cares. The committee also beg leave to observe, that the constitution proposed for public approbation, was formed by gentlemen, who, at the same time, had a large share in conducting an important war, and who were employed in carrying into execution almost all the various powers of government.

The committee however proceeded in attempting the task assigned them, and the success of that attempt is now reported.

The reason and understanding of mankind, as well as the experience of all ages, confirm the truth of this proposition, that the benefits resulting to individuals from a free government, conduce much more to their happiness, than the retaining of all their natural rights in a state of nature. These benefits are greater or less, as the form of government, and the mode of exercising the supreme power of the State, are more or less conformable to those principles of equal impartial liberty, which is the property of all men from their birth as the gift of their Creator, compared with the manners and genius of the people, their occupations, customs, modes of thinking, situation, extent of country, and numbers. If the constitution and form of government are wholly repugnant to those principles, wretched are the subjects of that State. They heve surrendered a portion of their natural rights, the enjoyment of which was in some degree a blessing, and the consequence is, they find themselves stripped of the remainder. As an anodyne to compose the spirits of these slaves, and to lull them into a passively obedient state, they are told, that tyranny is preferable to no government at all; a proposition which is to be doubted, unless considered under some limitation. Surely a state of nature is more excellent than that, in which men are meanly submissive to the haughty will of an imperious tyrant, whose savage passions are not bounded by the laws of reason, religion, honor, or a regard to his subjects, and the point to which all his movements center, is the gratification of a brutal appetite. As in a state of nature much happiness cannot be enjoyed by individuals, so it has been conformable to the inclinations of almost all men, to enter into a political society so constituted, as to remove the inconveniences they were obliged to submit to in their former state, and, at the same time, to retain all those natural rights, the enjoyment of which would be consistent with the nature of a free government, and the necessary subordination to the supreme power of the state. . . .

The freemen inhabiting the territory of the Massachusetts-Bay are now forming a political society for themselves. Perhaps their situation is more favorable in some respects, for erecting a free government, than any other people were ever favored with. That attachment to old forms, which usually embarrasses, has no place amongst them. They have the history and experience of all States before them. Mankind have been toiling through ages for their information; and the philosophers and learned men of antiquity have trimmed their midnight lamps, to transmit to them instruction. We live also in an age, when the principles of political liberty, and the foundation of governments, have been freely canvassed, and fairly settled. Yet some difficulties we have to encounter. Not content with removing our attachment to the old government, perhaps we have contracted a prejudice against some part of it without foundation. The idea of liberty has been held up in so dazzling colours, that some of us may not be willing to submit to that subordination necessary in the freest States. Perhaps we may say further, that we do not consider ourselves united as brothers, with an united interest, but have fancied a clashing of interests amongst the various classes of men, and have acquired a thirst of power, and a wish of domination, over some of the community. We are contending for freedom—Let us all be equally free—It is possible, and it is just. Our interests when candidly considered are one. Let us have a constitution founded, not upon party or prejudice—not one for to-day or to-morrow—but for posterity. . . .

A republican form is the only one consonant to the feelings of the generous and brave Americans. Let us now attend to those principles, upon which all republican governments, who boast any degree of political liberty, are founded, and which must enter into the spirit of a FREE republican constitution. For all republics are not FREE.

All men are born equally free. The rights they possess at their births are equal, and of the same kind. Some of those rights are alienable, and may be parted with for an equivalent. Others are unalienable and inherent, and of that importance, that no equivalent can be received in exchange. Sometimes we shall mention the surrendering of a power to controul our natural rights, which perhaps is speaking with more precision, than when we use the expression of parting with natural rights—but the same thing is intended. Those rights which are unalienable, and of that importance, are called the rights of conscience. We have duties, for the discharge of which we are accountable to our Creator and benefactor, which no human power can cancel. What those duties are, is determinable by right reason, which may be, and is called, a well informed conscience. What this conscience dictates as our duty, is so; and that power which assumes a controul over it, is an usurper; for no consent can be pleaded to justify the controul, as any consent in this case is void. The alienation of some rights, in themselves alienable, may be also void, if the bargain is of that nature, that no equivalent can be received. Thus, if a man surrender all his alienable rights, without reserving a controul over the supreme power, or a right to resume in certain cases, the surrender is void, for he becomes a slave; and a slave can receive no equivalent. Common equity would set aside this bargain.

When men form themselves into society, and erect a body politic or State, they are to be considered as one moral whole, which is in possession of the supreme power of the State. This supreme power is composed of the powers of each individual collected together, and VOLUNTARILY parted with by him. No individual, in this case, parts with his unalienable rights, the supreme power therefore cannot controul them. Each individual also surrenders the power of controuling his natural alienable rights, ONLY WHEN THE GOOD OF THE WHOLE REQUIRES it. The supreme power therefore can do nothing but what is for the good of the whole; and when it goes beyond this line, it is a power usurped. If the individual receives an equivalent for the right of controul he has parted with, the surrender of that right is valid; if he receives no equivalent, the surrender is void, and the supreme power as it respects him is an usurper. If the supreme power is so directed and executed that he does not enjoy political liberty, it is an illegal power, and he is not bound to obey. . . .

Over the class of unalienable rights the supreme power hath no controul, and they ought to be clearly defined and ascertained in a BILL of RIGHTS, previous to the ratification of any constitution. The bill of rights should also contain the equivalent every man receives, as a consideration for the rights he has surrendered. This equivalent consists principally in the security of his person and property, and is also unassailable by the supreme power: for if the equivalent is taken back, those natural rights which were parted with to purchase it, return to the original proprietor, as nothing is more true, than that ALLEGIANCE AND PROTECTION ARE RECIPROCAL. . . .

That state, (other things being equal) which has reposed the supreme power in the hands of one or a small number of persons, is the most powerful state. An union, expedition, secrecy and dispatch are to be found only here. Where power is to be executed by a large number, there will not probably be either of the requisites just mentioned. Many men have various opinions: and each one will be tenacious of his own, as he thinks it preferable to any other; for when he thinks otherwise, it will cease to be his opinion. From this diversity of opinions results disunion; from disunion, a want of expedition and dispatch. And the larger the number to whom a secret is entrusted, the greater is the probability of it's disclosure. This inconvenience more fully strikes us when we consider that want of secrecy may prevent the successful execution of any measures, however excellently formed and digested.

But from a single person, or a very small number, we are not to expect that political honesty, and upright regard to the interest of the body of the people, and the civil rights of each individual, which are essential to a good and free constitution. For these qualities we are to go to the body of the people. The voice of the people is said to be the voice of God. No man will be so hardy and presumptuous, as to affirm the truth of that proposition in it's fullest extent. But if this is considered as the intent of it, that the people have always a disposition to promote their own happiness, and that when they have time to be informed, and the necessary means of information given them, they will be able to determine upon the necessary measures therefor, no man, of a tolerable acquaintance with mankind, will deny the truth of it. . . .

Yet, when we are forming a Constitution, by deductions that follow from established principles, (which is the only good method of forming one for futurity,) we are to look further than to the bulk of the people, for the greatest wisdom, firmness, consistency, and perseverance. These qualities will most probably be found amongst men of education and fortune. From such men we are to expect genius cultivated by reading, and all the various advantages and assistances, which art, and a liberal education aided by wealth, can furnish. From these result learning, a thorough knowledge of the interests of their country, when considered abstractedly, when compared with the neighbouring States, and when with those more remote, and an acquaintance with it's produce and manufacture, and it's exports and imports. All these are necessary to be known, in order to determine what is the true interest of any state; and without that interest is ascertained, impossible will it be to discover, whether a variety of certain laws may be beneficial or hurtful. From gentlemen whose private affairs compel them to take care of their own household, and deprive them of leisure, these qualifications are not to be generally expected, whatever class of men they are enrolled in.

Let all these respective excellencies be united. Let the supreme power be so disposed and ballanced, that the laws may have in view the interest of the whole; let them be wisely and consistently framed for that end, and firmly adhered to; and let them be executed with vigour and dispatch.

Before we proceed further, it must be again considered, and kept always in view, that we are not attempting to form a temporary constitution, one adjusted only to our present circumstances. We wish for one founded upon such principles as will secure to us freedom and happiness, however our circumstances may vary. One that will smile amidst the declensions of European and Asiatic empires, and survive the rude storms of time. It is not therefore to be understood, that all the men of fortune of the present day, are men of wisdom and learning, or that they are not. Nor that the bulk of the people, the farmers, the merchants, the tradesmen, and labourers, are all honest and upright, with single views to the public good, or that they are not. In each of the classes there are undoubtedly exceptions, as the rules laid down are general. The proposition is only this. That among gentlemen of education, fortune and leisure, we shall find the largest number of men, possessed of wisdom, learning, and a firmness and consistency of character. That among the bulk of the people, we shall find the greatest share of political honesty, probity, and a regard to the interest of the whole, of which they compose the majority. That wisdom and firmness are not sufficient without good intentions, nor the latter without the former. The conclusion is, let the legislative body unite them all. The former are called the excellencies that result from an aristocracy; the latter, those that result from a democracy.

The supreme power is considered as including the legislative, judicial, and executive powers. The nature and employment of these several powers deserve a distinct attention.

The legislative power is employed in making laws, or prescribing such rules of action to every individual in the state, as the good of the whole requires, to be conformed to by him in his conduct to the governors and governed, with respect both to their persons and property, according to the several relations he stands in. What rules of action the good of the whole requires, can be ascertained only by the majority, for a reason formerly mentioned. Therefore the legislative power must be so formed and exerted, that in prescribing any rule of action, or, in other words, enacting any law, the majority must consent. This may be more evident, when the fundamental condition on which every man enters into society, is considered. No man consented that his natural alienable rights should be wantonly controuled: they were controulable, only when that controul should be subservient to the good of the whole; and that subserviency, from the very nature of government, can be determined but by one absolute judge. The minority cannot be that judge, because then there may be two judges opposed to each other, so that this subserviency remains undetermined. Now the enacting of a law, is only the exercise of this controul over the natural alienable rights of each member of the state; and therefore this law must have the consent of the majority, or be invalid, as being contrary to the fundamental condition of the original social contract. In a state of nature, every man had the sovereign controul over his own person. He might also have, in that state, a qualified property. Whatever lands or chattels he had acquired the peaceable possession of, were exclusively his, by right of occupancy or possession. For while they were unpossessed he had a right to them equally with any other man, and therefore could not be disturbed in his possession, without being injured; for no man could lawfully dispossess him, without having a better right, which no man had. Over this qualified property every man in a state of nature had also a sovereign controul. And in entering into political society, he surrendered this right of controul over his person and property, (with an exception to the rights of conscience) to the supreme legislative power, to be exercised by that power, *when the good of the whole demanded it.* This was all the right he could surrender, being all the alienable right of which he was possessed. The only objects of legislation therefore, are the person and property of the individuals which compose the state. If the law affects only the persons of the members, the consent of a majority of any members is sufficient. If the law affects the property only, the consent of those who hold a majority of the property is enough. If it affects, (as it will very frequently, if not always,) but the person and property, the consent of a majority of the members, and of those members also who hold a majority of the property, is necessary. If the consent of the latter is not obtained, their interest is taken from them against their consent, and their boasted security of property is vanished. Those who make the law, in this case give and grant what is not theirs. The law, in it's principles, becomes a second stamp act. Lord Chatham very finely ridiculed the British house of commons upon that principle. "You can give and grant, said he, only your own. Here you give and grant, what? The property of the Americans." The people of the Massachusetts-Bay then thought his Lordship's ridicule well pointed. And would they be willing to merit the same? Certainly they will agree in the principle, should they mistake the application. The laws of the province of Massachusetts-Bay adopted the same principle, and very happily applied it. As the votes of proprietors of common and undivided lands in their meetings, can affect only their property, therefore it is enacted, that in ascertaining the majority, the votes shall be collected according to the respective interests of the proprietors. If each member, without regard to his property, has equal influence in legislation with any other, it follows, that some members enjoy greater benefits and powers in legislation than others, when these benefits and powers are compared with the rights parted with to purchase them. For the property-holder parts with the controul over his person, as well as he who hath no property, and the former also parts with the controul over his property, of which the latter is destitute. Therefore to constitute a perfect law in a free state, affecting the persons and property of the members, it is necessary that the law be for the good of the whole, which is to be determined by a majority of the members, and that majority should include those, who possess a major part of the property in the state.

The judicial power follows next after the legislative power; for it cannot act, until after laws are prescribed. Every wise legislator annexes a sanction to his laws, which is most commonly penal, (that is) a punishment either corporal or pecuniary, to be inflicted on the member who shall infringe them. It is the part of the judicial power (which in this territory has always been, and always ought to be, a court and jury) to ascertain the member who hath broken the law. Every man is to be presumed innocent, until the judicial power hath determined him guilty. When that decision is known, the law annexes the punishment, and the offender is turned over to the executive arm, by whom it is inflicted on him. The judicial power hath also to determine what legal contracts have been broken, and what member hath been injured by a violation of the law, to consider the damages that have been sustained, and to ascertain the recompense. The executive power takes care that this recompense is paid.

The executive power is sometimes divided into the external executive, and internal executive. The former comprehends war, peace, the sending and receiving ambassadors, and whatever concerns the transactions of the state with any other independent state. The confederation of the United States of America hath lopped off this branch of the executive, and placed it in Congress. We have therefore only to consider the internal executive power, which is employed in the peace, security and protection of the subject and his property, and in the defence of the state. The executive power is to marshal and command her militia and armies for her defence, to enforce the law, and to carry into execution all the orders of the legislative powers.

A little attention to the subject will convince us, that these three powers ought to be in different hands, and independent of one another, and so ballanced, and each having that check upon the other, that their independence shall be preserved—If the three powers are united, the government will be absolute, *whether these powers are in the hands of one or a large number*. The same party will be the legislator, accuser, judge and executioner; and what probability will an accused person have of an acquittal, however innocent he may be, when his judge will be also a party.

If the legislative and judicial powers are united, the maker of the law will also interpret it; and the law may then speak a language, dictated by the whims, the caprice, or the prejudice of the judge, with impunity to him—And what people are so unhappy as those, whose laws are uncertain. It will also be in the breast of the judge, when grasping after his prey, to make a retrospective law, which shall bring the unhappy offender within it; and this also he can do with impunity—The subject can have no peaceable remedy—The judge will try himself, and an acquittal is the certain consequence. He has it also in his power to enact any law, which may shelter him from deserved venegeance.

Should the executive and legislative powers be united, mischiefs the most terrible would follow. The executive would enact those laws it pleased to execute, and no others—The judicial power would be set aside as inconvenient and tardy—The security and protection of the subject would be a shadow—The executive power would make itself absolute, and the government end in a tyranny—Lewis the eleventh of France, by cunning and treachery compleated the union of the executive and legislative powers of that kingdom, and upon that union established a system of tyranny. France was formerly under a free government.

The assembly or representatives of the united states of Holland, exercise the executive and legislative powers, and the government there is absolute.

Should the executive and judicial powers be united, the subject would then have no permanent security of his person and property. The executive power would interpret the laws and bend them to his will; and, as he is the judge, he may leap over them by artful constructions, and gratify, with impunity, the most rapacious passions. Perhaps no cause in any state has contributed more to promote internal convulsions, and to stain the scaffold with it's best blood, than this unhappy union. And it is an union which the executive power in all states, hath attempted to form: if that could not be compassed, to make the judicial power dependent upon it. Indeed the dependence of any of these powers upon either of the others, which in all states has always been attempted by one or the other of them, has so often been productive of such calamities, and of the shedding of such oceans of blood, that the page of history seems to be one continued tale of human wretchedness.

The following principles now seem to be established.

1. That the supreme power is limited, and cannot controul the unalienable rights of mankind, nor resume the equivalent (that is, the security of person and property) which each individual receives, as a consideration for the alienable rights he parted with in entering into political society.

2. That these unalienable rights, and this equivalent, are to be clearly defined and ascertained in a BILL of RIGHTS, previous to the ratification of any constitution.

3. That the supreme power should be so formed and modelled, as to exert the greatest possible power, wisdom, and goodness.

4. That the legislative, judicial, and executive powers, are to be lodged in different hands, that each branch is to be independent, and further, to be so balanced, and be able to exert such checks upon the others, as will preserve it from a dependence on, or an union with them.

5. That government can exert the greatest power when it's supreme authority is vested in the hands of one or a few.

6. That the laws will be made with the greatest wisdom, and best intentions, when men, of all the several classes in the state concur in the enacting of them.

7. That a government which is so constituted, that it cannot afford a degree of political liberty nearly equal to all it's members, is not founded upon principles of

freedom and justice, and where any member enjoys no degree of political liberty, the government, so far as it respects him, is a tyranny, for he is controuled by laws to which he has never consented.

8. That the legislative power of a state hath no authority to controul the natural rights of any of it's members, unless the good of the whole requires it.

9. That a majority of the state is the only judge when the general good does require it.

10. That where the legislative power of the state is so formed, that a law may be enacted by the minority, each member of the state does not enjoy political liberty. And

11. That in a free government, a law affecting the person and property of it's members, is not valid, unless it has the consent of a majority of the members, which majority should include those, who hold a major part of the property in the state.

It may be necessary to proceed further, and notice some particular principles, which should be attended to in forming the three several powers in a free republican government.

The first important branch that comes under our consideration, is the legislative body. Was the number of the people so small, that the whole could meet together without inconvenience, the opinion of the majority would be more easily known. But, besides the inconvenience of assembling such numbers, no great advantages could follow. Sixty thousand people could not discuss with candor, and determine with deliberation. Tumults, riots, and murder would be the result. But the impracticability of forming such an assembly, renders it needless to make any further observations. The opinions and consent of the majority must be collected from persons, delegated by every freeman of the state for that purpose. Every freeman, who hath sufficient discretion, should have a voice in the election of his legislators. To speak with precision, in every free state where the power of legislation is lodged in the hands of one or more bodies of representatives elected for that purpose, the person of every member of the state, and all the property in it, ought to be represented, because they are objects of legislation. All the members of the state are qualified to make the election, unless they have not sufficient discretion, or are so situated as to have no wills of their own; persons not twenty one years old are deemed of the former class, from their want of years and experience. The municipal law of this country will not trust them with the disposition of their lands, and consigns them to the care of their parents or guardians. Women what age soever they are of, are also considered as not having a sufficient acquired discretion; not from a deficiency in their mental powers, but from the natural tenderness and delicacy of their minds, their retired mode of life, and various domestic duties. These concurring, prevent that promiscuous intercourse with the world, which is necessary to qualify them for electors. Slaves are of the latter class and have no wills. But are slaves members of a free government? We feel the absurdity, and would to God, the situation of America and the tempers of it's inhabitants were such, that the slave-holder could not be found in the land.

The rights of representation should be so equally and impartially distributed, that the representatives should have the same views, and interests with the people at large. They should think, feel, and act like them, and in fine, should be an exact miniature of their constituents. They should be (if we may use the expression) the whole body politic, with all it's property, rights, and priviledges, reduced to a smaller scale, every part being diminished in just proportion. To pursue the metaphor. If in adjusting the representation of freemen, any ten are reduced into one, all the other tens should be alike reduced: or if any hundred should be reduced to one, all the other hundreds should have just the same reduction. The representation ought also to be so adjusted, that it should be the interest of the representatives at all times, to do justice, therefore equal interest among the people, should have equal interest among the body of representatives. The majority of the representatives should also represent a majority of the people, and the legislative body should be so constructed, that every law affecting property, should have the consent of those who hold a majority of the property. The law would then be determined to be for the good of the whole by the proper judge, the majority, and the necessary consent thereto would be obtained: and all the members of the State would enjoy political liberty, and an equal degree of it. If the scale to which the body politic is to be reduced, is but a little smaller than the original, or, in other words, if a small number of freemen should be reduced to one, that is, send one representative, the number of representatives would be too large for the public good. The expences of government would be enormous. The body would be too unwieldy to deliberate with candor and coolness. The variety of opinions and oppositions would irritate the passions. Parties would be formed and factions engendered. The members would list under the banners of their respective leaders: address and intrigue would conduct the debates, and the result would tend only to promote the ambition or interest of a particular party. Such has always been in some degree, the course and event of debates instituted and managed by a large multitude.

For these reasons, some foreign politicians have laid it down as a rule, that no body of men larger than a hundred, would transact business well: and Lord Chesterfield called the British house of commons a mere mob, because of the number of men which composed it.

Elections ought also to be free. No bribery, corruption, or undue influence should have place. They stifle the free voice of the people, corrupt their morals, and introduce a degeneracy of manners, a supineness of temper, and an inattention to their liberties, which pave the road for the approach of tyranny, in all it's frightful forms. . . .

The rights of representation should also be held sacred and inviolable, and for this purpose, representation should be fixed upon known and easy principles; and the constitution should make provision, that recourse should constantly be had to those principles within a very small period of years, to rectify the errors that will creep in through lapse of time, or alteration of situations. The want of fixed principles of government, and a stated regular recourse to them, have produced the dissolution of all states, whose constitutions have been transmitted to us by history.

But the legislative power must not be trusted with one assembly. A single assembly is frequently influenced by the vices, follies, passions, and prejudices of an individual. It is liable to be avaricious, and to exempt itself from the burdens it lays upon it's constituents. It is subject to ambition, and after a series of years, will be prompted to vote itself perpetual. The long parliament in England voted itself perpetual, and thereby, for a time, destroyed the political liberty of the subject. Holland was governed by one representative assembly annually elected. They afterwards voted themselves from annual to septennial; then for life; and finally exerted the power of filling up all vacancies, without application to their constituents. The government of Holland is now a tyranny *though a republic.*

The result of a single assembly will be hasty and indigested, and their judgments frequently absurd and inconsistent. There must be a second body to revise with coolness and wisdom, and to controul with firmness, independent upon the first, either for their creation, or existence. Yet the first must retain a right to a similar revision and controul over the second.

Let us now ascertain some particular principles which should be attended to, in forming the executive power.

When we recollect the nature and employment of this power, we find that it ought to be conducted with vigour and dispatch. It should be able to execute the laws without opposition, and to controul all the turbulent spirits in the state, who should infringe them. If the laws are not obeyed, the legislative power is vain, and the judicial is mere pageantry. As these laws, with their several sanctions, are the only securities of person and property, the members of the state can confide in, if they lie dormant through failure of execution, violence and oppression will erect their heads, and stalk unmolested through the land. The judicial power ought to discriminate the offender, as soon after the commission of the offence, as an impartial trial will admit; and the executive arm to inflict the punishment immediately after the criminal is ascertained. This would have an happy tendency to prevent crimes, as the commission of them would awaken the attendant idea of punishment; and the hope of an escape, which is often an inducement, would be cut off. The executive power ought therefore in these cases, to be exerted with union, vigour, and dispatch. Another duty of that power is to arrest offenders, to bring them to trial. This cannot often be done, unless secrecy and expedition are used. The want of these two requisites, will be more especially inconvenient in repressing treasons, and those more enormous offences which strike at the happiness, if not existence of the whole. Offenders of these classes do not act alone. Some number is necessary to the compleating of the crime. Cabals are formed with art, and secrecy presides over their councils; while measures the most fatal are the result, to be executed by desperation. On these men the thunder of the state should be hurled with rapidity; for if they hear it roll at a distance, their danger is over. When they gain intelligence of the process, they abscond, and wait a more favourable opportunity. If that is attended with difficulty, they destroy all the evidence of their guilt, brave government, and deride the justice and power of the state.

It has been observed likewise, that the executive power is to act as Captain-General, to marshal the militia and armies of the state, and, for her defence, to lead them on to battle. These armies should always be composed of the militia or body of the people. Standing armies are a tremendous curse to a state. In all periods in which they have existed, they have been the scourge of mankind. In this department, union, vigour, secrecy, and dispatch are more peculiarly necessary. Was one to propose a body of militia, over which two Generals, with equal authority, should have the command, he would be laughed at. Should one pretend, that the General should have no controul over his subordinate officers, either to remove them or to supply their posts, he would be pitied for his ignorance of the subject he was discussing. It is obviously necessary, that the man who calls the militia to action, and assumes the military controul over them in the field, should previously know the number of his men, their equipments and residence, and the talents and tempers of the several ranks of officers, and their respective departments in the state, that he may wisely determine to whom the necessary orders are to be issued. Regular and particular returns of these requisites should be frequently made. Let it be enquired, are these returns to be made only to the legislative body, or a branch of it, which necessarily moves slow?—Is the General to go to them for information? intreat them to remove an improper officer, and give him another they shall chuse? and in fine is he to supplicate his orders from them, and constantly walk where their leading-strings shall direct his steps? If so, where are the power and force of the militia—where the union—where the dispatch and profound secrecy? Or shall these returns be made to him?—when he may see with his own eyes—be his own judge of the merit, or demerit of his officers—discern their various talents and qualifications, and employ them as the service and defence of his country demand. Besides, the legislative body or a branch of it is local—they cannot therefore personally inform themselves of these facts, but must judge upon trust. The General's opinion will be founded upon his own observations—the officers and privates of the militia will act under his eye: and, if he has it in his power immediately to promote or disgrace them, they will be induced to noble exertions. It may further be observed here, that if the subordinate civil or military executive officers are appointed by the legislative body or a branch of it, the former will become dependent upon the latter, and the necessary independence of either the legislative or executive powers upon the other is wanting. The legislative power will have that undue influence over the executive which will amount to a controul, for the latter will be their creatures, and will fear their creators.

One further observation may be pertinent. Such is the temper of mankind, that each man will be too liable to introduce his own friends and connexions into office, without regarding the public interest. If one man or a small number appoint, their connexions will probably be introduced. If a large number appoint, all their connexions will receive the same favour. The smaller the number appointing, the more contracted are their connexions, and for that reason, there will be a greater probability of better officers, as the connexions of one man or a very small number can fill but a very few of the offices. When a small number of men have the power of appointment, or the management in any particular department, their conduct is accurately noticed. On any miscarriage or imprudence the public resentment lies with weight. All the eyes of the people are converted to a point, and produce that attention to their censure, and that fear of misbehaviour, which are the greatest security the state can have, of the wisdom and prudence of its servants. This observation will strike us, when we recollect that many a man will zealously promote an affair in a public assembly, of which he is but one of a large number, yet, at the same time, he would blush to be thought the sole author of it. For all these reasons, the supreme executive power should be rested in the hands of one or of a small number, who should have the appointment of all subordinate executive officers. Should the supreme executive officer be elected by the legislative body, there would be a dependence of the executive power upon the legislative. Should he be elected by the judicial body, there also would be a dependence. The people at large must therefore designate the person, to whom they will delegate this power. And upon the people, there ought to be a dependence of all the powers in government, for all the officers in the state are but the servants of the people.

We have not noticed the navy-department. The conducting of that department is indisputably in the supreme executive power: and we suppose, that all the observations respecting the Captain-General, apply to the Admiral.

We are next to fix upon some general rules which should govern us in forming the judicial power. This power is to be independent upon the executive and legislative. The judicial power should be a court and jury, or as they are commonly called, the Judges and jury. The jury are the peers or equals of every man, and are to try all facts. The province of the Judges is to preside in and regulate all trials, and ascertain the law. We shall only consider the appointment of the Judges. The same power which appoints them, ought not to have the power of removing them, not even for misbehavior. That conduct only would then be deemed misbehavior which was opposed to the will of the power removing. A removal in this case for proper reasons, would not be often attainable: for to remove a man from an office, because he is not properly qualified to discharge the duties of it, is a severe censure upon that man or body of men who appointed him—and mankind do not love to censure themselves. Whoever appoints the judges, they ought not to be removable at pleasure, for they will then feel a dependence upon that man or body of men who hath the power of removal. Nor ought they to be dependent upon either the executive or legislative power for their salaries; for if they are, that power on whom they are thus dependent, can starve them into a compliance. One of these two powers should appoint, and the other remove. The legislative will not probably appoint so good men as the executive, for reasons formerly mentioned. The former are composed of a large body of men who have a numerous train of friends and connexions, and they do not hazard their reputations, which the executive will. It has often been mentioned that where a large body of men are responsible for any measures, a regard to their reputations, and to the public opinion, will not prompt them to use that care and precaution, which such regard will prompt one or a few to make use of. Let one more observation be now introduced to confirm it. Every man has some friends and dependents who will endeavor to snatch him from the public hatred. One man has but a few comparatively, they are not numerous enough to protect him, and he falls a victim to his own misconduct. When measures are conducted by a large number, their friends and connexions are numerous and noisy—they are dispersed through the State—their clamors stifle the execrations of the people, whose groans cannot even be heard. But to resume, neither will the executive body be the most proper judge when to remove. If this body is judge, it must also be the accuser, or the legislative body, or a branch of it, must be—If the executive body complains, it will be both accuser and judge—If the complaint is preferred by the legislative body, or a branch of it, when the judges are appointed by the legislative body, then a body of men who were concerned in the appointment, must in most cases complain of the impropriety of their own appointment. Let therefore the judges be appointed by the executive body—let their salaries be independent—and let them hold their places during good behaviour—Let their misbehaviour be determinable by the legislative body—Let one branch thereof impeach, and the other judge. Upon these principles the judicial body will be independent so long as they behave well and a proper court is appointed to ascertain their mal-conduct.

The Committee afterwards proceeded to consider the Constitution framed by the Convention of this State. They have examined that Constitution with all the care the shortness of the time would admit. And they are compelled, though reluctantly to say, that some of the principles upon which it is founded, appeared to them inconsonant, not only to the natural rights of mankind, but to the fundamental condition of the original social contract, and the principles of a free republican government. In that form of government the governor appears to be the supreme executive officer, and the legislative power is in an house of representatives and senate. It may be necessary to descend to a more particular consideration of the several articles of that constitution.

The second article thereof appears exceptionable upon the principles we have already attempted to establish, because the supreme executive officer hath a seat and voice in one branch of the legislative body, and is assisting in originating and framing the laws, the Governor being entitled to a seat and voice in the Senate, and to preside in it, and may thereby have that influence in the legislative body, which the supreme executive officer ought not to have.

The third article among other things, ascertains the qualifications of the Governor, Lieutenant Governor, Senators and Representatives respecting property—The estate sufficient to qualify a man for Governor is so small, it is hardly any qualification at all. Further, the method of ascertaining the value of the estates of the officers aforesaid is vague and uncertain as it depends upon the nature and quantity of the currency, and the encrease of property, and not upon any fixed principles. This article therefore appears to be exceptionable.

The sixth article regulates the election of representatives. So many objections present themselves to this article, we are at a loss which first to mention. The representation is grossly unequal, and it is flagrantly unjust. It violates the fundamental principle of the original social contract, and introduces an unwieldy and expensive house. Representation ought to be equal upon the principles formerly mentioned. By this article any corporation, however small, may send one representative, while no corporation can send more than one, unless it has three hundred freemen. Twenty corporations (of three hundred freemen in each) containing in the whole six thousand freemen, may send forty representatives, when one corporation, which shall contain six thousand two hundred and twenty, can send but nineteen. One third of the state may send a majority of the representatives, and all the laws may be enacted by a minority—Do all the members of the state then, enjoy political liberty? Will they not be controuled by laws enacted against their consent? When we go further and find, that sixty members make an house, and that the concurrence of thirty one (which is about one twelfth of what may be the present number of representatives) is sufficient to bind the persons and properties of the members of the State, we stand amazed, and are sorry that any well disposed Americans were so inattentive to the consequences of such an arrangement.

The number of representatives is too large to debate with coolness and deliberation, the public business will be protracted to an undue length and the pay of the house is enormous. As the number of freemen in the state encreases, these inconveniences will encrease; and in a century, the house of representatives will, from their numbers, be a mere mob. Observations upon this article croud upon us, but we will dismiss it, with wishing that the mode of representation there proposed, may be candidly compared with the principles which have been already mentioned in the course of our observations upon the legislative power, and upon representation in a free republic.

The ninth article regulates the election of Senators, which we think exceptionable. As the Senators for each district will be elected by all the freemen in the state properly qualified, a trust is reposed in the people which they are unequal to. The freemen in the late province of Main, are to give in their votes for senators in the western district, and so, on the contrary. Is it supposeable that the freemen in the county of Lincoln can judge of the political merits of a senator in Berkshire? Must not the several corporations in the state, in a great measure depend upon their representatives for information? And will not the house of representatives in fact chuse the senators? That independence of the senate upon the house, which the constitution seems to have intended, is visionary, and the benefits which were expected to result from a senate, as one distinct branch of the legislative body, will not be discoverable.

The tenth article prescribes the method in which the Governor is to be elected. This method is open to, and will introduce bribery and corruption, and also originate parties and factions in the state. The Governor of Rhode-Island was formerly elected in this manner, and we all know how long a late Governor there, procured his re-election by methods the most unjustifiable. Bribery was attempted in an open and flagrant manner.

The thirteenth article ascertains the authority of the general court, and by that article we find their power is limited only by the several articles of the constitution. We do not find that the rights of conscience are ascertained and defined, unless they may be thought to be in the thirty fourth article. That article we conceive to be expressed in very loose and uncertain terms. What is a *religious* profession and worship of God, has been disputed for sixteen hundred years, and the various sects of christians have not yet settled the dispute. What is a free exercise and enjoyment of religious worship has been, and still is, a subject of much altercation. And this free exercise and enjoyment is said to be *allowed* to the protestants of this state by the constitution, when we suppose it to be an unalienable right of all mankind, which no human power can wrest from them. We dō not find any bill of rights either accompanying the constitution, or interwoven with it, and no attempt is made to define and secure that protection of the person and property of the members of the state, which the legislative and executive bodies cannot withhold, unless the general words *of confirming the right to trial by jury,* should be considered as such definition and security. We think a bill of rights ascertaining and clearly describing the rights of conscience, and that security of person and property, the supreme power of the state is bound to afford to all the members thereof, ought to be fully ratified, before, or at the same time with, the establishment of any constitution.

The fifteenth article fixes the number which shall constitute a quorum in the senate and house of representatives—We think these numbers much too small—This constitution will immediately introduce about three hundred and sixty members into the house. If sixty make a quorum, the house may totally change its members six different times; and it probably will very often in the course of a long session, be composed of such a variety of members, as will retard the public business, and introduce confusion in the debates, and inconsistency in the result. Besides the number of members, whose concurrence is necessary to enact a law, is so small, that the subjects of the state will have no security, that the laws which are to controul their natural rights, have the consent of a majority of the freemen. The same reasoning applies to the senate, though not so strikingly, as a quorum of that body must consist of nearly a third of the senators.

The eighteenth article describes the several powers of the Governor or the supreme executive officer. We find in comparing the several articles of the constitution, that the senate are the only court to try impeachments. We also conceive that every officer in the state ought to be amenable to such court. We think therefore that the members of that court ought never to be advisory to any officer in the state. If their advice is the result of inattention or corruption, they cannot be brought to punishment by impeachment, as they will be their own judges. Neither will the officer who pursues their advice be often, if ever, punishable, for a similar reason. To condemn this officer will be to reprobate their own advice—consequently a proper body is not formed to advise the Governor, when a sudden emergency may render advice expedient: for the senate advise, and are the court to try impeachments. We would now make one further observation, that we cannot discover in this article or in any part of the constitution that the executive power is entrusted with a check upon the legislative power, sufficient to prevent the encroachment of the latter upon the former—Without this check the legislative power will exercise the executive, and in a series of years the government will be as absolute as that of Holland.

The nineteenth article regulates the appointment of the several classes of officers. And we find that almost all the officers are appointed by the Governor and Senate. An objection formerly made occurs here. The Senate with the Governor are the court to remove these officers for misbehaviour. Those officers, in general, who are guilty of male-conduct in the execution of their office, were improper men to be appointed. Sufficient care was not taken in ascertaining their political military or moral qualifications. Will the senators therefore if they appoint, be a proper court to remove. Will not a regard to their own characters have an undue bias upon them. This objection will grow stronger, if we may suppose that the time will come when a man may procure his appointment to office by bribery. The members of that court therefore who alone can remove for misbehaviour, should not be concerned in the appointment. Besides, if one branch of the legislative body appoint the executive officers, and the same branch alone can remove them, the legislative power will acquire an undue influence over the executive.

The twenty second article describes the authority the Governor shall have in all business to be transacted by him and the Senate. The Governor by this article must be present in conducting an impeachment. He has it therefore in his power to rescue a favourite from impeachment, so long as he is Governor, by absenting himself from the Senate, whenever the impeachment is to be brought forwards.

We cannot conceive upon what principles the twenty third article ascertains the speaker of the house to be one of the three, the majority of whom have the power of granting pardons. The speaker is an officer of one branch of the legislative body, and hourly depends upon them for his existence in that character—he therefore would not probably be disposed to offend any leading party in the house, by consenting to, or denying a pardon. An undue influence might prevail and the power of pardoning be improperly exercised.—When the speaker is guilty of this improper exercise, he cannot be punished but by impeachment, and as he is commonly a favourite of a considerable party in the house, it will be difficult to procure the accusation; for his party will support him.

The judges by the twenty fourth article are to hold their places during good behaviour, but we do not find that their salaries are any where directed to be fixed. The house of representatives may therefore starve them into a state of dependence.

The twenty-eighth article determines the mode of electing and removing the delegates for Congress. It is by joint ballot of the house and Senate. These delegates should be some of the best men in the State. Their abilities and characters should be thoroughly investigated. This will be more effectually done, if they are elected by the legislative body, each branch having a right to originate or negative the choice, and removal. And we cannot conceive why they should not be elected in this manner, as well as all officers who are annually appointed with annual grants of their sallaries, as is directed in the nineteenth article. By the mode of election now excepted against, the house may choose their delegates, altho' every Senator should vote against their choice.

The thirty-fourth article respecting liberty of conscience, we think exceptionable, but the observations necessary to be made thereon, were introduced in animadverting upon the thirteenth article.

The Committee have purposely been as concise as possible in their observations upon the Constitution proposed by the Convention of this State—Where they thought it was non-conformable to the principles of a free republican government, they have ventured to point out the non-conformity—Where they thought it was repugnant to the original social contract, they have taken the liberty to suggest that repugnance—And where they were persuaded it was founded in political injustice, they have dared to assert it. . . .

[There follows a detailed scheme for the legislative, executive and judicial branches of government.][1]

The committee have only further to report, that the inhabitants of the several towns who deputed delegates for this convention, be seriously advised, and solemnly exhorted, as they value the political freedom and happiness of themselves and of their posterity, to convene all the freemen of their several towns in town meeting, for this purpose regularly notified, and that they do unanimously vote their disapprobation of the constitution and form of government, framed by the convention of this state; that a regular return of the same be made to the secretary's office, that it may there remain a grateful monument to our posterity of that consistent, impartial and persevering attachment to political, religious, and civil liberty, which actuated their fathers, and in defence of which, they bravely fought, chearfully bled, and gloriously died.

The above report being read was accepted.

Attest, PETER COFFIN, *Chairman.*

1. Proposed franchise qualifications for electing senators were, "Let every freeman whose estate pays such a proportion of the state-tax that had been assessed previous to his electing, as three pounds is to an hundred thousand pounds, be an elector. . . ." For governor, "Every freeman in the State should have a voice in this formation; for as the executive power hath no controul over property, but in pursuance of established laws, the consent of the property-holders need not be considered as necessary."

CHAPTER V

THE CONSTITUTIONALISTS DEMAND ACTION

After the rejection of the Constitution of 1778, most parts of the state were content to await further developments. Only the Constitutionalists continued systematic pressure on the provisional government. When the General Court early in 1778 had ordered the re-opening of Berkshire's Quarter Sessions courts, Pittsfield had remained defiant, and in August the town called a convention for a formal vote to decide whether the county should permit courts to operate. At this convention the Constitutionalists won a clear victory over their opponents, and the courts in the county remained closed.

From the very beginning the Constitutionalists had insisted that no government could exist without the direct sanction of the people. Keeping the courts closed was their way of forcing political authority to legitimatize itself. In a petition to the General Court, the Pittsfield convention suggested that it might have been well had the courts elsewhere not re-opened "rather than to have Law dealt out by piece meal as it is this Day, without any Foundation to support it, for We doubt not we should before this time have had a Bill of rights, and a Constitution" (No. 34). Unquestionably some of the Constitutionalists stood to benefit from closed courts, for, as long as the courts did not function, hard-pressed farmers could escape suits for debt. Indeed, a debtor outlook was apparent in the earliest petitions from Pittsfield (see Chapter II). Still, there is no reason to doubt the Constitutionalists' concern with issues larger than selfish ones. In the petition of August 1778 they pleaded for a convention specially elected to form a constitution, thus adding their weight to the growing demand for a true constitutional convention. Somewhat petulantly, perhaps, their petition wound up threatening secession: "If this our request is rejected We shall endeavour by addressing the first Committee of Safety etc. in this State & others, that there be a State Convention formed for the purpose aforesaid—And if this Honourable Court are for dismembering there are other States, which have Constitutions who will We doubt not, as bad as we are, gladly receive Us. . . ." But no one can mistake the ring of sincerity in their petition expressing a fear of "being thrown into confusion & divisions by delaying the formation of a new Constitution" (No. 36).

The Pittsfield convention of August informed neighboring counties of its action in petitioning the General Court. Northampton, acknowledged leader of the committees of Hampshire towns, made no response; courts had already begun to operate in that county. But the town of Worcester in the central part of the state responded tartly, finding it incredible that a minority could defy the majority in the name of liberty (No. 35). The General Court decided to send out an investigating committee empowered to call together representatives of Berkshire towns to state their grievances. When the committee arrived in the county on November 17, 1778, Pittsfield had already lined up its support and was ready with a long defense of its position (No. 36). In it the Constitutionalists reiterate their belief that only the "approbation of the Majority" can breathe life into a constitution, which must be the foundation of legislation, and that "the Compact in this state is not yet formed." After this, the address assumes a mollifying tone: "Nor will any of those consequences follow on this supposition, that we have no Law, or that the Honourable Council & House of Representatives are Usurpers & Tyrants. Far from it. We consider our case as very Extraordinary. We do not consider this state in all Respects as in a state of Nature though destitute of such fundamental Constitution." Possibly the Constitutionalists here are taking into account an "Address to the Inhabitants of Berkshire" (No. 37), published in October 1778, which castigated the Constitutionalists for their seditious committees and mob violence. The author, following the fashion of many theorists on natural rights, distinguishes three conditions: a state of nature, organized society based on majority rule, and full constitutional government.

During its investigation, the General Court's committee asked the delegates from Berkshire towns whether they regarded the "present constitution as valid" and themselves as bound to abide by it until a new one was adopted. The number of *yeas* caused the committee to report that "if proper Civil Officers Should soon be Appointed in such County of Berksheir . . . the Clamours about Executive Courts there, would very soon subside."[1] In accordance with this view, the General Court passed an act to pardon past riots, and the Council proceeded to appoint four judges for the court of common pleas. For good measure, the Superior Court was to meet in Berkshire annually.

It turned out that the optimism of the investigating committee was unwarranted. The Constitutionalists saw the re-opening of the county courts and the meeting of the Superior Court as a threat to their cause. Riots and turmoil continued in Berkshire, and the issue of whether or not Massachusetts had a government that should be obeyed remained a burning one. Submission to orders from Boston would give a sanction to the provisional government

1. *Acts and Resolves of the Province of Massachusetts-Bay,* V, 1032.

that the Constitutionalists desired to avoid at all costs. Moreover, with the General Court now asking the towns for a new vote on calling a constitutional convention (see Chapter VI), the Constitutionalists feared a weakening in their ranks. Consequently a convention meeting in Pittsfield requested Berkshire towns to vote on whether they thought Massachusetts had indeed a constitution binding on the people and whether the orders of the General Court should be accepted.

Two different groups in Stockbridge sought action on the Pittsfield proposal (Nos. 38A and B). To give some idea of the economic status of these two sets of petitioners, an assessors' list for 1778 is included (No. 39). Assessment on "faculty" was an assessment made on one's trade or profession. Both groups of petitioners received recognition in the warrant calling a town meeting for March 22, 1779 (No. 40); but one will observe that constitutional issues did not completely overshadow matters of local concern. Among other things, the question of whether swine should be permitted to run at large continued to be a perennial problem. Stockbridge voted twice on the question that Pittsfield had raised (Nos. 41 and 42). In the neighboring county of Hampshire, Pittsfield still had some support, but that county was by no means unanimous (Nos. 43 and 44). Chesterfield's call for action reveals rather vividly a fear of "designing men" delaying a bill of rights and a constitution for their wicked ends—a theme that ran through the writings of the Constitutionalists from the beginning. In May 1779, when the Superior Court arrived in Berkshire to hold a session recently authorized by the General Court, a polite but firm crowd successfully persuaded the justices not to sit. The crowd's address to the court (No. 45) examines once again the question of whether the advice of the Continental Congress could sanction the provisional government.

QUESTIONS

1. Why was the petition of August 26 from Berkshire more likely to get action than the earlier petitions from Pittsfield? Are there any notable differences in content between this and the earlier ones?

2. What various reasons does Worcester advance for opposing the views of Pittsfield?

3. To what degree does Pittsfield answer Worcester in its letter to the committee sent out by the General Court? Does Pittsfield leave any of Worcester's points unanswered?

4. What telling points does an "Address to the Inhabitants of Berkshire" make against the theoretical position of the Constitutionalists?

5. Which article submitted for inclusion in the warrant for a Stockbridge town meeting was prepared by supporters of the Constitutionalists? Which by their opponents?

6. Compare the names on the tax list with the names attached to the articles meant to be included in the warrant. Is there evidence here for possible class conflict? Are there suggestions of class conflict elsewhere in this group of documents?

7. Where is it implied that delay in securing a constitution is deliberate and with evil intent?

8. What attitude did the majority in Hampshire County apparently take toward the Constitutionalists?

9. What argument is now advanced by the Constitutionalists regarding Congressional sanction for the existing government of Massachusetts?

Berkshire Insists on Constitutional Government

34. A Berkshire Petition to the General Court, Pittsfield, August 26, 1778

[*Acts and Resolves, Public and Private, of the Province of Massachusetts Bay,* V, 1028-29]

We the subscribers Delegates from the several Towns in the County of Berkshire, chosen & appointed for the Special purpose of Petitioning the Great and General Court to call a special convention of Delegates from each Town in this State, for the purpose of forming a Bill of rights & a Constitution or form of Government—Humbly shew——

That your Memorialists have from the time of the Stamp Act to this present Day, manifested a constant and uniform Abhorrence and Destestation (not only in Sentiment but overt Actions) of all the Unconstitional Measures taken by the British Parliament to tax, depauperate and Subjugate these now United and Independent States of America——

That they can Vie with any County in this State not only in Voluntarily appearing in Arms upon the least notice, when their Brethren in Distress needed their Assistance as at the Massacre at Lexington, the Fight at Bunkers Hill &c. &c. But also in filling up their Quotas of Men from time to time, demanded either by this State or the Commanding Officer in these Parts: although our Situation has been such, as might have justified the General Court had they called upon Us for no such supplies, over and above which our Zeal in the Common Cause has carried Us beyond our Ability in the frequent Excursions against the Common Enemy, as in the Battle of Bennington, in assisting Colonel Brown in the Capture of so many Hundreds at the Carrying place at Tyconderoga, in the quelling the Tories at divers times in a Neighbouring States, which otherwise, might have suffered amazingly, and in instances of the like Nature too many to enumerate——

Notwithstanding this Our Fidelity to the State and our exertions for the Common Cauze. We have by designing and disaffected Men been represented as a Mobbish, Ungovernable refractory, licentious and dissolute People, by means whereof have been threatned with Dismemberment, more especially, as we conceive, on Account of our not admitting the Course of common Law——

It is true we were the first County that put a Stop to Courts, and were soon followed by many others, Nay in effect by the whole State—And we are not certain but that it might have been as well (if not better) had they continued so, rather than to have Law dealt out by piece meal as it is this Day, without any Foundation to support it, for We doubt not we should before this time have had a Bill of rights, and a Constitution which are the only things, We at this time are empowered to pray for—And We do now with the greatest Deference Petition your Honors, that you would issue your Precepts to all the Towns and places within this State (called upon to pay public Taxes) requiring them to choose Delegates to set as soon as may be in some suitable place to form a Bill of Rights and a Constitution for this State, without which We shall retain the aforesaid Character, if grounded upon the Non-admission Law, as abundantly appears to Us this Day by the Yeas and Nays, brought in from the respective Towns We represent, taken in Town Meeting, especially called for that purpose, there being four fifths of the Inhabitants of said County against supporting the Courts of Law, untill a Constitution be formed and Accepted by the people——

If this our request is rejected We shall endeavour by addressing the first Committee of Safety &c. in this State & others, that there be a State Convention formed for the purpose aforesaid—And if this Honourable Court are for dismembering there are other States, which have Constitutions who will We doubt not, as bad as we are, gladly receive Us; And We shall to the utmost of our Ability support and defend authority and Law as we should with greater Cheerfulness in this State to which We belong was there any proper Foundation for it——

We are with all Submission your Honors youngest Child and are determined to the utmost of our Power to protect and secure our just Inheritance, and hope our parent will graciously concur and assist by granting this our request. And as in Duty bound will ever pray—

Ezra Fellows,—	Sheffield
William Whiting—	G. Barrington
Joseph Chaffee Daniel Kenne	Partridgefield
Elisha Baker.	Williamston
Jabez Ward Caleb Wright	N. Marlboro'
Jonathan Smith James Harris	Lanesborough
William Williams Valentine Rathbone Enoch Root—	Pittsfield
Caleb Hyde William Walker	Lenox
Asa Bement	Stockbridge
Jabez Holden—	Sandisfield
Joseph Pierce John Burrows	Gageboro'
William Douglas—	Hancock,
Benjamen Pierson—	Richmond
Smith Marcy	Loudon
Eusebius Bushnell George Sloan—	Washington
Joseph Gilbert—	Alfred
Jesse Bradley—	Lee
Benjamen Taylor—	New Ashford—

35. Worcester Answers Pittsfield, October 8, 1778

[William Williams Collection, Berkshire Athenaeum, 376-79]

To the Committee of Correspondence &c for the town of Pittsfield in the County of Berkshire,

Gentlemen:

William Young Esqr delivered us a Letter for our Consideration from you, by which we are informed that a Convention of the Several Committees of that County sat there on the 12th of August last, in order to know and determine, whether that County was for opening and supporting the Courts of Quarter Sessions and Common Pleas, untill a new Constitution should be formed and accepted by the people: and that you were by them appointed to write to the Committees in Hampshire and this County.

We are told that by the reccommendation of that Convention, the Several towns in your County met and determined the Question by Yeas and Nays, and that four fifths were against supporting the Courts under the present Constitution. Likewise, that the several towns, at the same time chose delegates, who met there on the 26th of the same month, and petitioned the General Court, that they would issue their precepts to all the towns and places, within this State (called upon to pay public taxes) requiring them to chuse delegates to set as soon as may be, in some convenient place, to form a bill of Rights and a Constitution for this State; assuring them that if this request should be rejected, they should endeavour by advising the first Commissioner of Safety in this State and others, that there be a State Convention formed for that purpose &c. The import of which appears to us to be of such Consequence to the Public, that we think it our duty to write you our sentiments upon it, which we request you to communicate to your next County Convention. As Corporate parts of the same Community, or as individuals, we consider ourselves entitled to no preheminence, as an "elder Brother," but as having at all times an equal and common right to offer each other our opinions; we shall, therefore, speek with the freedom of independent Americans. We cannot agree with you, Gentlemen, with respect to the non-admission of the Courts of Quarter Sessions and Common Pleas, untill the formation and acceptance of a new Constitution. Our opinion, we hope will appear to be founded in reason, and consistant with the interest of America and the liberties of Mankind. That Power, which declared these States independent, by whose wisdom, patriotism and prudence we find ourselves in a situation, which perhaps no people on earth were ever in before, that of forming for ourselves a Constitution from the formation, reccommended it to this State to adhere, as near as possible to their antient forms and Constitution, untill a new one should be formed and established. In consequence of which reccommendation, the authority of this State immediately restored the Several executive Courts of Justice, which by law were before appointed to be held in it. The people sanctified the measure by their consent, it therefor is constitutional so long as such consent shall continue, as the Consent of a Majority of the State: For it is a principal laid down by some of the best political writers, that what ever, in government, is publicly allowed at any perticular period, has been regularly and openly introduced and established by the approbation of the majority of those who have the power of establishing it is constitutional at that period. Now that so small a minority as four fifths of one County in this State which cannot possibly be supposed to be more than one fourteenth of the whole, should not only oppose such a great majority of a State, but act directly contrary to the sense & reccommendation of the whole Continent, in our opinion is acting like persons that do not understand the true principals of Liberty and are durating from the end this Country had in view in commencing the Contest with Great Britain. The reason that is given for stoping the Courts of Quarter Sessions and Common Pleas, will be equally conclusive for stoping the Superior Courts, the consequence of which will be, that, untill the formation & acceptance and establishment of a new Constitution which will require time and ought not to be done in a hurry without due consideration all treasons and misprisions of treasons, murders and felons of what kind soever, committed in your County, cannot be tried; for the Law makes it necessary that these Crimes shall be tried in the same County they were Committed. Every member of Society must dread the consequence of suffering such offences to pass with impunity; our Lives, liberties and Estates would become insecure, and we should soon be in a situation worse than that of a State of nature; and such criminal offences cannot be supposed to be less frequent in your County or in any other, but rather increase in proportions as the operation of the laws are suspended; for it is absolutely necessary that punishment should be held forth as motives to restrain and counter ballance the effects of the passions of many individuals in all societies. It is our opinion, that the operation of the executive Courts, rather than be an abstraction, will be an assistance and of great advantage to us, while we are forming a Constitution it will tend to establish that order and regularity among the people which is necessary for that cool dispassionate deliberation which such important a matter requires. And we are apprehensive, that the powers of Government in the meantime, should be suffered by stoping the Courts of Justice, the concursion of jarring these ties would throw the State into anarchy and confusion, it is the wish and endeavour of our internal enemies, those canker worms among us, who desparing of devouring our liberties by open force, are secretly and subtlely seeking the opportunity of knawing assunder the Cords of our Union (on) which alone our political salvation depends, The idea of Committees forming County Conventions, and these County Conventions advising State Conventions to act in opposition to, or in conformity with the General Court, the supreme authority of the State, seems to us at present to involve in it the greatest absurdity and to be intirely inconsistant with the best and most established maxims of government. The supposition of two different powers in a State assuming the right of controling the people, whose doings are liable to interfere with each other, forms that great political solecism imperium in imperio, a head within a head, and the State in which a monster of this denomination of a kingdom divided against itself, which cannot stand.

When the talons of Slavery were about to fasten upon us, when tyranny was shaking over us his iron rod, and those in power were assisting and endeavouring to reduce us to absolute subjection, it was necessary for the people to bestir themselves and invent some method to prevent the fatal catastrophe; the Committees of the several towns in each County did then assemble together and form County Conventions, which were at that time very favourable, & tended greatly to the Salvation of America. But when we had repelled the fatal blow . . . . their places those in power that were endeavouring our distruction, and; agreeable to the reccommendation of the Continental Congress, assumed the forms and execution of legislative, and executive government the reason and necessity of the Convention ceased.

At this day, it appears to us, they can do no good, but may be productive of great and lasting mischief and for Committees to take to themselves such power is, we conseive, without the line of their duty; they are made by the Law, and the Law has limited and defined their power and jurisdiction, every step beyond which is an illegal arrogation. Our government is now placed in an assembly, that is annually and freely chosen by the people, and if they find any, to whom it was intrusted, exert it to the prejudice of their constituents, they have it in their power, in the short revolution of one year, to remedy the evil by leaving out such and chusing others. In such an assembly where their own and the peoples interest is so interwoven, that if they act for themselves, they must act for the common interest of the whole, we can have no fear of placing our influence in these, we conceive, are the proper persons to point out a method of forming a bill of rights and a Constitution, and of obtaining the consent and approbation of the people. In the petition of your Convention to the General Court, an extract of which we have in your letter, you say that you assured them that if your request was rejected "You should endeavor, by advising the first Committee of safety in this State and others, that there be a State Convention formed for that purpose." who this first Committee is, we acknowledge we cannot determine, but it appears to us that the convention take upon themselves, by this to controll the doings of the General Court, they put them under duress and obliged them to grant their request, or they will put their designs in execution themselves, which is in fact governing the Court & not being governed by them.

If we set up in this way to controll the established authority of the State, we cannot but think we should act contrary to the principles and motives that first induced us to oppose the authority of Great Britain—and "will give just occassion to our adversaries to reproach us, as being men of turbulent dispositions and licentious principles, that cannot bear to be restrained by good and wholesome Laws, even tho they are of our own making, nor submit to rulers of our own chusing." And in truth such intestine divisions and opposition to legal government will give more advantage to our enemy than all their fleets and armies, It was not the laws, then in being, we complained of as the motive of our resistance, but the executors of the laws, who instead of using them for the end they were designed, prostituted them to flaginous purposes. The executive authority is now deposited in those that have the confidence of the people men of virtue and knowledge, whose doings and decisions meet with universal approbation. We in this County, and we will venture to say those of other counties in this State, that have had the experience, are perfectly satisfied, and well pleased, that the laws are once more regularly executed. We feel the good effects of it. We know how and where to apply for the redress of injuries. We cannot be deprived of our personal liberty or our property, by the capricious and arbital decision of a body of men who are guided by no rule, are not bound even with the tie of an oath, but judge and determine just as their passions and prejudices lead them but among us "the laws bear sway." These, Gentlemen, are our sentiments, which we submit to your consideration. We hope they will be received with all that candor and impartiality, which our good intention may claim. We wish not to inflame & excite passions but to promote & cement Union & harmony among us, which at present we conceive necessary to save the States from ruin.

We are, Gentlemen, with all due respect yours &c., Daniel Bigelow, Nath^{ll} Heywood, William Dana, Joseph Barber, Jonathan Rice. Committee of Correspondence, Inspec^{n}. and Safety for town of Worcester
Worcester, October 8th 1778.

The General Court Investigates Berkshire's Grievances

36. Pittsfield Addresses the Committee of the General Court, November 1778

[*Acts and Resolves,* V, 1030-32]

To The Honourable Committee from the General Court of Massachusetts Bay now convened at Pittsfield——

Mr. Chairman, Sir

We whose Names are underwritten indulging some Apprehensions of the Importance of Civil & religious Liberty, the destructive Nature of Tyranny & lawless power, & the absolute necessity of legal Government, to prevent Anarchy & Confusion; have taken this method to indulge our own Feelings & Sentiments respecting the important matters that have for some Time been the Subject of debate in this present Meeting—Political Disquisitions, if managed with Decency, Moderation & Candor are a good preservative against Ignorance & Servility & such a state of perfect Quietude as would endanger the Rights of Mankind united in the Bands of Society. We wish to preserve this Character in what we have now to offer in the Defence of our Constituents in opposing, in times past, the executive Courts of Justice in this County.

We wish with the least Delay to come to the Merits of the cause, & shall now proceed to make those observations on the Nature of Government which are necessary to bring into view the Apprehensions we indulge respecting the present Condition of this state, whether we have a fundamental Constitution or not; & how far we have Government duly organized & how far not; In free States the people are to be considered as the fountain of power. And the social Tie as founded in Compact. The people at large are endowed with alienable & unalienable Rights. Those which are unalienable, are those which belong to Conscience respecting the worship of God & the practice of the Christian Religion, & that of being determined or governed by the Majority in the Institution or formation of Government. The alienable are those which may be delegated for the Common good, or those which are for the common good to be parted with. It is of the unalienable Rights, particularly that of being determined or governed by the Majority in the Institution or formation of Government of which something further is necessary to be considered at this Time. That the Majority should be governed by the Minority in the first Institution of Government is not only contrary to the common apprehensions of Mankind in general, but it contradicts the common Law of Justice & benevolence.

Mankind being in a state of nature equal, the larger Number (Caeteris paribus) is of more worth than the lesser, & the common happiness is to be preferred to that of Individuals. When Men form the social Compact, for the Majority to consent to be governed by the Minority is down right popery in politicks, as submission to him who claims Infallibility, & of being the only Judge of Right & rong, is popery in Religion. In all free Governments duly organized there is an essential Distinction to be observed between the fundamental Constitution, & Legislation. The fundamental Constitution is the Basis & ground work of Legislation, & asscertains the Rights Franchises, Immunities & Liberties of the people, However & how often officers Civil & military shall be elected by the people, & circumscribing and defining the powers of the Rulers, & so affoarding a sacred Barrier against Tyranny & Despotism. This in antient &

corrupt Kingdoms when they have woke out of Slavery to some happy dawnings of Liberty, has been called a Bill of Rights, Magna Charta etc. which must be considered as imperfect Emblems of the Securities of the present grand period. Legislators stand on this foundation, & enact Laws agreeably to it. They cannot give Life to the Constitution: it is the approbation of the Majority of the people at large that gives Life & being to it. This is the foundation of Legislation that is agreeable to true Liberty, it is above the whole Legislature of a free state, it being the foundation upon which the Legislature stands. A Representative Body may form but cannot impose said Constitution upon a free people. The giving Existence to the fundamental Constitution of a free state is a Trust that cannot be delegated. For any rational person to give his vote for another person to aid and assist in forming said Constitution with a view of imposing it on the people without reserving to himself a Right of Inspection Approbation rejection or Amendment, imports, if not impiety, yet real popery in politicks. We could bring many Vouchers for this Doctrine sufficient for our present purpose is the following Extract from a Noted Writer. in answer to that assertion of another respectable writer that 'The bare Idea of a State without a power some where vested to alter every part of its Laws is the height of political Absurdity.' He remarks upon it, 'A position, which I apprehend, ought to be, in some Measure limited & explained. For if it refers to those particular Regulations, which take place in Consequence of Immemorial Custom, or are enacted by positive Statue, & at the same Time, are subordinate to the fundamental Constitution from which the Legislature itself derives its Authority; it is admitted to be within the power or Trust vested in the Legislature to alter these, pro, Re nata, as the good of Society may require. But this power or Authority of the Legislature to make Alterations cannot be supposed to extend to the Infringement of those essentials Rights & previleges, which are reserved to the Members of a free state at large, as their undoubted Birthright & unalienable property. I say, in every free State there are some Liberties & previleges, which the Society has not given out of their own Hands to their Governors, not even to the Legislature: & to suppose the contrary would be the height of political absurdity; for it is saying that a state is free & not free at the same Time; or which is the same thing, that its Members are possessed of Liberties, of all which they may be divested at the will of the Legislature; that is, they enjoy them during pleasure, but can claim no property in them

In a word nothing is more certain than that Government in the general nature of it is a Trust in behalf of the people. And there cannot be a Maxim, in my opinion, more ill grounded, than that there must be an arbitrary power lodged somewhere in every Government. If this were true, the different kinds of Government in the world would be more alike, & on a level, than they are generally supposed to be. In our own Government in particular, though no one thinks with more respect of the powers which the Constitution hath vested in every branch of the Legislature; yet I must be excused in saying what is strictly true, that the whole Legislature is so far from having an absolute power, that it hath not power in several Cases that might be mentioned. For instance, their Authority does not extend to making the house of Commons perpetual, or giving that house a power to fill up their own vacancies: the house of Commons being the representatives of all the Commons of England & in that Capassity only a branch of the Legislature; & if they concur in destroying the foundation on which they themselves stand; & if they annihilate the Rights of their Constituents & claim a share in the Legislature upon any other footing than that upon which the Constitution hath given it to them; they subvert the very Trust under which alone they act, &

thereby forfeit all their Authority. In short they cannot dispence with any of those essential Rights of the people which it ought to be the great object of Government as it is of our Constitution in particular to preserve.'——

These reasonings tend abundantly to evince, that the whole Legislature of any state is insufficient to give Life to the fundamental Constitution of such state, it being the foundation on which they themselves stand & from which the Legislature derives its Authority.——

May it be considered, further, that to suppose the Representative Body capable of forming & imposing this Compact or Constitution without the Inspection & Approbation Rejection or Amendment of the people at large would involve in it the greatest Absurdity. This would make them greater than the people who send them, this supposes them their own Creators, formers of the foundation upon which they themselves stand. This imports uncontroulable Dominion over their Constituents for what should hinder them from making such a Constitution as invests them & their successors in office with unlimited Authority, if it be admitted that the Representatives are the people as to forming & imposing the fundamental Constitution of the state upon them without their Approbation & perhaps in opposition to their united sense—In this the very essence of true Liberty consists, viz in every free state the Consitution is adopted by the Majority.

It is needful to be observed that we are not to Judge of true Liberty by other Nations of the Earth, darkness has overspread the Earth, Tyranny Triumps through the world. The Day light of Liberty, only begins to dawn upon these Ends of the Earth. To measure the freedom, the Rights & previleges of the American Empire by those enjoyed by other Nations would be folly.

It is now both easy & natural to apply these reasonings to the present State of Massachusetts Bay. We think it undeniably follows from the preceeding Reasonings that the Compact in this state is not yet formed: when did the Majority of the people at large assent to such Constitution, & what is it? if the Majority of the people of this state have adopted any such fundamental Constitution it is unknown to us & we shall submit to it as we always mean to be governed by the Majority——

Nor will any of those consequences follow on this supposition, that we have no Law, or that the Honourable Council & House of Representatives are Usurpers & Tyrants. Far from it. We consider our case as very Extraordinary. We do not consider this state in all Respects as in a state of Nature though destitute of such fundamental Constitution. When the powers of Government were totally dissolved in this state, we esteemed the State Congress as a necessary & useful body of Men suited to our Exigencies & sufficiently authorized to levy Taxes, raise an Army & do what was necessary for our common defence & it is Sir in this light that we view our present Honourable Court & for these and other reasons *have inculcated* a careful Adherence to their orders. Time will not permit to argue this Matter any longer, for your Honors patience must have been tryed already. These have been some of the reasons we have indulged, & Sentiments we have cultivated respecting Constitution, & for these Reasons we have been looking forward towards a new Constitution—But we must further add

That a fear of being finally deprived of a Constitution & of being thrown into confusion & divisions by delaying the formation of a new Constitution, has caused our Constituents so early & invariably to oppose the executive Courts—We have feared, we now realize those fears, that upon our submission we shall sink down into a dead Calm & never transmit to posterity a single Right nor leave them the least Knowledge of so fair an Inheritance, as we may now convey to them.——

We & our Constituents have also indulged some fears respecting some of the particular persons appointed for our Rulers least in the future Execution of Law they should execute their own private Resentments, we are willing to hope the best——

We have been ready to consider some of them as indulging an unnatural temper in vilifying & reproaching their own County but we hope they will do better for the future, & that we shall do better, & we wish to give them our confidence—We are determined to cultivate a spirit of meekness forbearance & Love & to study the Things that shall make for peace and order.

It has appeared to us & those we are appointed to represent that in an early opposition to the executive Courts, such opposition would become general through the state, which in our opinion would bring on a new Constitution without Delay. Our hope of which is now very weakened, & such are the Dissentions of this state that we are now ready to fear we shall never obtain any other than what is called our present Constitution our Apprehensions of which have been already explained——

It is with Gratitude we reflect on the Appointment of this Honourable Committee by the General Court for the purpose of peace Reconciliation & order through this County, & their impartial & faithful Execution of their Commission. We are persuaded by the Temper and Moderation exhibited that they will not embibe any prejudices against this County, by what they have seen & heared, & that they will make a Just Representation of our state to the General Court.——

To evince to your Honors our Love of peace Reconciliation & legal Government, & that we have been actuated not by personal Prejudices or Motives of Ambition, notwithstanding the powerful Reasons we have had for a Suspension of the Executive Courts we are willing to forego our own opinions & if it shall be thought best by our Constituents to submit to the establishment of the Executive Courts in this County——

	VALENTINE RATHBUN
Pittsfield	JOSIAH WRIGHT
	JAMES NOBLE

We the Subscribers Delagates from the Several Towns in the County of Berksheir Approveing of and consenting to the foregoing letter have hereunto Set our hands.

Town Hancock	REUBEN ELY
	ASA DOUGLAS
New Providence	JOAB STAFFORD
Lanesborough	JAMES BARKER
Partridgefield	EBENEZER PEIRCE
	DANIEL KINNE
Windsor	ARNOLD LEWIS
Washenton	EUSUBIUS BUSHNELL
	JONATHAN SMITH

37. Address to the Inhabitants of Berkshire, 1778

[(William Whiting), *Address to the Inhabitants of Berkshire* (1778), 9-16, 25-27]

Let us now, my brethren . . . consider those mighty objections which are so zealously urged against the introduction of law into this country. And I think they may be substantially comprehended in these words, viz. "We have no constitution of government. And how can we have government without a constitution, or a foundation for it to stand upon?"

Here let me call up your best and most careful attention, while we take a short view of what is termed a state of nature, and afterwards that of civil society.

In a state of nature, each individual has a right, not only to dispose of, order, and direct, his property, his person, and all his own actions, within the bounds of the law of nature, as he thinks fit, but he also has a right in himself, not only to defend, but to judge and to punish the person who shall make any assault or encroachment, either upon his person or property, without asking leave, or depending on the will of any other man, or any set of men whatever,

Now when any number of men enter into a state of society with each other, they resign into the hands of the society, the right they had, in a state of nature. of disposing, directing and ordering their own persons and properties, so far as the good of the whole may require it. And as to the right of judging and punishing injuries done to any of the individuals, that is to be wholly given up to the society. Hence, it is obvious, there can be no medium between being, in a state of nature, and in a state of civil society.

Again, in all societies of men, united together for mutual aid, support and defence, there exists one supreme, absolute, and rightful judge over the whole, one, who has a right, at all times, to order, direct, and dispose of the persons, actions and properties of the individuals of the community, so far as the good of the community shall require it; and this judge is no other than the majority of the whole.

The great Mr. Locke tells us, "That when men enter into a community, they just give up all the powers necessary for, the purposes for which they entered into society, to the majority of the community; and this is done barely by agreeing to enter into political society; which is all the compact there is, or need be, between the individuals to make up a commonwealth. And this is that, and that only, which gives beginning to any lawful government in the world."

Here let it be carefully observed, that when men emerge from a state of nature, and unite in society, in order to forming a political government; the first step necessary is, for each individual to give up his alienable natural rights and privileges, to be ordered, directed, and disposed of, as the major part of the community shall think fit; so far as shall be necessary for the good of the whole, of which the majority must be the judges. And this must necessarily take place previous to the community's forming any particular constitution, mode, or form of government whatever: For, to be in a state of society, so far as to be under obligation to obey the rules and orders prescribed by the major part of the society, is one thing; and for that society to be under any particular constitution or form of government, is another. The latter is necessarily subsequent to the former, and must depend intirely on the pleasure of the supreme judge; that is, the major part of the community, who have an undoubted right to enter upon, or postpone that matter, when, and so long as they see fit; and no individual can, on that account, be justified in withdrawing their allegiance, or refusing to submit to the rules and orders of the society.

Here my brethren, let me call upon you to consider, what an absurd and rediculous figure those men cut, who cry out vehemently for a *new Constitution,* while, at the same time, by refusing to make that resignation of their alienable rights which is the necessary condition on which men enter into civil society, they positively declare, that they do not even belong to the political society of the State of *Massachusetts-Bay.*

I know some will object, that on the declaration of Independence, all civil government was annihilated; consequently, that we are under no obligation to submit to government, till we have a constitution that we approve of. To which I answer, That even admitting the declaration of Independence did actually annihilate the *Constitution* of the province of the *Massachusetts-Bay;* yet it did not annihilate, or materially affect, the *union* or *compact* existing among the people: For, as I have already show'd, that for a people to be so in a state of political society, as to be under indispensable obligation to obey the rules and orders prescribed by the major part of the society, and to be under any particular constitution or form of government, are things intirely distinct; and, that the latter is subsequent to, and wholly dependent on, the former. This being the case, it follows, that no revolution in, or dissolution of, particular constitutions or forms of government, can absolve the members of the society from their allegiance to the major part of the community. And I can hardly conceive how it is possible for such a society to be dissolved, unless by their being dispersed abroad as the Jews are, so that the will of the major part cannot be, either known or obeyed, or by the usurpation and deadly breath of an absolute tyrant.

It is true, when the majority of a society do not act, or when their will and orders cannot be known to the members; during such suspension, the natural right of defending and protecting himself, reverts back to each individual; and on this principle only, can those salutary mobs, and necessary exertions of the people, in the beginning of the present contest, be justified. But after congress and assemblies, composed of the free representatives of the people, had prescribed rules for ordering and conducting the public affairs of the community, whatever has taken place of that sort since, has generally, if not universally, been unnecessary, unwarrantable and seditious.

But should we admit for once, that on the declaration of independence, not only all modes and forms of government were dissolved, but also, that civil society was annihilated at the same time: Yet, as it plainly appears from what has been said, that previous, and in order to the forming a constitution or mode of government, it is essentially necessary that the people enter into society, and give up their alienable natural rights, and submit to be governed by the major part of the community; I ask, with what face you can pretend to the least colour of right to give your voices in, or to say any thing about, a constitution, while you utterly refuse to comply with the necessary preliminaries? This is really no less preposterous than it would be for the savages of the wilderness to run together, and take upon them, in hideous yells, to frame, and enact, a constitution and form of government for the state of Massachusetts-Bay.

It is a fact which needs no proof, that whatever state the inhabitants of the Massachusetts-Bay might be in at the time independence was declared, they are now in a state of civil society, and (the county of *Berkshire* excepted) enjoy the blessings of a free and equal government.

And now my brethren, let me ask you this very plain, tho' pertinent and important question,—Are you members of the political society of the state of Massachusetts-Bay? Or are you not? If you answer in the affirmative; then let me ask you again, why do you refuse to submit to those rules which the community have prescribed? And not only this; but why, by threats and violence, do you deter the servants of the community, in this county, from redressing injuries and insults offered to others, and like the fable of the dogy in the manger, neither enjoy the blessings of government yourselves, nor suffer othersto enjoy them? Or how will you exculpate yourselves from the charge of being in a state of rebellion against the community?

But should you say that you do not belong to the community, that you do not mean to give up any of your natural rights till you know what constitution you are to be governed by: Then let me tell you, that you must be considered, as being, at lest, in a state of nature, and that you can have no right to join, or give your voice in forming a constitution of government,

But perhaps you will say, that you do not act, in this affair, as individuals, but, as a community: For, when the minds of the inhabitants of the county were lately taken upon the expediency or inexpedency of setting up courts, there appeared to be a very great majority against it.—Here let me repeat a former question: Are the inhabitants of the county of *Berkshire* members of the political society of the Massachusetts Bay? Or are they not? Your conduct, in sending members to the general court, answers this question in the affirmative.—A majority of the inhabitants of the county therefore, can be of no more real avail in this matter, than a majority of any particular town, or, than even a majority of any particular family in any particular town in the county. For, it is only a major part of the *community* that have a right to determine matters of this kind, and they have ordered that courts of sessions be held in this county. The friends of government therefore cannot consider themselves as being, in any measure, included in this vote of the county. The truth of the fact is, that should ninety-nine out of an hundred thro' the county, vote against law, yet, that hundredth part would, as loyal subjects of the community, have a right to enjoy the benifits of government, and the major part of the community are under absolute obligation, therein to protect and support them. Otherwise the community could have no right to punish them, should they even commit treason against the state: For, no maxim can stand on firmer ground than this, *That protection and allegiance are reciprocal:* and that, *where protection is wanting, allegiance is not due.*———Let me entreat you, my brethren, seriously to consider, how shockingly unreasonable, as well as grossly immoral your conduct is, while by threats and violence, you deprive the peaceable and loyal inhabitants of this county, of that inextimable previlege of having their grevances redressed in that ancient and equal way, of tryal by jurors, as well as of all other benefits of a free and lawful government. And all this, upon the most frivolous pretences, as I have already show'd, and shall further evince in the course of these observations.

You loudly proclaim yourselves to be *Sons of liberty.* Pray, what kind of liberty is it you contend for, against Great-Britain? Does not your conduct testify against you, that you contend for the same thing, for which all tyrants contend with each other, viz. that each one may monopolize the whole empire of tyranny to himself? But left, ere I am aware, I should catch the epidemic disease my self, and a flame of passion, begin to rage in my own breast, I will dismiss this head, and proceed to notice some other objections that are made against the introduction of law into this country. . . .

And now, my brethren, from the foregoing observations, I think it evident to a demonstration, that the common cry in this county, *that we have no foundation of government,* is altogether groundless. For, even admitting that we have no particular constitution yet, it hath been shown, that such a constitution is not so essential to government, that there can be no foundation of government without it; but, on the contrary, that a compact or union among the people, by which they agree to submit themselves to be governed by the major part of the community, is itself, a sufficient and substantial foundation of government. And this being the case, how surprising is your conduct, that while you profess to belong to the community, by joining with it in making all the laws and rules for the government thereof, by your representatives; you, at the same time, refuse to submit to these very laws and rules; because, say you, we have no foundation of government. Although the great Mr. Loc. tells you, and common sense tells you the same, that this, and this only, is that which can lay a foundation for any lawful government in the world.

I have shewn, that the common cry of danger of being enslaved, and again bro't under the British yoke of bondage, by introducing (for present convenience) the old constitution, as now practised upon, is perfectly idle and rediculous. I have shewn that our conduct, in refusing to submit to law, till we have a new form of government established, instead of bringing forward, will have a direct and powerful tendency to retard and embarrass, that desirable and important object.—I have shewn, that the people of this county, who at present oppose the due execution of law, have intirely mistook the true meaning and import of the words, *constitution* and form of government. I have shewn, that for a people to give up their alienable natural rights, and to agree to be directed by the major part of the society, so far as the good of the whole shall require it, is the only foundation of lawful government; and that this is absolutely necessary, previous to their forming any particular mode of government; and therefore, that as the people of this county refuse to comply with these preliminaries, they do thereby exclude themselves from all just rights to give their voices in forming a constitution.

NOTWITHSTANDING the pains I have taken to set these matters in a just point of view, it will be to no good purpose, so long as the people are determined that they will retain all the rights of a state of nature. Let me tell you, my brethren, you cannot retain these rights, and at the same time enjoy the protection of society. It is therefore high time to away with these shocking inconsistencies, in which you have gone on for several years past—pretending to belong to the community of Massachusetts-Bay, by sending representatives, or rather spies, to the general court, and, at the same time, refusing to obey those laws and rules which they prescribe, unless in some particular instances, wherein they happen to coincide with your fancies! And here I can't but take notice, how shamefully that antient maxim, *vox populi* est vox Dei (the voice of the people is the voice of God) has been prostituted in this county. When the major part of a free and independent community, by their representatives, declare to the individual members, and the world, their acts and resolutions, this being considered as the greatest power on earth, nothing can more fitly resemble *the voice of God*. But when a small number of individuals, who ought to be members of the society, inflamed with passion (if not with strong drink) collect together for the avowed purpose of opposing the true *vox populi,* let any one say whether their voice is not rather that of blasphemy and treason, than god like.

I shall close my address by repeating my most serious advice to you to act a part more consistent. And as you are now erecting little democracies in several of your towns, you ought to withdraw your representatives from the general assembly of the Massachusetts-Bay; for it is highly unreasonable they should sit there as spies. You ought to send them as ambassadors, or commissioners plenipotentiary, and in that character they ought to be received, if received at all, and not as representatives. You ought to send the like officers to the American Congress, and to have your independence confirmed by that august body, before you proceed further in the exercise of your novel government; otherwise, it is more than possible you may meet with difficulty: For, should you compel any one to submit to your assumed authority, he will have a right to demand satisfaction, and the state is bound to see him redressed. And you may be assured that the supreme authority of the state will not be easily convinced that those trifling objections against law, which are so easily confuted, are sufficient to justify you in setting up independent governments in your several towns, unless you can obtain a ratification of your independence from Congress, which, I dare say, in your most extravagant excursions of fancy, you never once thought of.

Western Massachusetts Discusses the Legality of the Provincial Government

38. The Views of Some Stockbridge People

A. Petition of March 8, 1779

[Town Papers, 1770-1885, Stockbridge Library]

To the Selectmen of the Town of Stockbridge

Gentlemen:

We the Subscribers being Freeholders in the said Town Request that you Insert in the Warrant for the Annual March Meeting to be held this month the following Article as the first after the Moderator is Chosen To be Determined by yeas & Nays (viz)——

Wheather the Inhabitants of the Town of Stockbridge consider the Constitution as now Practiced upon in the Eastern Part of this State is Binding upon the Inhabitants of said Town; and whether the Acts and Resolves of the General Court of this State are obligatory upon said Inhabitants——

Stockbridge
March 8 1779

Erastus Sergeant
Stephen Nash
Elihu Parsons
Sam Brown
Tim[y] Edwards

Jah[l] Woodbridge
John Bacon
Sam Brown, Jun
Elijah Brown
Joseph Woodbridge

B. Petition of March 15, 1779

[Town Papers, 1770-1885, Stockbridge Library]

To the Selectmen of the Town of Stockbridge—

We the Subscribers do hereby Petition that you would insert the following articles in the Warrant for the Annual Town Meeting to be holden this Instant March viz—

1st To see whether the Town will take into consideration the doings of the late County Convention which set at Pittsfield and act thereon

2nd To take the minds of this Town by Yeas and Nays whether they consider that old Form of a Constitution which by some is held up to view, and by which the General Court are said to act, be really a Constitution established by the Freemen of this State directly and binding of the Inhabitants of this Town

3[dly] To see if the Town will call upon their Representative to the General Court for the present year, to produce and lay before the Town a copy of the Constitution of the State if any there by, that the Town may act understandingly for the Future.

Stockbridge March 15th 1779

John Whedon
Robert Train
Jn. Fiske
Isaac Curtis
Stephen Pearl
Peter Pixley
W Goodrich

Silas Bingham
Moses Nash
Simeon Porter
Ephm. Foot
Wm. Woodbridge
Samuel Hatch

39. From a Stockbridge Assessor's List for 1778

[Town Papers, 1770-1885, Stockbridge Library]

[For the convenience of the student, each man's name is preceded by the letter of document No. 38 on which his name appears. The faculty rating in pounds listed £500 for Silas Bingham and Dr. E. Sergeant, £180 for Stephen Nash, £100 for Ephraim Foot, and £11 for John Whedon.]

	Poll	Real Estate £	Personal Estate £	Total
A John Bacon	2	636	770	1336
B Silas Bingham	2	896	17	1413
A Elijah Brown	1	1524	391	1915
A Samuel Brown	1	597	—	597
A Samuel Brown, Jr.	1	2258	1014	3273
B Isaac Curtis	1	503	272	775
A Timothy Edwards	2	2956	1525	4481
B John Fiske	1	893	100	993
B Ephraim Foot	1	105	118	323
B Wm. Goodrich	1	538	119	657
B Samuel Hatch	3	828	190	1018
B Moses Nash	1	434	220	654
A Stephen Nash	3	395	134	710
A Elihu Parsons	3	1574	572	2146
B Stephen Pearl	1	216	—	216
B Peter Pixley	1	288	—	288
B Simeon Porter	—	150	—	150
A Dr. E. Sergeant	1	1300	1047	2847
B Robert Train	1	—	—	—
	13			
B John Whedon	2	785	326	1111
A Jahleel Woodbridge	1	1368	496	1864
A Jos. Woodbridge	2	818	386	1204
B Wm. Woodbridge	1	660	119	779

40. A Warrant for a Stockbridge Town Meeting, March 16, 1779

[Town Papers, 1770-1885, Stockbridge Library]

Stockbridge To Moses Barnam one of the constables of the Town of Stockbridge greeting——

In the name of the Government & People of the State of Massachusetts Bay you are hereby required to warn all the freeholders and other inhabitants of the Town of Stockbridge (excepting Indians) qualified to vote in town meetings to meet at the meeting house in said Stockbridge on Monday the 22 day of March warrant at nine o'clock in the morning then & there to consider of and act on the following articles viz.

1 To chose a moderator.

2 To chose all Town officers as the law directs

3 To see whether the Town will Make & repair the Highways by a vote and grant a sum of money for the same and whether the Town will discontinue or confirm any highways——

4 To see whether the town will grant a sum of money for schooling

5 To see whether the Town will set of a school district in the south west part and another in the westerly part of the Town

6 To see if the swine shall run at large under the regulations of the law

7 To see if the Town will grant a sum of money to rebuild the orphan Bridge so called

8 To see if the Town will raise a sum of money for contingent charges

9 To see if the Town will take into consideration certain matters contained in a request made in writing to the Selectmen by the Honorable Tim[y] Edwards Esq & others to take into consideration the validity of the present constitution, &c, &c and act thereon

10 To see if the Town will take into consideration certain matters contained in a request made in writing to the Selectmen by Stephen Pearl & others to take into consideration the doings of the late county convention, &c, &c and act thereon and to act on any other matter the Town shall think proper.

Hereof fail not But make due return of this warrant with your doings there to some one of us at or before said time for said meeting Given under our hands & seal this sixteenth day of March 1779

Elnathan Curtis
Asa Bement
Elisha Bradley
Elias Gilbert
David Pixley
} Selectmen of Stockbridge

41. Stockbridge Votes on the Validity of the Provisional Government, March 26, 1779

[Stockbridge Town Book, 1760-1835, 115, Stockbridge Library]

Friday
26th of March AD 1779

The inhabitants that according to adjournment & Past the following Votes (Viz)

49 Voted that the Request of Timothy Edwards Esq & others be now considered Said Request may be seen on File the matter being Debated Largley

50 Voted to put the following Question & to be answered by yeas & nays

Is the present mode of Government as now Practiced upon the Major part of the State of Massachusetts Bay for the present necessity only & untill a nother may be obtained Binding on the Inhabitants of this Town as also the Laws & orders of the General Council

Yeas 54

Nays 54

42. Stockbridge Reconsiders its Vote, March 29, 1779

[Stockbridge Town Book, 1760-1835, 116, Stockbridge Library]

Monday March 29 AD 1779 Then met according to adjournment & Past the following votes (viz)

52 Voted that the Doings of the Late Convention held att Pittsfield be read

52 Voted that the following Question be put & to be answered by yeas and nays (viz) Whether we the Inhabitants of the Town of Stockbridge Do acknowledge our Selves Bound by the Doings of the General Court of this State.

Yeas 66

Nays None

43. Resolutions of a Hampshire Convention, March 30, 1779

[Hawley Papers, Box I, N.Y. Public Lib.]

Chesterfield March 30th 1779

At a Meeting holden by the Committees of a Number of Towns In the Western Part of the County of Hampshire——

Capt. Thomas Weeks in the Chair
Capt. William White Clerk

Have Given our Opinion viz as Follows

1st It is the Opinion of this Convention That all men are Born Equally Free and Independant, and that no man Can be bound by a Law that he has not Given his Consent to, Either by his Person, or Legal Representative——

2ndly We are of Opinion that the Power is originally in the People and that no Select Body of men can Lawfully Legislate for them, unless the People have by Some mode or form Delagated their Power to them as their Representatives, which form of Government we Call a Constitution of a State or Kingdom; by which there should be Proper Bounds set to the Legislative, and Executive Authority, without which the People Cannot be Saf, Free, or Happy.——

3rdly We are of Opinion That as the People at Large in this County & State Authorized the Congress to Declare us Independant to Great Britain, & as we have under God maintained our Independance with our Blood & Treasure to this Day: It is Our Opinion we are free from any Charter Law, or Laws Derived from Britain, and that we know of no Constitution in this State Consented to by the People at Large.——

4thly We are of opinion that a Legal Representative is a Creature of the Constitution of a State, or Kingdom; but we Desire to know how such a Creature Can Exist In a Legal Sense Prior to that Constitution on which his being and Existance Depends——

5thly We are of Opinion that by Delaying and Putting off the Forming a Bill of Rights and a free Constitution for this State, we are Deprived of a Great Blessing viz Civil Government and Good wholsom Laws—Founded thereon, whereby the Virtuous may be Protected in their Liberty and Property, and Transgressors Brought to proper Punishment——

6thly We are not without Fear that there is Designing men in this State that Intends by Delaying the Forming a Bill of Rights and a free Constitution to Lull People to Sleep, or Fatigue them other ways so as to obtain a Constitution to their minds, Calculated to Answer their own Ends and wicked Purposes. By which means the People will Loose the Benefit of their Independance, and may further be said to have changed Masters than Measures——

7thly We are of opinion that it is the Duty of Virtuous Leaders to Preserve the Liberty of the People over whom they Preside, and whenever from a desire to Agrandize Themselves they Endeaver to Persuade the People to submit to Arbitrary Infringments of their Rights, they not only forfeit their Title to the Respect which is Due to a Virtuous Member of Society, But Deserves to be Treated with the Severity Due to a Traitor——

8thly Whereas there is a General Uneasiness in the People in the western Part of this State with Regard to the Execution of Law Derived from the Old Constitution (So Called) and to Prevent the Difficulties we fear will arrise by Intestine Broils and Mobs, we think it Expedient without Loss of Time to Call upon the Committees of the Several Towns in this County in a Convention that they may Give their Opinion with us on such Matters as shall be Laid before them for the General Good of the State at Large, In uniting & forming a Bill of Rights & Constitution, and Bear Testimony against a Constitution without a Name & Legislation without Law——

Therefore Resolved

That a Coppy of the foregoing Votes be sent to the Select men or Committees of the several Towns in this County: and they are hereby Desired to Assemble by their Respective Committees at the Court House at Northampton on Tuesday the Twentieth Day of April Next at Ten oClock A.M. then & there to act upon any Matter or Matters of Importance Relative to the State that may be Laid before them——

Also Resolved that the Chairman be, and he is hereby Directed to send Attested Coppies of the forgoing Votes to the several Towns in the County as aforesaid.——

44. Petition of Hampshire Towns, April 20, 1779

[Massachusetts Archives, CLXXV, 147]

At a Convention properly notified held at Northampton in the County of Hampshire on the 20th of April 1779 To consider of important matters relative to the state of Massachusetts Bay particularly respecting the forming a bill of rights and a free Constitution.

Notwithstanding the Handbills lately issued by the Great and General Court to the several Towns in this state for the purpose of instructing their Representatives for the year ensuing relative to the forming a Constitution

It is the opinion of this Convention, That whereas there is an uneasiness in the people of this County with respect to the execution of Law, that the great and General Court of this State be, and they are hereby desired in the present session forthwith to Issue their handbills to the several towns in this state to appoint a state Convention for the sole purpose of forming a bill of rights and free Constitution for this state to be sent back to the several towns for their approbation disapprobation or amendment; at the same time appointing a time and place for the meeting of such Convention.

Joseph Smith Charman

Northampton April 21st. 1779

No. of Towns Present 23

45. A Berkshire Convention Addresses the Superior Court, May 3, 1779

[*Acts and Resolves*, V, 1275-76]

County of Berkshire, State of Massachusetts-Bay.

To the Honorable the Judges of the superior Court appointed to sit at Great Barrington on Tuesday the fourth of May 1779—

May it please your Honors

We being a Convention formed by the Delegates from several Towns in the County of Berkshire, beg leave to lay before your Honors the sense of our Constituents, which is as follows viz. that it is creating a dangerous President to admit or consent to the operation of Law untill there is a Constitution or Form of Government with a Bill of Rights explicitly approved of and firmly established by a Majority of the Freemen of this State, for which reason the good People of this County are oposed to the seting of Courts at this or any future time untill a Constitution be formed and approved of by the People of this State—And here we beg leave to give some account of ourselves, and the reasons of our Conduct and in the first place would premise That we always had a sense of the Necessity of Law, especially in time of War, that we feel the Want of a due Exercise of it, and in many instances the sad effects of not enjoying of it, and as we have heretofore observed to a former Assembly, will do all in our power to uphold Authority and Law settled upon a good foundation—But to our supprise in the seting of the first General Assembly in 1775 contrary to any Charter that we ever yet saw, The Members of each County were called upon to nomenate suitable persons in the civil and Military Line which were chosen by the House and commissioned by the Councill, in which effectual care was taken that those then present should be in the Nomenation, which procedure roused our attention that such persons should nomenate and vote for themselves or be elected in a form that the Charter knew nothing of—We have further reasons for the non admission of Law of the present foundation, we keep our Eye on the Origin of the present mode of Government, which as it is acknowledged by our Oponents, stands on the advice of the Continental Congress in 1775, which advice as may be seen had a special reference to a reconciliation to the Crown of Great Britain and in the exercise of such a mode mode [*sic*] of Government all our Officers civil and military were appointed and still hold their Authority, but when the Revolution took place by the subsequent Declaration of Independence that advice certainly ceased, and although there was a Proclamation from the general Court dated January 23[d] 1776 congratulating the People on a new form of Government, yet this was before the declaration of Independence, every Law therefore exercised at that time must have the Crown for its Index, yet the general Plea is by our Oponents that we hold our Authority and Government consequent upon said Advice from Congress, it is a Truth too well known to be denied, that since the Declaration of Independence there has been no social Compact or fundamental Constitution formed and adopted by the great Majority of the People of this State therefore the Basis and foundation of the present mode of Government is what we dislike, together with the Spirit & Principle which actuates many of the men who would inforce it—And considering all those Reasons (which appear to us of weight) we are fearfull of the Consequences should the operation of Law take place upon the present Foundation, especially if it should be attempted to be enforced by Violence, as some have intimated, which intimations we hope will appear to be groundless, as they have very much exasperated the People; We must therefore in Duty to ourselves to our Country and Constituents earnestly desire that your Honors would desist from attempting to set in this County untill the explicit voice of the great Majority of the Freemen of this State may be taken by Yeas and Nays respecting the Validity of the present Form of Government, by whoes Determination when explicitly and regularly known we are determined chearfully and religiously to abide by——

The above being read and duly considered was unanimously approved of signed per Order of said Convention

Stockbridge May 3[d] 1779—

JONATHAN YOUNGLOVE Chairman

CHAPTER VI

THE CONSTITUTION OF 1780

CONCEDING THE inevitable, the General Court in February 1779 recognized the demand for a constitutional convention and passed a joint resolution requesting town selectmen to call together those qualified to vote for representatives and obtain answers to two questions: whether the people wanted a constitution made and whether they would empower their representatives to call a state convention to draft one (No. 46). By this time there were about 270 towns in the state, and returns from 134 of them are preserved in the Archives. The totals show a better than 2 to 1 majority in favor of the resolution, one town recording a unanimous vote in the affirmative "except one person who is an old insignifant Torey and never ought to vote in any case."[1] Still, thirty-eight towns did reject the resolution without much explanation. The strongest support came from the two western counties, where not a single town opposed having a constitution drafted.

In June 1779, the General Court issued the call for the election of a state constitutional convention, stipulating that each town could choose as many delegates as it was entitled to elect representatives. Delegates were to be chosen by all freemen over twenty-one, and the work of the convention had to have the approval of two-thirds of those voting before the constitution could become effective (No. 47). A ratifying convention would examine the returns and count the votes. The action of the General Court thus settled the procedural question in favor of those demanding a grant of constituent power.

Selections 48-50 are instructions adopted by the towns as a guide for their delegates to the drafting convention. Since the Archives contain very few such sets of instructions, these cannot be called typical; they are illustrative only. However, almost all of them stress the importance of guarantees for man's basic rights, thus revealing their concern over the omission of a bill of rights from the draft constitution of 1778. Stoughton (No. 50) recommends a Council of Censors to determine periodically whether the three branches of government have violated the constitution in any way, a scheme reminiscent of the Pennsylvania Constitution of 1776.

1. Oakham, Worcester County, Massachusetts Archives, CLX, 98.

On September 1, 1779, the constitutional convention met in Cambridge. Although a committee of thirty was named to draft the constitution, the real work was assigned to a subcommittee of three—James Bowdoin, Samual Adams, and John Adams—and the basic draft was worked out by John Adams. Preceded by an elaborate Declaration of Rights, the Constitution was one of the most comprehensive drawn up during the Revolutionary era. Anticipating some of the objections bound to be raised by the towns, the Address of the convention to the people stresses that limited government has been secured through a system of checks and balances, including a two-house legislature and a strong executive. The Address also explains the hard work behind the writing of the article on religion—Article III in the Declaration of Rights—and expounds upon the desirability of property qualifications for voters. The Address (No. 51) and the Declaration of Rights and Frame of Government (No. 52) appear just as they did in printed handbills sent to each of the towns.

The Archives contain 181 returns from the towns out of a possible total of 290. While the returns are virtually complete for a number of counties, they are entirely lacking for several others, notably for Essex, Cumberland (in Maine), Dukes, and Nantucket, the latter two being islands. The decision of the ratifying convention not to accept returns after June 13 may explain some of these gaps. Although the town clerks did not always keep careful tallies on each article, nearly all of them did so for the highly controversial Article III of the Declaration of Rights. Judging by the returns now available, this article fell some 600 votes short of the necessary two-thirds majority for ratification. In fact, the ratifying convention resorted to manipulation of the totals to secure the required assent. In the tally sheet for Hampshire County, for example, some towns which voted against Article III have their totals listed as favorable, and in some instances unfavorable votes are not recorded at all or are scratched out. Boston (No. 53) and Ashby (No. 54) illustrate objections raised against Article III.

It is also probable that two other provisions of the Constitution did not achieve the necessary majority: Chapter II, Section I, Article II, which required the governor to be of the Christian religion; and Chapter VI, Article X, which required the General Court in fifteen years to ask the people whether they wanted the Constitution amended. Sixty-three towns, among them Springfield (No. 60), demanded that the governor be a Protestant, unimpressed apparently by the assurances of the Address to the people. New Marlborough (No. 57) was one of sixty-seven towns that wanted the Constitution subject to amendment sooner than fifteen years, and twelve others insisted that amendments be automatically considered at the end of the fifteen-year period.

A number of other features of this Constitution were opposed by sizable minorities. The convention had eliminated from Adams' draft of Article XVI a guarantee of free speech. After Boston (No. 53) published its objections to Article XVI in the Declaration of Rights and to Chapter VI, Article VII, thus demanding greater protection for free speech and the right of habeas corpus, a dozen or more towns entered similar complaints. Braintree (No. 55), mindful perhaps of British violations of natural law, sought to have breaches of this law tried in equity courts. Thirty towns wanted a smaller senate, and five wanted no senate at all—Rehoboth (No. 56), for example. Twenty-six towns would have eliminated property qualifications for voting, twelve additional ones wanted no property qualifications to vote for representatives, and four towns wanted to reduce property qualifications for voting. The views of New Marlborough (No. 57), Mansfield (No. 58) and Dorchester (No. 59) on property qualifications for voting and office-holding present interesting contrasts. Forty-six towns, including Springfield (No. 60), found fault with the method of apportionment of representatives, many fearing a large and thus expensive House in which small and distant towns would be overshadowed by large ones near the capital. Finally, various objections were made to the appointive power of the governor and to the tenure of judicial officers. See Middleborough (No. 61), Barnstable (No. 62) and Belchertown (No. 63). Again material from Pittsfield (Nos. 64 and 65) has been included to give a complete picture of that town's actions.

The Constitution was duly declared ratified by the convention on June 16, 1780, and it went into effect on October 25, 1780. Not quite satisfied with the results, Theophilus Parsons (No. 66), author of the Essex Result (see Chapter IV), reasoned that too many concessions had been made to the popular temper, that a more conservative—in his view, a more nearly perfect—constitution could have won the people's assent. Plainly his was a minority report, and certainly he erred in his notions of what were the greatest objections to it. But the detailed criticisms and revisions of the towns should not obscure the fact that the Constitution as a whole was a notable achievement. It was praised even by officers of the Massachusetts line, although they were displeased not to have participated in the voting on it (No. 67). The members of the General Court heaped extravagant praise on the new Constitution (No. 68), but the last word is reserved for an early leader of the Revolutionary cause in Massachusetts, Sam Adams (No. 69). Appropriately enough, he addressed the man who more than any other was the architect of Massachusetts' fundamental law—John Adams.

The story of the struggle for a constitution in Massachusetts exemplifies that cardinal principle of the American Revolution, that government shall be by consent of the governed. From the first this was the fixed idea of the Constitutionalists, and the implementation of it gradually became the concern of men all over the state. Their determination bore fruit in a bill of rights and a written constitution drafted by a convention elected for the purpose and ratified by instructed delegates chosen by manhood suffrage. The method of a special convention to draft a constitution and of the popular election of delegates to ratify it was used a few years later to create a new government for the United States. In its provisions the Massachusetts Constitution also anticipated to a degree the federal one. The clearly defined separation of powers and the checks and balances provided by a bicameral legislature and a very strong executive were well in advance of the practice of the other states in that day.

QUESTIONS

1. In this section are Pittsfield's instructions to its delegate to the constitutional convention, its return on the Constitution of 1780, and its instructions to its delegate to the ratifying convention. Earlier are found various petitions, letters, and memorials from Pittsfield. Taking all this material into consideration, how well were Pittsfield's hopes and expectations satisfied?

2. What unique provisions are found in the instructions given by the towns to their delegates to the constitutional convention?

3. In what respects does the Constitution of 1780 meet objections made by the towns earlier to the Constitution of 1778?

4. A number of towns complained that the very wording of Article III of the Declaration of Rights was inconsistent within itself and with other parts of the Declaration. Does this seem a valid point to you?

5. What important changes did Boston make in Article III?

6. How would you compare the objections of Boston and Ashby to this article?

7. How sound are Boston's other criticisms of the Declaration of Rights?

8. What is unusual about Braintree's use of natural law?

9. How is the convention's defense of property qualifications for voting answered by the towns?

10. What are the various objections made to the appointive power of the governor and council?

11. While many towns objected to Article III in the Declaration of Rights, many of the same towns took the position of Springfield (No. 62) on the religion of the governor. Why did they see no inconsistency here? Compare the "Address" of the convention on this point also.

12. What fears are expressed concerning the mode of representation? To what extent were these really justified? To what extent might they be rationalizations?

The Call for a Constitutional Convention

46. The General Court Asks Whether the People Want a Constitutional Convention, February 1779

[Massachusetts Archives, CLX, 32]

State of *Massachusetts-Bay*
In the House of REPRESENTATIVES,
February 19, 1779

WHEREAS *the Constitution or Form of Civil Government, which was proposed by the late Convention of this State to the People thereof, hath been disapproved by a Majority of the Inhabitants of said State:*

And whereas it is doubtful, from the Representations made to this Court what are the Sentiments of the major Part of the good People of this State as to the Expediency of now proceeding to form a new Constitution of Government:

Therefore, *Resolved,* That the Selectmen of the several Towns within this State cause the Freeholders, and other Inhabitants in their respective Towns duly qualified to vote for Representatives, to be lawfully warned to meet together in some convenient Place therein, on or before the last Wednesday of *May* next, to consider of and determine upon the following Questions.

First, Whether they chuse at this Time to have a new Constitution or Form of Government made.

Secondly, Whether they will impower their Representatives for the next Year to vote for the calling a State Convention, for the sole Purpose of forming a new Constitution, provided it shall appear to them, on Examination, that a major Part of the People present and voting at the Meetings called in the Manner and for the Purpose aforesaid, shall have answered the first Question in the affirmative.

And in Order that the Sense of the People may be known theron: Be it further *Resolved,* That the Selectmen of each Town be and hereby are directed to return into the Secretary's Office, on or before the first Wednesday in *June* next, the Doings of their respective Towns on the first Question above mentioned, certifying the Numbers voting in the Affirmative, and Numbers voting in the Negative, on the said Question.

Sent up for Concurrence,
JOHN PICKERING, *Speaker*

In COUNCIL, February 20, 1779
Read and concurred, JOHN AVERY, *Dep. Sec'ry*

Consented to by the Major Part of the Council

47. The General Court Issues a Call for a Convention, June 1779

[Massahcusetts Archives, CLX, 125]

State of *Massachusetts-Bay.*
In the House of REPRESENTATIVES,
June 15, 1779.

WHEREAS *by the Returns made into the Secretary's Office from more than two thirds of the Towns belonging to this State, agreeably to a Resolve of the General Court of the 20th of* February *last, it appears that a large majority of the inhabitants of such Towns, as have made return as aforesaid, think it proper to have a new Constitution or Form of Government, and are of opinion that the same ought to be formed by a Convention of Delegates who should be specially authorized to meet for this Purpose:* Therefore,

RESOLVED, That it be and it hereby is recommended to the several Inhabitants of the several towns in this State to form a Convention for the sole purpose of framing a new Constitution, consisting of such Number of Delegates from each town throughout the State, as every different town is intitled to send Representatives to the General Court, to meet at *Cambridge,* in the county of *Middlesex,* on the first day of *September* next.

And the Selectmen of the several towns and places in this State, impowered by the laws thereof to send Members to the General Assembly, are hereby authorized and directed to call a Meeting of their respective towns at least fourteen days before the meeting of the said Convention, to elect one or more Delegates to represent them in said Convention, at which Meeting for the election of such Delegate or Delegates, every Freeman, inhabitant of such town, who is twenty one years of age, shall have a right to vote.

Be it also *Resolved,* That it be and hereby is recommended to the inhabitants of the several towns in this State to instruct their respective Delegates to cause a printed copy of the Form of a Constitution they may agree upon in Convention, to be transmitted to the Selctmen of each town, and the Committee of each plantation, and the said Selectmen and Committees are hereby impowered and directed to lay the same before their respective towns and plantations at a regular meeting of the Male inhabitants thereof being free and twenty one years of age, to be called for that purpose, in order to its being duly considered and approved or disapproved by said towns and plantations; and it is also recommended to the several towns within this State to instruct their respective Representatives to establish the said Form of a Constitution as the Constitution and Form of Government of the State of *Massachusetts-Bay,* if upon a fair Examination it shall appear that it is approved of by at least two thirds of those who are free and twenty one years of age, belonging to this State, and present in the several Meetings.

Sent up for Concurrence,

JOHN HANCOCK, *Speaker*

In COUNCIL, June 21, 1779. Read and concurred.

JOHN AVERY, *Dep. Secr'y.*

Consented to by the Major Part of the COUNCIL.

The Towns Instruct Their Delegates to the Constitutional Convention

48. The Instructions of Pittsfield, 1779

[Smith, *History of Pittsfield,* I, 66-67]

Report of the Committee appointed by the Town to draw up Instructions for their Representatives in State Convention is as follows:——

To Col. Williams.

Sir,—As you have been duly elected by the town of Pittsfield their representative to meet in a convention of this State at Cambridge, the 1st of September next, for the purpose of forming a new Constitution for the people of this State, which we view as a matter of the greatest consequence to the present and future generations, it will doubtless be agreeable to you to understand their sentiments for the government of your deportment. You are therefore hereby instructed to unite with said convention in drawing up a Bill of Rights and in forming a new Constitution for the people of this State. We wish you to oppose all unnecessary delay in this great work, and to proceed in it with the utmost wisdom and caution.

In the Bill of Rights, you will endeavor that all those unalienable and important rights which are essential to true liberty, and form the basis of government in a free State, shall be inserted: particularly, that this people have a right to adopt that form of government which appears to us most eligible, and best calculated to promote the happiness of ourselves and posterity; that as all men by nature are free, and have no dominion one over another, and all power originates in the people, so, in a state of civil society, all power is founded in compact; that every man has an unalienable right to enjoy his own opinion in matters of religion, and to worship God in that manner that is agreeable to his own sentiments without any control whatsoever, and that no particular mode or sect of religion ought to be established, but that every one be protected in the peaceable enjoyment of his religious persuasion and way of worship; that no man can be deprived of liberty, and subjected to perpetual bondage and servitude, unless he has forfeited his liberty as a malefactor; that the people have a right peaceably to assemble, consider of their grievances, and petition for redress; that, as civil rulers derive their authority from the people, so they are accountable to them for the use of it; that elections ought to be free, equal, and annual; that, as all men are equal by nature, so, when they enter into a state of civil government, they are entitled precisely to the same rights and privileges, or to an equal degree of political happiness; that the right of trial by jury ought to be perpetual; that no man's property of right can be taken from him without his consent, given either in person or by his representative; that no laws are obligatory on the people but those that have obtained a like consent, nor are such laws of any force, if, proceeding from a corrupt majority of the legislature, they are incompatible with the fundamental principles of government, and tend to subvert it; that the freedom of speech and debates and proceedings in the House of Representatives ought not to be questioned or impeached in any court, or place out of the General Court; that excessive bail shall not be required, nor excessive fines imposed, nor cruel and unjust punishments inflicted; that jurors ought to be duly impanelled and returned, and all jurors ought to be freeholders. These, and all other liberties which you find essential to true liberty, you will claim, demand, and insist upon, as the birthrights of this people.

In respect to the Constitution, you will use your best endeavors that the following things may be inserted in it amongst others: That the election of the representative body be annual; that no representative on any occasion shall absent himself from said House without leave first had from said body, but shall constantly attend on the business during the sessions. All taxes shall be levied with the utmost equality on polls, faculty, and property. You may consent to government by a Governor, Council, and House of Representatives. The Governor and Council shall have no negative voice upon the House of Representatives; but all disputed points shall be settled by the majority of the whole legislative body. The supreme judges of the executive courts shall be elected by the suffrages of the people at large, and be commissioned by the Governor. That all grants of money shall originate in the House of Representatives. The judges of the maritime courts, the attorney-general, and high sheriffs of each county, are to be appointed by the suffrages of people at large, and commissioned by the Governor. The justices of the Common Pleas and Quarter Sessions of the Peace in each county be elected by the suffrages of the people of said counties. That no person, unless of the Protestant religion, shall be Governor, Lieutenant-governor, or member of the Council or the House of Representatives.

The said Bill of Rights and Constitution you will move may be printed, and sent abroad for the approbation of the people of this State at large, and that each town be requested by said convention to show their approbation or disapprobation of every paragraph in said Bill of Rights and Constitution, and that it be not sent abroad for their approbation or disapprobation in the lump; and that the objectionable parts, if any such shall be, shall be pointed out by each town.

You are not to dissolve the convention, but to adjourn from time to time, as you shall find necessary, till said form of government is approved by the majority of the people.

On the whole, we empower you to act agreeable to the dictates of your own judgment after you have heard all the reasonings upon the various subjects of disquisition, having an invariable respect to the true liberty and real happiness of this State throughout all generations, any instructions herein contained to the contrary notwithstanding.

THOMAS ALLEN,
ELI ROOT,
JAMES NOBLE,
LEBBEUS BACKUS. } *Committee.*

Accepted.

49. The Instructions of Gorham (Maine), 1779

[Massachusetts Archives, CLX, 288]

as God hath made of one blood all the Nations That dwell on the Earth all men that come into the world are in a state of Equality no one Higher or lower but all upon a par, this gives [——?] and stimulates the benevolent Social portion of the Soul to exercise and inclines individuals to form into civil societiy as the surest way to their protection and mutual happiness, and as civil society without without [*sic*] Rulers is like a body without a head, it is necessary that there be a first magistrate vested with so much power and no more, as is Necessary for the Due execution of the Laws and the Protection and [care ?] of the people under his Charge, which is the sole End of his Choice. The Legislative Body to consist of a President and representatives of the People without Governour and without Council as not only unnessesary but inconveinent, and perhaps Dangerous, there are so many objections against both that might be offered, that it is hoped they will never exist in this state, one Assembly as a Legislator is thought to be much the best to dispatch publick business and the affairs of state. the Jewish [system?] approved by heaven was an Excellent Institution of Goverment and the Jews happy under that goverment while wise and Good men Constituted the same[.] the Roman Senate was a happy Constitution of Goverment and the Roman a happy People while the Patricians considered their interest the same with that of the Plebiens, but when the Patricians made their insterests distinct from the Plebiens Confusion and misery insued The President in his Legislative Capacity to be speaker of the House and to have Voice with the Rest, considered as Primus inter pares——

In his Executive Capacity to sign all Commissions of Persons Chosen into office, and in the recess of the House of Representatives to conduct the weighty affairs of the Government, with the aid and assistance of a privy Council of five or seven of the best men of the state. To Command the Militia the Assembly of Representatives to Chuse the Generals of the Army Brigadiers &c and also the superiour Judges &c The several Counties in the state to chuse their field officers viz Colonels majors &c and the Justices of the Court, Justices of the Peace, Coroner, &c Every Town to Chuse their Captains Lieutenants and Ensigns

That No Qualification be required of any officer or Ruler but merit viz a sufficient knowledge and understanding in matters relative to the office, and fidelity and firmness in the Cause of Liberty. Pecuniary Qualifications can never give a Good understanding or Good Heart. That no Restriction be lade on any Profession of Christianity or denomination of Christians, but all Equally inteleled to protection of the Laws

The sense of Gorham relative to a mode of Goverment the more simple, the less danger of the loss of Liberty and most tending to happiness with the least expence Humbly addressed to the Honourable Committy on the mode of goverment

50. From the Instructions of Stoughton (Suffolk County), 1779

[Massachusetts Archives, CLX, 266-77]

As the Great End & Design of all goverment ought to be the Safety & Happiness of the people or for the Security & Protection of the Community as Such & to inable Individuals Equally to Enjoy all the Blessings & benefits resulting there from:——You are therefore Instructed to make this Fundamental Principle the Grand Object of your Study & the Ultimate end of your Exertion, thus far in General but to be more particular——

You are directed to use & employ your most assiduous Endeavors as Soon as the Convention meets that a Bill of Rights be in the first place compiled; wherin the inherent & unalienable Rights of Conscience & all those alienable rights that are not necessary to be given up in to the hand of government together with the equivalent Individuals ought undoubtedly to Recive from Government for their relinquishing a part of their natural & alienable rights for the nesessary Support of the Same; shall be clearly, fully & unequivocally ascertained defined & explained. The following Mode or plan for Collecting the wisdom of the State in framing the Constitution, appearing to your Constituents the most Eligible; you are to endeavour that the Same be adopted by the Convention, viz Let the whole Convention be divided into as many parts as there are Counties; & Let the Delegats of Each County Choose a Commitee to frame a Constitution; & when framed let them meet in County Convention with in the limits of each County at time & place agreed on to Consider alter or amend their respective forms & when So done as to be approved by a majority Let them be published for the consideration of the people Then let the Smallest County choose one Commitee Man from among their own number of Delegates to Carry in their form of Goverment to be Considered with the Rest; —& let each County that have not Double the number of inhabitants do Likewise;—those that have double to Choose two, & so on in the Same proportion with all;——

Let a sufficient length of time be allowed to Effect the Purposes afore said; —then let the Commitee Choosen to carry in & Compair their thoughts together meet in one grand Commitee at time & place agreed on & then let them proceed to frame out of the above Materials the best Constitution of Goverment in the world.——

As soon as the Grand Commitee have Compleated this task let all the delegates in the State Reassemble in one Convention to Consider alter or amend or otherwise approve of the Same;

Then Transmitt it to the Town agreeable to a Resolve of the General Court for their approbation in whole or in part, & that return be made to the Convention for examination & ratification if the Towns Direct the Same For it is apparent to your Constituents that the mode recommended by the General Court for the Establishment of Constitution will institue a president dangerous to the liberties of the people. ————

As you must be fully Satisfied that a republican form of Goverment is the most agreeable to the Genius of the people; therefore you are Directed Carefully to investigate the true principles of Such a form

And where as their are various opinions in the world respecting these principles, it must be agreeable to you to know the Sentiments of your Constituents on these Important points, therefore they will attempt to enumerate & adjust Some of them & Leave the rest to the exercise of your Superiour Talents

1[t] That man in a State of Nature, unconected with society Cannot Justly be Controuled by any Earthly power whatever but when united to Society he is under the Controul of the Supreme power thereof in a Certain limited degree.——

2[d] That the Design of man in entering into society & Submitting himself to Controul of the Supreme Power of the State is to obtain greater benefitts & advantages than he Could possiblely enjoy by being out of it that is he expects, Lays Claim & is justly entitled to the Protection and Security of his person & property together with the enjoyment of all those natural Rights whether alienable or unalienable that that [*sic*] he has not explicitly given up to the Controul of the Supreme power in the Social Contract

3[d] That in the Social Contract every individual is bound with each other to the Supreme Power to Submit to its Controul where the good of the whole Requirest it; & also to contribute his full & equal propotion of power according to his best abilities for the Support & Defence of the Power;——And the Supreme power is Likewise bound to every individual that is a Good Subject & peacefull member of Society to protect his Person Secure his property & defend his indefeasable Rights & liberties against the violence & opposition of the wicked

4th That the Supreme Power of the State is Composed of the power of individuals united Together & Exercised by the Consent of the Majority of the Members of the State for the good of the whole

5th That the Supreme power is limited & cannot Controul the unalienable Rights of mankind, or those that are alienable, if not expressly Given up the Social Contract, nor resume the equivalent that is the Security of the person & property which each individual Receives as a Consideration for those alienable Rights he parted with in entering into political society;——

6th That the Supreme power Should be So ajusted & balanced as to exert the Greatest possible energy wisdom & Goodness;——

7th That the Supreme power is divisible into Several Deparments, viz the legislative Judicial & executive; & that the powers particular to each may & ought to be delegated to Certain Disstinct and seperate Bodies of men in Such Manner that the power belonging to all or either two of the branches may not be exercised by any one of them,——

8th That the Majority of the people wherein the Supreme power is vested has a Controul over all the delegated Powers of the State; or other words, that all persons entrusted with any of the Delegated powers of the State are Servants of the people & as Such are elected by them & accountable to them & removable for breach of Trust incapacity or misbehaviour,——

9th That all the Delegated Powers of the State are to be Considered as so many Streams issuing out or flowing from the Grand fountain of Supreme power & that the people ought with care, jealouscy & circumspection to prevent these Streams from flowing too copious & rapid least in time the Grand fountain be exhausted & their Liberties Deluged in a flood of Tyranny; or other wise that every degree or portion of power is or ought to be instituted & delegated by the people to promote their Safty & happyness; and that no greater degree or portion of power ought to be Given to any man or any Body of men in any Deparment than what is absolutely Necessary to promote & Secure there Safty & happyness:——

10th That the legislative department ought to be restricted & confined wholly to the Business & duty of Making Just & equal laws agreeable to the Constitution & impossing Just & equal Taxes to be appropriated by them for the Good of the whole,—& that the Subjects of Legislation & taxation are person & that where Polittical & republican Liberty fully Subsists no law can be enacted or tax imposed that Shall be binding on any person whether property holder or not with out his consent; therefore the Consequence is this; that in order that political Liberty should fully Subsist, & the freeman Give his Consent to the Making a Law or the imposing a tax;—every free man & all the property in the State Should be Equally Represented as nearly as the nature of the thing will admitt and that the Legislature Should Consist of two Branches the one to Represent persons the other the property of the State

These, Sir, appear to your Constituents to be Some of the essential leading principles of a free Goverment & you are directed to Endeavour that no article in the Constitution be repugnant to them;—but the general use & improvment that ought to be made of the foregoing & the other Principles of a free Goverment not here mentioned your Constituents refer to your wisdom & Distinction; yet not with standing there are Some Rights & Priviledges that the Towns as Such are justly intitled to which they are not allowed to enjoy under the old Constitution and your are instructed to do your best Endeavours to have them inserted in the Proposed new Constitution

viz That Courts of equity be established in each Town for trial of civil causes to prevent the unecessary expences attending the usual Course & process of Common Law in County Courts also that the probate business & Recording of Deeds be done in Each town. Likewise that each Town choose their own magistrates & other officers Requisite to effect the purposes affore said & that the Statute & Common Laws of England as they have usually been practiced in the Courts of Law be excluded from any part of the Constitution; ———

And you are further enjoined to Spare no pain to have the following articles inserted in the Constitution in order that the freedome of the State may be preserved inviolate for ever & that the Majority of the People wherein the supreme power exist may retain their inherent controul over the Legislative judicial & executive Powers of the State viz.

That their Shall be Chosen by ballet, & every freeman to be a voter one person in the Smallest County two Persons in each County that have Double the number of inhabitants to the Smallest & So on in the Same proportion, to Sitt in State Congress to be Stiled the Council of Censors & Controul;—who Shall meet together for the first time in three years after the establishment of the Constitution & that said Council be Chosen & set once in three years for ever after the majority of whom shall be a quorum in every Case ecept as to Caling a Convention, in which two thirds of the whole Number elected Shall agree & all Persons belonging to the Legislative, judicial or executive departments to be disqualifyed for Sitting in Said Council,—And the Duty & business of Said Council shall be, in the behalf of the people to enquire whether the Constitution has been preserved inviolate, and whether the legislative juditial & executive branches of Goverment have performed their duty as guardians of the people or asumed to themselves or exercised other or Greater powers than they are intitled to by the Constitution they are also to Enquire whether the publick taxes have been justly Laid & collected in all parts of the State in what mannor the publick monies have been Disposed of & whether the Laws have been Duly executed; for these purposes they Shall have power to Send for persons papers & records they Shall have authority to pass publick Censures to order impeachments & negative Laws enacted contrary to the principles of the Constitution: these powers they Shall Continue to have & during the Space of one year from the Day of their election and no Longer.———

The Said Council of Censors & Controul Shall also have power to Call a Convention, to meet with in two years after their Sitting if their appear to them an absolute necessity of amending any article of the Constitution which may be Defective Explaining Such as may be thought not Clearly Expressed or ading Such as are necessary for the Preservation of the Rights & happiness of the people but the article to be amended & the amendments proposed and such Articles as are proposed to be added or abolished Shall be promulgated at Least Six Months before the Day appointed for the Election of Such Convention for the previous Consideration of the people That they may have an oppertunity of instructing their Delegats on the Subject, ———

The Constitutional Convention

51. An Address of the Constitutional Convention, to Their Constituents, 1780

[Massachusetts Archives, CCLXXVI, 9]

Friends and Countrymen,

Having had your Appointment and Instruction, we have undertaken the arduous Task of preparing a civil Constitution for the People of the Massachusetts Bay; and we now submit it to your candid Consideration. It is your *Interest* to revise it with the greatest Care and Circumspection, and it is your undoubted *Right,* either to propose such Alterations and Amendments as you shall judge proper, or, to give it your own Sanction in its present Form, or, totally to reject it.

In framing a Constitution, to be adapted as far as possible to the Circumstances of Posterity yet unborn, you will conceive it to be exceedingly difficult, if not impracticable, to succeed in every part of it, to the full Satisfaction of all. Could the *whole Body* of the People have Conven'd for the same Purpose, there might have been equal Reason to conclude, that a perfect Unanimity of Sentiments would have been an Object not to be obtain'd. In a Business so universally interesting, we have endeavor'd to act as became the Representatives of a wise, understanding and free People; and, as we have Reason to believe you would *yourselves* have done, we have open'd our Sentiments to each other with Candor, and made such mutual Concessions as we could consistently, and without marring the only Plan, which in our most mature Judgment we can at present offer to you.

The Interest of the Society is common to all its Members. The great Enquiry is, wherein this Common Interest consists. In determining this Question, an Advantage may arise from a Variety of Sentiments offer'd to public Examination concerning it. But wise Men are not apt to be obstinately tenacious of their own Opinions: They will always pay a due Regard to those of other Men and keep their minds open to Conviction. We conceive, that in the present Instance, by accommodating ourselves to each other, and individually yielding particular and even favorite Opinions of smaller moment, to essential Principles, and Considerations of general Utility, the public Opinion of the Plan now before you may be consolidated. —But without such mutual Condescention in unimportant Matters, we may almost venture to predict, that we shall not soon, if ever, be bless'd with such a Constitution as those are intitled to, who have struggled hard for Freedom and Independence. You will permit us on this Occasion, just to hint to you our own Apprehension, that there may be amongst us, some Persons disaffected to that great Cause for which we are contending, who may be secretly instructed by our common Enemy to divide and distract us; in hopes of preventing our Union in any Form of Government whatever, and by this Means of depriving us of the most honorable Testimony, as well as the greatest Security of our Freedom and Independence.—If there be such Men, it is our Wisdom to mark them, and guard ourselves against their Designs.

We may not expect to agree in a perfect System of Government: This is not the Lot of Mankind. The great End of Government, is, to promote the Supreme Good of human Society: Every social Affection should therefore be interested in the Forming of a Government and in judging of one when it is Formed. Would it not be prudent for Individuals to cast out of the Scale, smaller Considerations and fall in with an evident Majority, unless in Matters in which their Consciences shall constrain them to determine otherwise? Such a Sacrifice, made for the sake of Union, would afford a strong Evidence of public Affection; and Union, strengthened by the social Feeling, promise a greater Stability to any Constitution, and, in its operation, a greater Degree of Happiness to the Society. It is here to be remembered, that on the Expiration of Fifteen Years a new Convention may be held, in order that such Amendments may be made in the Plan you may now agree to, as Experience, that best Instructor, shall then point out to be expedient or necessary.

A Government without Power to exert itself, is at best, but an useless Piece of Machinery. It is probable, that for the want of Energy, it would speedily lose even the Appearance of Government, and sink into Anarchy. Unless a due Proportion of Weight is given to each of the Powers of Government, there will soon be a Confusion of the whole. An Overbearing of any one of its Parts on the rest, would destroy the Balance and accelerate its Dissolution and Ruin: And, a Power without any restraint is Tyranny. The Powers of Government must then be balanced: To do this accurately requires the highest Skill in political Architecture. Those who are to be invested with the Administration, should have such Powers given to them, as are requisite to render them useful in their respective Places; and such *Checks* should be aded to every Branch of Power as maybe sufficient to prevent its becoming formidable and injurious to the Common wealth. If we have been so fortunate as to succeed in this point of the greatest Importance, our Happiness will be compleat, in the Prospect of having laid a good Foundation for many

Generations. *You* are the Judges how far we have succeeded; and whether we have raised our Superstructure, agreeably to our profess'd Design; upon the Principles of a *Free Common Wealth.*

In order to assist your Judgments, we have thought it necessary, briefly to explain to you the Grounds and Reasons upon which we have formed our Plan. In the third article of the Declaration of Rights, we have, with as much Precision as we were capable of, provided for the free exercise of *the Rights of Conscience:* We are very sensible that our Constituents hold those Rights infinitely more valuable than all others; and we flatter ourselves, that while we have considered Morality and the public Worship of GOD, as important to the happiness of Society, we have sufficiently guarded the rights of Conscience from every possible infringement. This Article underwent long debates, and took Time in proportion to its importance; and we feel ourselves peculiarly happy in being able to inform you, that though the debates were managed by persons of various denominations, it was finally agreed upon with much more Unanimity than usually takes place in disquisitions of this Nature. We wish you to consider the Subject with Candor, and Attention. Surely it would be an affront to the People of Massachusetts Bay to labour to convince them, that the Honor and Happiness of a People depend upon Morality; and that the Public Worship of GOD has a tendency to inculcate the Principles thereof, as well as to preserve a People from forsaking Civilization, and falling into a state of Savage barbarity.

In the form now presented to you; there are no more Departments of Government than are absolutely necessary for the free and full Exercise of the Powers thereof. The House of Representatives is intended as the Representative of the Persons and the Senate, of the property of the Common Wealth. These are to be annually chosen, and to sit in seperate Bodies, each having a Negative upon the Acts of other. This Power of a Negative in each must ever be necessary; for all Bodies of Men, assembled upon the same occasion and united by one common Interest of Rank, Honor, or Estate, are liable, like an individual, to mistake bias and prejudice. These two Houses are vested with the Powers of Legislation, and are to be chosen by the Male Inhabitants who are Twenty one Years of age, and have a Freehold of the small annual income of Three Pounds or Sixty Pounds in any Estate. Your Delegates considered that Persons who are Twenty one Years of age, and have no Property, are either those who live upon a part of a Paternal estate, expecting the Fee thereof, who are but just entering into business, or those whose Idleness of Life and profligacy of manners will forever bar them from acquiring and possessing Property. And we will submit it to the former Class, whether they would not think it safer for them to have their right of Voting for a Representative suspended for small space of Time, than forever hereafter to have their Privileges liable to the control of Men, who will pay less regard to the Rights of Property because they have nothing to loose.

The Power of Revising, and stating objections to any Bill or Resolve that shall be passed by the two Houses, we were of opinion ought to be lodged in the hands of some *one* person; not only to preserve the Laws from being unsystematical and innaccurate, but that a due balance may be preserved in the three capital powers of Government. The Legislative, the Judicial and Executive Powers naturally exhist in every Government: And the History of the rise and fall of the Empires of the World affords us ample proof, that when the Man or Body of Men enact, interpret and execute the Laws, property becomes too precarious to be valuable, and a People are finally borne down with the force of corruption resulting from the Union of those Powers. The Governor is emphatically the Representative of the whole People, being chosen not by one Town or County, but by the People at large. We have therefore thought it safest to rest this Power in his hands; and as the Safety of the Common wealth requires, that there should be one Commander in Chief over the Militia, we have given the Governor that Command for the same reason, that we thought him the only proper Person that could be trusted with the power of revising the Bills and Resolves of the General Assembly; but the People may if they please choose their own Officers.

You will observe that we have resolved, that Representation ought to be founded on the Principle of equality; but it cannot be understood thereby that each Town in the Commonwealth shall have Weight and importance in a just proportion to its Numbers and property. An exact Representation would be unpracticable even in a System of Government arising from the State of Nature, and much more so in a state already divided into nearly three hundred Corporations. But we have agreed that each Town having One hundred and fifty Rateable Poles shall be entitled to send one Member, and to prevent an advantage arising to the greater Towns by their numbers, have agreed that no Town shall send two unless it hath three hundred and seventy five Rateable Poles, and then the still larger Towns are to send one Member for every two hundred and twenty-five Rateable Polls over and above Three hundred and seventy-five. This method of calculation will give a more exact Representation when applied to all the Towns in the State than any that we could fix upon.

We have however digressed from this Rule in admiting the small Towns now incorporated to send Members. There are but a few of them which will not from their continual increase, be able to send one upon the above plan in a very little Time. And a few who will never probably have that number have been heretofore in the exercise of this privilege, and will now be very unwilling to relinquish it.

To prevent the governor from abusing the Power which is necessary to be put into his hands we have provided that he shall have a Council to advise him at all Times and upon all important Occasions, and he with the advice of his Council is to have the Appointment of Civil Officers. This was very readily agreed to by your Delegates, and will undoubtedly be agreeable to their Constituents; for if those Officers who are to interpret and execute the Laws are to be dependent upon the Election of the people it must forever keep them under the Controul of ambitious, artful and interested men, who can obtain most Votes for them.—If they were to be Appointed by the Two Houses or either of them, the persons appointing them would be too numerous to be accountable for putting weak or wicked Men into Office. Besides the House is designed as the Grand Inquest of the Common Wealth, and are to impeach Officers for male Conduct, the Senate are to try the Merits of such impeachments; it would be therefore unfit that they should have the Creation of those Officers which the one may impeach and the other remove: but we conceive there is the greatest propriety in Vesting the Governor with this Power, he being as we have before observed, the compleat representative of all the People, and at all Times liable to be impeached by the House before the Senate for male Administration. And we would here observe that all the Powers which we have given the Governor are necessary to be lodged in the hands of one Man, as the General of the Army and first Magistrate, and none can be entitled to it but he who has the Annual and United Suffrages of the whole Common Wealth.

You will readily conceive it to be necessary for your own Safety, that your Judges should hold their Offices during good behaviour; for Men who hold their places upon so precarious a Tenure as annual or other frequent Appointments will never so assiduously apply themselves to study as will be necessary to the filling their places with dignity. Judges should at all Times feel themselves independent and free.

Your Delegates have further provided that the Supreme Judicial Department, by fixed and ample Salaries, may be enabled to devote themselves wholly to the Duties of their important Office. And for this reason, as well as to keep this Department seperate from the others in Government have excluded them from a Seat in the Legislature; and when our Constituents consider that the final Desicion of their Lives and Property must be had in this Court, we conceive they will universally approve the measure. The Judges of Probate and those other officers whose presence is always necessary in their respective Counties are also excluded.

We have attended to the inconveniences suggested to have arisen from having but one Judge of Probate in each County; but the erecting and altering Courts of Justice being a mere matter of Legislation, we have left it with your future Legislature to make such Alterations as the Circumstances of the several Counties may require.

Your Delegates did not conceive themselves to be vested with Power to set up one Denomination of Christians above another; for Religion must at all Times be a matter between GOD and individuals: But we have, nevertheless, found ourselves obliged by a Solemn Test, to provide for the exclusion of those from Offices who will not disclaim those Principles of Spiritual Jurisdiction which Roman Catholicks *in some Countries* have held, and which are subversive of a free Government established by the People. We find it necessary to continue the former Laws, and Modes of proceeding in Courts of Justice, until a future Legislature shall alter them: For, unless this is done, the title to Estates will become precarious, Law-suits will be multiplied, and universal Confusion must take place. And least the Commonwealth for want of a due Administration of Civil Justice should be involved in Anarchy, we have proposed to continue the present Magistrates and Officers until new Appointments shall take place.

Thus we have, with plainess and sincerity, given you the Reasons upon which we founded the principal parts of the System laid before you, which appeared to us as most necessary to be explained: And we do most humbly beseech the Great Disposer of all Events, that we and our Posterity may be established in and long enjoy the Blessings of a well-ordered and free Government.

In the Name, and pursuant to a Resolution of the Convention,

JAMES BOWDOIN, *President,*

Attest

SAMUEL BARRETT, *Secretary.*

52. The Constitution of 1780

[Massachusetts Archives, CCLXXVI, 30]

CONSTITUTION OR FORM OF GOVERNMENT for the COMMONWEALTH OF MASSACHUSETTS.

PREAMBLE.

THE end of the institution, maintenance and administration of Government, is to secure the existence of the body-politic; and to furnish the individuals who compose it, with the power of enjoying, in safety and tranquillity, their natural rights and the blessings of life: And whenever these great objects are not obtained, the people have a right to alter the Government, and to take measures necessary for their safety, prosperity and happiness.

THE body politic is formed by a voluntary association of individuals: It is a social compact, by which the whole people covenants with each citizen, and each citizen with the whole people, that all shall be governed by certain laws for the common good. It is the duty of the people, therefore, in framing a Constitution of Government, to provide for an equitable mode of making laws, as well as for an impartial interpretation, and a faithful execution of them; that every man may, at all times, find his security in them.

WE, therefore, the people of Massachusetts, acknowledging, with grateful hearts, the goodness of the Great Legislator of the Universe, in affording us, in the course of his providence, an opportunity, deliberately and peaceably, without fraud, violence, or surprise, of entering into an original, explicit and solemn compact with each other; and of forming a new Constitution of Civil Government, for ourselves and posterity; and devoutly imploring His direction in so interesting a design, DO agree upon, ordain and establish, the following *Declaration of Rights,* and *Frame of Government,* as the CONSTITUTION OF THE COMMONWEALTH OF MASSACHUSETTS.

MASSACHUSETTS.

PART THE FIRST,

A DECLARATION OF THE RIGHTS of the Inhabitants of the Commonwealth of Massachusetts.

Art. I. ALL men are born free and equal, and have certain natural, essential, and unalienable rights; among which may be reckoned the right of enjoying and defending their lives and liberties; that of acquiring, possessing, and protecting property; in fine, that of seeking and obtaining their safety and happiness.

II. IT is the right as well as the duty of all men in society, publicly, and at stated seasons, to worship the SUPREME BEING, the great creator and preserver of the universe. And no subject shall be hurt, molested, or restrained, in his person, liberty, or estate, for worshipping GOD in the manner and season most agreeable to the dictates of his own conscience; or for his religious profession or sentiments; provided he doth not disturb the public peace, or obstruct others in their religious worship.

III. AS the happiness of a people, and the good order and preservation of civil government, essentially depend upon piety, religion and morality; and as these cannot be generally diffused through a community, but by the institution of the public worship of GOD, and of public instructions in piety, religion and morality: Therefore, to promote their happiness, and to secure the good order and preservation of their government, the people of this Commonwealth have a right to invest their legislature with power to authorize and require, and the legislature shall, from time to time, authorize and require, the several towns, parishes, precincts, and other bodies politic, or religious societies, to make suitable provision, at their own expense, for the institution of the public worship of GOD, and for the support and maintenance of public protestant teachers of piety, religion and morality, in all cases where such provision shall not be made voluntarily.

AND the people of this Commonwealth have also a right to, and do, invest their legislature with authority to enjoin upon all the subjects an attendance upon the instructions of the public teachers aforesaid, at stated times and seasons, if there be any on whose instructions they can conscienciously and conveniently attend.

PROVIDED notwithstanding, that the several towns, parishes, precincts, and other bodies politic, or religious societies, shall, at all times, have the exclusive right of electing their public teachers, and of contracting with them for their support and maintenance.

AND all monies paid by the subject to the support of public worship, and of the public teachers aforesaid, shall, if he require it, be uniformly applied to the support of the public teacher or teachers of his own religious sect or denomination, provided there be any on whose instructions he attends; otherwise it may be paid towards the support of the teacher or teachers of the parish or precinct in which the said monies are raised.

AND every denomination of christians, demeaning themselves peaceably, and as good subjects of the Commonwealth, shall be equally under the protection of the law; And no subordination of any one sect or denomination to another shall ever be established by law.

IV. THE people of this Commonwealth have the sole and exclusive right of governing themselves as a free, sovereign, and independent state; and do, and forever hereafter shall, exersice and enjoy every power, jurisdiction, and right, which is not, or may not hereafter, be by them expresly delegated to the United States of America, in Congress assembled.

V. ALL power residing originally in the people, and being derived from them the several magistrates and officers of Government, vested with authority, whether legislative, executive, or judicial, are their substitutes and agents, and are at all times accountable to them.

VI. NO man, nor corporation, or association of men, have any other title to obtain advantages, or particular and exclusive privileges, distinct from those of the community, than what arises from the consideration of services rendered to the public; and this title being in nature neither hereditary, nor transmissible to children, or descendents, or relations by blood, the idea of a man born a magistrate, lawgiver, or judge, is absurd and unnatural.

VII. GOVERNMENT is instituted for the common good; for the protection, safety, prosperity, and happiness of the people; and not for the profit, honour, or private interest of any one may, family or class of men: Therefore the people alone have an incontestable, unalienable, and indefeasible right to institute Government; and to reform, alter, or totally change the fame, when their protection, safety, prosperity and happiness require it.

VIII. IN order to prevent those, who are vested with authority, from becoming oppressors, the people have a right, at such periods and in such manner as they shall establish by their frame of government, to cause their public officers to return to private life; and to fill up vacant places by certain and regular elections and appointments.

IX. ALL elections ought to be free; and all the inhabitants of this Commonwealth, having such qualifications as they shall establish by their frame of government, have an equal right to elect officers, and to be elected, for public employments.

X. EACH individual of the society has a right to be protected by it in the enjoyment of his life, liberty and property, according to standing laws. He is obliged, consequently, to contribute his share to the expense of this protection; to give his personal service, or an equivalent, when necessary: But no part of the property of any individual, can, with justice, be taken from him, or applied to public uses, without his own consent, or that of the representative body of the people: In fine, the people of this Commonwealth are not controulable by any other laws, than those to which their constitutional representative body have given their consent. And whenever the public exigencies require, that the property of any individual should be appropriated to public uses, he shall receive a reasonable compensation therefor.

XI. EVERY subject of the Commonwealth ought to find a certain remedy, by having recourse to the laws, for all injuries or wrongs which he may receive in his person, property, or character. He ought to obtain right and justice freely, and without being obliged to purchase it; compleatly, and without any denial; promptly, and without delay; comformably to the laws.

XII. NO subject shall be held to answer for any crime or offence, until the same is fully and plainly, substantially and formally, described to him; or be compelled to accuse, or furnish evidence against himself. And every subject shall have a right to produce all proofs, that may be favourable to him; to meet the witnesses against him face to face; and to be fully heard in his defence by himself, or his council, at his election. And no subject shall be arrested, imprisoned, despoiled, or deprived of his property, immunities, or privileges, put out of the protection of the law, exiled, or deprived of his life, liberty, or estate, but by the judgment of his peers, or the law of the land.

AND the legislature shall not make any law, that shall subject any person to a capital or infamous punishment, excepting for the government of the army, and navy, without trial by jury.

XIII. IN criminal prosecutions, the verification of facts in the vicinity where they happen, is one of the greatest securities of the life, liberty, and property of the citizen.

XIV. EVERY subject has a right to be secure from all unreasonable searches, and seizures of his person, his houses, his papers, and all his possessions. All warrants, therefore, are contrary to this right, if the cause or foundation of them be not previously supported by oath or affirmation; and if the order in the warrant to a civil officer, to make search in suspected places, or to arrest one or more suspected persons, or to seize their property, be not accompanied with a special designation of the persons or objects of search, arrest, or seizure: and no warrant ought to be issued but in cases, and with the formalities, prescribed by the laws.

XV. IN all controversies concerning property, and in all suits between two or more persons, except in cases in which it has heretofore been otherways used and practised, the parties have a right to a trial by a jury; and this method of procedure shall be held sacred, unless, in causes arising on the high-seas, and such as relate to mariners wages, the legislature shall hereafter find it necessary to alter it.

XVI. THE liberty of the press is essential to the security of freedom in a state; it ought not, therefore, to be restrained in this Commonwealth.

XVII. THE people have a right to keep and to bear arms for the common defence. And as in time of peace armies are dangerous to liberty, they ought not to be maintained without the consent of the legislature; and the military power shall always be held in an exact subordination to the civil authority, and be governed by it.

XVIII. A FREQUENT recurrence to the fundamental principles of the constitution, and a constant adherence to those of piety, justice, moderation, temperance, industry, and frugality, are absolutely necessary to preserve the advantages of liberty, and to maintain a free government: The people ought, consequently, to have a particular attention to all those principles, in the choice of their officers and representatives: And they have a right to require of their law-givers and magistrates, an exact and constant observance of them, in the formation and execution of the laws necessary for the good administration of the Commonwealth.

XIX. THE people have a right, in an orderly and peaceable manner, to assemble to consult upon the common good; give instructions to their representatives; and to request of the legislative body, by the way of addresses, petitions, or remonstrances, redress of the wrongs done them, and of the grievances they suffer.

XX. THE power of suspending the laws, or the execution of the laws, ought never to be exercised but by the legislature, or by authority derived from it, to be exercised in such particular cases only as the legislature shall expressly provide for.

XXI. THE freedom of deliberation, speech and debate in either house of the legislature, is so essential to the rights of the people, that it cannot be the foundation of any accusation or prosecution, action or complaint, in any other court or place whatsoever.

XXII. THE legislature ought frequently to assemble for the redress of grievances, for correcting, strengthening, and confirming the laws, and for making new laws, as the common good may require.

XXIII. NO subsidy, charge, tax, impost, or duties ought to be established, fixed, laid or levied, under any pretext whatsoever, without the consent of the people, or their representatives in the legislature.

XXIV. LAWS made to punish for actions done before the existence of such laws, and which have not been declared crimes by preceeding laws, are unjust, oppressive, and inconsistent with the fundamental principles of a free government.

XXV. NO subject ought, in any case, or in any time, to be declared guilty of treason or felony by the legislature.

XXVI. NO magistrate or court of law, shall demand excessive bail or sureties, impose excessive fines, or inflict cruel or unusual punishments.

XXVII. IN time of peace no soldier ought to be quartered in any house without the consent of the owner; and in time of war such quarters ought not to be made but by the civil magistrate, in a manner ordained by the legislature.

XXVIII. NO person can, in any case, be subjected to law-martial, or to any penalties or pains, by virtue of that law, except those employed in the army or navy, and except the militia in actual service, but by authority of the legislature.

XXIX. IT is essential to the preservation of the rights of every individual, his life, liberty, property and character, that there be an impartial interpretation of the laws, and administration of justice. It is the right of every citizen to be tried by judges as free, impartial and independent as the lot of humanity will admit. It is therefore not only the best policy, but for the security of the rights of the people, and of every citizen, that the judges of the supreme judicial court should hold their offices as long as they behave themselves well; and that they should have honourable salaries ascertained and established by standing laws.

XXX. IN the government of this Commonwealth the legislative department shall never exercise the executive and judicial powers, or either of them: The executive shall never exercise the legislative and judicial powers, or either of them: The judicial shall never exercise the legislative and executive powers, or either of them: To the end it may be a government of laws and not of men.

PART the SECOND.

The Frame of Government.

THE people inhabiting the territory formerly called the Province of Massachusetts Bay, do hereby solemnly and mutually agree with each other, to form themselves into a free, sovereign, and independent body-politic or state, by the name of THE COMMONWEALTH OF MASSACHUSETTS.

CHAPTER I.

The Legislative Power

SECTION I.

The General Court

Art. I. THE department of legislation shall be formed by two branches, *a Senate* and *House of Representatives:* each of which shall have a negative on the other.

THE legislative body shall assemble every year on the last Wednesday in May, and at such other times as they shall judge necessary; and shall dissolve and be dissolved on the day next preceeding the said last Wednesday in May; and shall be styled, THE GENERAL COURT *of* MASSACHUSETTS.

II. NO bill or resolve of the Senate or House of Representatives shall become a law, and have force as such, until it shall have been laid before the Governor for his revisal: And if he, upon such revision, approve thereof, he shall signify his approbation by signing the same. But if he have any objection to the passing of such bill or resolve, he shall return the same, together with his objections thereto, in writing, to the Senate or House of Representatives, in which soever the same shall have originated; who shall enter the objections sent down by the Governor, at large, on their records, and proceed to reconsider the said bill or resolve: But if after such reconsideration, two thirds of the said Senate or House of Representatives, shall, notwithstanding the said objections, agree to pass the same, it shall, together with the objections, be sent to the other branch of the legislature, where it shall also be reconsidered, and if approved by two thirds of the members present, it shall have the force of a law: But in all such cases, the votes of both houses shall be determined by yeas and nays; and the names of the persons voting for, or against, the said bill or resolve, shall be entered upon the public records of the Commonwealth.

AND in order to prevent unnecessary delays, if any bill or resolve shall not be returned by the Governor within five days after it shall have been presented, the same shall have the force of a law.

III. THE General Court shall forever have full power and authority to erect and constitute judicatories and courts of record, or other courts, to be held in the name of the Commonwealth, for the hearing, trying, and determining of all manner of crimes, offences, pleas, processes, plaints, actions, matters, causes and things, whatsoever, arising or happening within the Commonwealth, or between or concerning persons inhabiting, or residing, or brought within the same; whether the same be criminal or civil, or whether the said crimes be capital or not capital, and whether the said pleas be real, personal, or mixt; and for the awarding and making out of execution thereupon: To which courts and judicatories are hereby given and granted full power and authority, from time to time, to administer oaths or affirmations, for the better discovery of truth in any matter in controversy or depending before them.

IV. AND further, full power and authority are hereby given and granted to the said General Court, from time to time, to make, ordain, and establish, all manner of wholesome and reasonable orders, laws, statutes and ordinances, directions and instructions, either with penalties or without; so as the same be not repugnant or contrary to this Constitution, as they shall judge to be for the good and welfare of this Commonwealth, and for the government and ordering thereof, and of the subjects of same, and for the necessary support and defence of the government thereof; and to name and settle annually, or provide by fixed laws, for the naming and settling all civil officers within the said Commonwealth; the election and constitution of whom are not hereafter in the Form of Government otherwise provided for; and to set forth the several duties, powers and limits, of the several civil and military officers of this Commonwealth, and the forms of such oaths or affirmations as shall be respectively administered unto them for the execution of their several offices and places, so as the same be not repugnant or contrary to this Constitution; and to impose and levy proportional and reasonable assessments, rates, and taxes, upon all the inhabitants of, and persons resident, and estates lying, within the said Commonwealth; and also to impose, and levy, reasonable duties and excises, upon any produce, goods, wares, merchandize, and commodities whatsoever, brought into, produced, manufactured, or being within the same; to be issued and disposed of by warrant, under the hand of the Governor of this Commonwealth for the time being, with the advice and consent of the Council, for the public service, in the necessary defence and support of the government of the said Commonwealth, and the protection and preservation of the subjects thereof, according to such acts as are or shall be in force within the same.

AND while the public charges of government, or any part thereof, shall be assessed on polls and estates, in the manner that has hitherto be practised; in order that such assessments may be made with equality, there shall be a valuation of estates within the Commonwealth taken anew once in every ten years at the least, and as much oftener as the General Court shall order.

CHAPTER I.

SECTION II.

SENATE

Art. I. THERE shall be annually elected by the freeholders and other inhabitants of this Commonwealth, qualified as in this Constitution is provided, forty persons to be Counsellors and Senators for the year ensuing their election; to be chosen by the inhabitants of the districts, into which the Commonwealth may from time to time be divided by the General Court for that purpose: And the General Court, in assigning the numbers to be elected by the respective districts, shall govern themselves by the proportion of the public taxes paid by the said districts; and timely make known to the inhabitants of the Commonwealth, the limits of each district, and the number of Counsellors and Senators to be chosen therein; provided that the number of such districts shall be never less than thirteen; And that no district be so large as to entitle the same to choose more than six Senators.

AND the several counties in this Commonwealth shall, until the General Court shall determine it necessary to alter the said districts, be districts for the choice of Counsellors and Senators, (except that the counties of Duke's County and Nantucket shall form one district for that purpose) and shall elect the following number for Counsellors and Senators, viz.

Suffolk	Six
Essex	Six
Middlesex	Five
Hampshire	Four
Plymouth	Three
Barnstable	One
Bristol	Three
York	Two
Duke's County and Nantucket	One
Worcester	Five
Cumberland	One
Lincoln	One
Berkshire	Two

II. THE Senate shall be the first branch of the legislature; and the Senators shall be chosen in the following manner, viz. There shall be a meeting on the first Monday in April annually, forever, of the inhabitants of each town in the several counties of this Commonwealth; to be called by the Selectmen, and warned in due course of law, at least seven days before the first Monday in April, for the purpose of electing persons to be Senators and Counsellors: And at such meetings every male inhabitant of twenty-one years of age and upwards, having a freehold estate within the Commonwealth, of the annual income of three pounds, or any estate of the value of sixty pounds, shall have a right to give in his vote for the Senators for the district of which he is an inhabitant. And to remove all doubts concerning the meaning of the word "inhabitant" in this Constitution, every person shall be considered as an inhabitant, for the purpose of electing and being elected into any office, or place within this State, in that town, district or plantation, where he dwelleth, or hath his home.

THE Selectmen of the several towns shall preside at such meetings impartially; and shall receive the votes of all the inhabitants of such towns present and qualified to vote for Senators, and shall sort and count them in open town meeting, and in presence of the Town Clerk, who shall make a fair record, in presence of the Selectmen, and in open town meeting, of the name of every person voted for, and of the number of votes against his name; and a fair copy of this record shall be attested by the Selectmen and the Town-Clerk, and shall be sealed up, directed to the Secretary of the Commonwealth for the time being, with a superscription, expressing the purport of the contents thereof, and delivered by the Town-Clerk of such towns, to the Sheriff of the county in which such town lies, thirty days at least before the last Wednesday in May annually; or it shall be delivered into the Secretary's office seventeen days at least before the said last Wednesday in May; and the Sheriff of each county shall deliver all such certificates by him received into the Secretary's office seventeen days before the said last Wednesday in May.

AND the inhabitants of plantations unincorporated, qualified as this Constitution provides, who are or shall be empowered and required to assess taxes upon themselves toward the support of government, shall have the same privilege of voting for Counsellors and Senators in the plantations where they reside, as town inhabitants have in their respective towns; and the plantation-meetings for that purpose shall be held annually on the same first Monday in April, at such place in the plantations respectively, as the Assessors thereof shall direct; which Assessors shall have like authority for notifying the electors, collecting and returning the votes, as the Selectmen and Town-Clerks have in their several towns, by this Constitution. And all other persons living in places unincorporated (qualified as aforesaid) who shall be assessed to the support of government by the Assessors of an adjacent town, shall have the privilege of giving in their votes for Counsellors and Senators, in the town where they shall be assessed, and be notified of the place of meeting by the Selectmen of the town where they shall be assessed, for that purpose accordingly.

III. AND that there may be a due convention of Senators on the last Wednesday in May annually, the Governor, with five of the Council, for the time being, shall, as soon as may be, examine the returned copies of such records; and fourteen days before the said day he shall issue his summons to such persons as shall appear to be chosen by a majority of voters, to attend on that day, and take their seats accordingly: Provided nevertheless, that for the first year the said returned copies shall be examined by the President and five of the Council of the former Constitution of Government; and the said President shall, in like manner, issue his summons to the persons so elected, that they may take their seats as aforesaid.

IV. THE Senate shall be the final judge of the elections, returns and qualifications of their own members, as pointed out in the Constitution; and shall, on the said last Wednesday in May annually, determine and declare who are elected by each district, to be Senators by a majority of votes: And in case there shall not appear to be the full number of Senators returned elected by a majority of votes for any district, the deficiency shall be supplied in the following manner, viz. The members of the House of Representatives, and such Senators as shall be declared elected, shall take the names of such persons as shall be found to have the highest number of votes in such district, and not elected, amounting to twice the number of Senators wanting, if there be so many voted for; and out of these, shall elect by ballot a number of Senators sufficient to fill up the vacancies in such district: And in this manner all such vacancies shall be filled up in every district of the Commonwealth; and in like manner all vacancies in the Senate, arising by death, removal out of the State, or otherwise, shall be supplied as soon as may be, after such vacancies shall happen.

V. PROVIDED nevertheless, that no person shall be capable of being elected as a Senator who is not seized in his own right of a freehold within this Commonwealth, of the value of three hundred pounds at least, or possessed of personal estate to the value of six hundred pounds at least, or of both to the amount of the same sum, and who has not been an inhabitant of this Commonwealth for the space of five years immediately preceeding his election, and at the time of his election, he shall be an inhabitant in the district, for which he shall be chosen.

VI. THE Senate shall have power to adjourn themselves, provided such adjournments do not exceed two days at a time.

VII. THE Senate shall choose its own President, appoint its own officers, and determine its own rules of proceedings.

VIII. THE Senate shall be a court with full authority to hear and determine all impeachments made by the House of Representatives, against any officer or officers of the Commonwealth, for misconduct and mal-administration in their offices. But previous to the trial of every impeachment, the members of the Senate shall respectively be sworn, truly and impartially to try and determine the charge in question, according to evidence. Their judgment, however, shall not extend further than to removal from office, and disqualification to hold or enjoy any place of honour, trust, or profit under this Commonwealth: But the party so convicted, shall be nevertheless, liable to indictment, trial, judgment, and punishment, according to the laws of the land.

IX. NOT less than sixteen members of the Senate shall constitute a quorum for doing business.

CHAPTER I.

SECTION III.

House of Representatives.

Art. I. THERE shall be in the Legislature of this Commonwealth, a representation of the people, annually elected, and founded upon the principle of equality.

II. AND in order to provide for a representation of the citizens of this Commonwealth, founded upon the principle of equality, every corporate town containing one hundred and fifty rateable polls, may elect one Representative: Every corporate town, containing three hundred and seventy-five rateable polls, may elect two Representatives: Every corporate town, containing six hundred rateable polls, may elect three Representatives; and proceeding in that manner, making two hundred and twenty-five rateable polls the mean increasing number for every additional Representative.

PROVIDED nevertheless, that each town now incorporated, not having one hundred and fifty rateable polls, may elect one representative: but no place shall hereafter be incorporated with the privilege of electing a Representative, unless there are within the same one hundred and fifty rateable polls.

AND the House of Representatives shall have power from time to time to impose fines upon such towns as shall neglect to choose and return members to the same, agreeably to this Constitution.

THE expenses of travelling to the General Assembly, and returning home, once in every session, and no more, shall be paid by the government, out of the public treasury, to every member who shall attend as seasonably as he can, in the judgment of the House, and does not depart without leave.

III. EVERY member of the House of Representatives shall be chosen by written votes; and for one year at least next preceeding his election, shall have been an inhabitant of, and have been seized in his own right of a freehold of the value of one hundred pounds within the town he shall be chosen to represent, or any rateable estate to the value of two hundred pounds; and he shall cease to represent the said town immediately on his ceasing to be qualified as aforesaid.

IV. EVERY male person, being twenty-one years of age, and resident in any particular town in this Commonwealth for the space of one year next preceeding, having a freehold estate within the same town, of the annual income of three pounds, or any estate of the value of sixty pounds, shall have a right to vote in the choice of a Representative or Representatives for the said town.

V. THE members of the House of Representatives shall be chosen annually in the month of May, ten days at least before the last Wednesday of that month.

VI. THE House of Representatives shall be the Grand Inquest of this Commonwealth; and all impeachments made by them shall be heard and tried by the Senate.

VII. ALL money-bills shall originate in the House of Representatives; but the Senate may propose or concur with amendments, as on other bills.

VIII. THE House of Representatives shall have power to adjourn themselves; provided such adjournment shall not exceed two days at a time.

IX. NOT less than sixty members of the House of Representatives, shall constitute a quorum for doing business.

X. THE House of Representatives shall be the judge of the returns, elections, and qualifications of its own members, as pointed out in the constitution; shall choose their own Speaker; appoint their own officers, and settle the rules and orders of proceeding in their own house: They shall have authority to punish by imprisonment, every person, not a member, who shall be guilty of disrespect to the House, by any disorderly, or contemptuous behaviour, in its presence; or who, in the town where the General Court is sitting, and during the time of its sitting, shall threaten harm to the body or estate of any of its members, for any thing said or done in the House; or who shall assault any of them therefor; or who shall assault, or arrest, any witness, or other person, ordered to attend the House, in his way in going or returning; or who shall rescue any person arrested by the order of the House.

AND no member of the House of Representatives shall be arrested, or held to bail on mean process, during his going unto, returning from, or his attending, the General Assembly.

XI. THE Senate shall have the same powers in the like cases; and the Governor and Council shall have the same authority to punish in like cases. Provided that no imprisonment on the warrant or order of the Governor, Council, Senate, or House of Representatives, for either of the above-described offenses, be for a term exceeding thirty days.

AND the Senate and House of Representatives may try, and determine, all cases where their rights and privileges are concerned, and which, by the Constitution, they have authority to try and determine, by committees of their own members, or in such other way as they may respectively think best.

CHAPTER II.

Executive Power

SECTION I.

Governor

Art. I. THERE shall be a supreme executive Magistrate, who shall be styled, THE GOVERNOR OF THE COMMONWEALTH OF MASSACHUSETTS; and whose title shall be —HIS EXCELLENCY.

II. THE Governor shall be chosen annually: And no person shall be eligible to this office, unless at the time of his election, he shall have been an inhabitant of this Commonwealth for seven years next preceeding; and unless he shall, at the same time, be seized in his own right, of a freehold within the Commonwealth, of the value of one thousand pounds; and unless he shall declare himself to be of the christian religion.

III. THOSE persons who shall be qualified to vote for Senators and Representatives within the several towns of this

Commonwealth, shall, at a meeting to be called for that purpose, on the first Monday of April annually, give in their votes for a Governor, to the Selectmen, who shall preside at such meetings; and the Town-Clerk, in the presence and with the assistance of the Selectmen, shall, in open town-meeting, sort and count the votes, and form a list of the persons voted for, with the number of votes for each person against his name; and shall make a fair record of the same in the town books, and a public declaration thereof in the said meeting; and shall, in the presence of the inhabitants, seal up copies of the said list, attested by him and the Selectmen, and transmit the same to the Sheriff of the county, thirty days at least before the last Wednesday in May; and the Sheriff shall transmit the same to the Secretary's office, seventeen days at least before the said last Wednesday in May; or the Selectmen may cause returns of the same to be made to the office of the Secretary of the Commonwealth seventeen days at least before the said day; and the Secretary shall lay the same before the Senate and the House of Representatives, on the last Wednesday in May, to be by them examined: And in case of an election by a majority of all the votes returned, the choice shall be by them declared and published: But if no person shall have a majority of votes, the House of Representatives shall, by ballot, elect two out of four persons who had the highest number of votes, if so many shall have been voted for; but, if otherwise, out of the number voted for; and make return to the Senate of the two persons so elected; on which, the Senate shall proceed, by ballot, to elect one, who shall be declared Governor.

IV. THE Governor shall have authority, from time to time, at his discretion, to assemble and call together the Counsellors of this Commonwealth, for the time being; and the Governor, with the said Counsellors, or five of them at least, shall, and may, from time to time, hold and keep a Council, for the ordering and directing the affairs of the Commonwealth, agreeably to the Constitution and the laws of the land.

V. THE Governor, with advice of Council, shall have full power and authority, during the session of the General Court, to adjourn or prorogue the same to any time the two Houses shall desire; and to dissolve the same on the day next preceeding the last Wednesday in May; and, in the recess of the said court, to prorogue the same from time to time, not exceeding ninety days in any one recess; and to call it together sooner than the time to which it may be adjourned or prorogued, if the welfare of the Commonwealth shall require the same: And in case of any infectious distemper prevailing in the place where the said court is next at any time to convene, or any other cause happening whereby danger may arise to the health or lives of the members from their attendance, he may direct the session to be held at some other the most convenient place within the State.

AND the Governor shall dissolve the said General Court on the day next preceeding the last Wednesday in May.

VI. IN cases of disagreement between the two Houses, with regard to the necessity, expediency or time of adjournment, or prorogation, the Governor, with advice of the Council, shall have a right to adjourn or prorogue the General Court, not exceeding ninety days, as he shall determine the public good shall require.

VII. THE Governor of this Commonwealth for the time being, shall be the commander in chief of the army and navy, and of all the military forces of the State, by sea and land; and shall have full power by himself, or by any commander, or other officer or officers, from time to time, to train, instruct, exercise and govern the militia and navy; and, for the special defence and safety of the Commonwealth, to assemble in martial array, and put in warlike posture, the inhabitants thereof, and to lead and conduct them and with them, to encounter, repel, resist, expel and pursue, by force of arms, as well by sea as by land, within or without the limits of this Commonwealth, and also to kill, slay and destroy, if necessary, and conquer by all fitting ways, enterprises and means whatsoever, all and every such person and persons as shall, at any time hereafter, in a hostile manner attempt or enterprise the destruction, invasion, detriment, or annoyance of this Commonwealth; and to use and exercise, over the army and navy, and over the militia in actual service, the law-martial, in time of war or invasion, and also in time of rebellion, declared by the legislature to exist, as occasion shall necessarily require; and to take and surprise by all ways and means whatsoever, all and every such person or persons, with their ships, arms, ammunition and other goods, as shall, in a hostile manner, invade or attempt the invading, conquering, or annoying this Commonwealth; and that the Governor be intrusted with all these and other powers, incident to the offices of Captain-General and Commander in Chief, and Admiral, to be exercised agreeably to the rules and regulations of the Constitution, and the laws of the land, and not otherwise.

PROVIDED, that the said Governor shall not, at any time hereafter, by virtue of any power by this Constitution granted, or hereafter to be granted to him by the legislature, transport any of the inhabitants of this Commonwealth, or oblige them to march out of the limits of the same, without their free and voluntary consent, or the consent of the General Court; except so far as may be necessary to march or transport them by land or water, for the defence of such part of the State, to which they cannot otherwise conveniently have access.

VIII. THE power of pardoning offences, except such as persons may be convicted of before the Senate by an impeachment of the House, shall be in the Governor, by and with the advice of Council: But no charter of pardon, granted by the Governor, with advice of the Council, before conviction, shall avail the party pleading the same, notwithstanding any general or particular expressions contained therein, descriptive of the offence, or offences intended to be pardoned.

IX. ALL judicial officers, the Attorney-General, the Solicitor-General, all Sheriffs, Coroners, and Registers of Probate, shall be nominated and appointed by the Governor, by and with the advice and consent of the Council; and every such nomination shall be made by the Governor, and made at least seven days prior to such appointment.

X. THE Captains and subalterns of the militia, shall be elected by the written votes of the trainband and alarm list of their respective companies, of twenty-one years of age and upwards: The field-officers of regiments shall be elected by the written votes of the Captains and subalterns of their respective regiments: The Brigadiers shall be elected in like manner, by the field-officers of their respective brigades: And such officers, so elected, shall be commissioned by the Governor, who shall determine their rank.

THE Legislature shall, by standing laws, direct the time and manner of convening the electors, and of collecting votes, and of certifying to the Governor the officers elected.

THE Major-Generals shall be appointed by the Senate and House of Representatives, each having a negative upon the other; and be commissioned by the Governor.

AND if the electors of Brigadiers, field-officers, Captains or subalterns, shall neglect or refuse to make such elections, after being duly notified according to the laws for the time being, then the Governor, with advice of Council, shall appoint suitable persons to fill such offices.

AND no officer, duly commissioned to command in the militia, shall be removed from his office, but by the address of both

Houses to the Governor; or by fair trial in court-martial, pursuant to the laws of the Commonwealth for the time being.

THE commanding officers of regiments shall appoint their Adjutants and Quartermasters; the Brigadiers their Brigade Majors; and the Major-Generals their Aids; and the Governor shall appoint the Adjutant-General.

THE Governor, with advice of Council, shall appoint all officers of the continental army, whom by the confederation of the United States it is provided that this Commonwealth shall appoint,—as also all officers of forts and garrisons.

THE divisions of the militia into brigades regiment and companies, made in pursuance of the militia laws now in force, shall be considered as the proper divisions of the militia of this Commonwealth, until the same shall be altered in pursuance of some future law.

XI. NO monies shall be issued out of the treasury of this Commonwealth, and disposed of (except such sums as may be appropriated for the redemption of bills of credit or Treasurer's notes, or for the payment of interest arising thereon) but by warrant under the hand of the Governor for the time being, with the advice and consent of the Council, for the necessary defence and support of the Commonwealth; and for the protection and preservation of the inhabitants thereof, agreeably to the acts and resolves of the General Court.

XII. ALL public boards, the Commissary-General, all superintending officers of public magazines and stores, belonging to this Commonwealth, and all commanding officers of forts and garrisons within the same, shall once in every three months officially and without requisition, and at other times, when required by the Governor, deliver to him an account of all goods, stores, provisions, ammunition, cannon with their appendages, and small arms with their accoutrements, and of all other public property whatever under their care respectively; distinguishing the quantity, number, quality and kind of each, as particularly as may be; together with the condition of such forts and garrisons: And the said commanding officer shall exhibit to the Governor, when required by him, true and exact plans of such forts, and of the land and sea or harbour or harbours adjacent.

AND the said boards, and all public officers, shall communicate to the Governor, as soon as may be after receiving the same, all letters, dispatches, and intelligences of a public nature, which shall be directed to them respectively.

XIII. AS the public good requires that the Governor should not be under the undue influence of any of the members of the General Court, by a dependence on them for his support—that he should in all cases, act with freedom for the benefit of the public—that he should not have his attention necessarily diverted from that object to his private concerns—& that he should maintain the dignity of the Commonwealth in the character of its chief magistrate—it is necessary that he should have an honorable stated salary, of a fixed & permanent value, amply sufficient for those purposes, & established by standing laws: And it shall be among the first acts of the General Court, after the commencement of this Constitution, to establish such salary by law accordingly.

PERMANENT and honorable salaries shall also be established by law for the Justices of the supreme judicial court.

AND if it shall be found, that any of the salaries aforesaid, so established, are insufficient, they shall, from time to time, be enlarged as the General Court shall judge proper.

CHAPTER II.

SECTION II.

Lieutenant-Governor

Art. I. THERE shall be annually elected a Lieutenant-Governor of the Commonwealth of Massachusetts, whose title shall be HIS HONOR—and who shall be qualified, in point of religion, property, and residence in the Commonwealth, in the same manner with the Governor: And the day and manner of his election, and the qualifications of the electors, shall be the same as are required in the election of a Governor. The return of the votes for this officer, and the declaration of his election, shall be in the same manner: And if no one person shall be found to have a majority of all the votes returned, the vacancy shall be filled by the Senate and House of Representatives, in the same manner as the Governor is to be elected, in case no one person shall have a majority of the votes of the people to be a Governor.

II. THE Governor, and in his absence the Lieutenant-Governor, shall be President of the Council, but shall have no vote in Council: And the Lieutenant-Governor shall always be a member of the Council, except when the chair of the Governor shall be vacant.

III. WHENEVER the chair of the Governor shall be vacant, by reason of his death, or absence from the Commonwealth, or otherwise, the Lieutenant-Governor, for the time being, shall, during such vacancy, perform all the duties incumbent upon the Governor, and shall have and exercise all the powers and authorities, which by this Constitution the Governor is vested with, when personally present.

CHAPTER II.

SECTION III.

Council, and the Manner of settling Elections by the Legislature.

Art. I. THERE shall be a Council for advising the Governor in the executive part of government, to consist of nine persons besides the Lieutenant-Governor, whom the Governor, for the time being, shall have full power and authority, from time to time, at his discretion, to assemble and call together. And the Governor, with the said Counsellors, or five of them at least, shall and may, from time to time, hold and keep a Council, for the ordering and directing the affairs of the Commonwealth, according to the laws of the land.

II. NINE Counsellors shall be annually chosen from among the persons returned for Counsellors and Senators, on the last Wednesday in May, by the joint ballot of the Senators and Representatives assembled in one room: And in case there shall not be found upon the first choice, the whole number of nine persons who will accept a seat in the Council, the deficiency shall be made up by the electors aforesaid from among the people at large; and the number of Senators left shall constitute the Senate for the year. The seats of the persons thus elected from the Senate, and accepting the trust, shall be vacated in the Senate.

III. THE Counsellors, in the civil arrangements of the Commonwealth, shall have rank next after the Lieutenant-Governor.

IV. NOT more than two Counsellors shall be chosen out of any one district of this Commonwealth.

V. THE resolutions and advice of the Council shall be recorded in a register, and signed by the members present; and this record may be called for at any time by either House of the legislature; and any member of the Council may insert his opinion contrary to the resolution of the majority.

VI. WHENEVER the office of the Governor and Lieutenant-Governor shall be vacant, by reason of death, absence, or otherwise, then the Council or the major part of them, shall, during such vacancy, have full power and authority, to do, and execute, all and every such acts, matters and things, as the Governor or the Lieutenant-Governor might or could, by virtue of this Constitution, do or execute, if they, or either of them, were personally present.

VII. AND whereas the elections appointed to be made by this Constitution, on the last Wednesday in May annually, by the two Houses of the legislature, may not be compleated on that day, the said elections may be adjourned from day to day until the same shall be compleated. And the order of elections shall be as follows; the vacancies in the Senate, if any, shall first be filled up; the Governor and Lieutenant-Governor shall then be elected, provided there should be no choice of them by the people: And afterwards the two Houses shall proceed to the election of the Council.

CHAPTER II.

SECTION IV.

Secretary, Treasurer, Commissary, &c.

Art. I. THE Secretary, Treasurer and Receiver-General, and the Commissary-General, Notaries Public, and Naval-Officers, shall be chosen annually, by joint ballot of the Senators and Representatives in one room. And that the citizens of this Commonwealth may be assured, from time to time, that the monies remaining in the public Treasury, upon the settlement and liquidation of the public accounts, are their property, no man shall be eligible as Treasurer and Receiver-General more than five years successively.

II. THE records of the Commonwealth shall be kept in the office of the Secretary, who may appoint his Deputies, for whose conduct he shall be accountable, and he shall attend the Governor and Council, the Senate and House of Representatives, in person, or by his deputies, as they shall respectively require.

CHAPTER III.

Judiciary Power.

Art. I. THE tenure, that all commission officers shall by law have in their officers, shall be expressed in their respective commissions. All judicial officers, duly appointed, commissioned and sworn, shall hold their offices during good behaviour, excepting such concerning whom there is different provision made in this Constitution: Provided nevertheless, the Governor, with consent of the Council, may remove them upon the address of both Houses of the Legislature.

II. EACH branch of the Legislature, as well as the Governor and Council, shall have authority to require the opinions of the Justices of the supreme judicial court, upon important questions of law, and upon solemn occasions.

III. IN order that the people may not suffer from the long continuance in place of any Justice of the Peace, who shall fail of discharging the important duties of his office with ability or fidelity, all commissions of Justices of the Peace shall expire and become void in the term of seven years from their respective dates; and upon the expiration of any commission, the same may, if necessary, be renewed, or another person appointed, as shall most conduce to the well-being of the Commonwealth.

IV. THE Judges of Probate of Wills, and for granting letters of administration, shall hold their courts at such place or places, on fixed days, as the convenience of the people shall require. And the Legislature shall, from time to time, hereafter appoint such times and places; until which appointments, the said courts shall be holden at the times and places which the respective Judges shall direct.

V. ALL causes of marriage, divorce and alimony, and all appeals from the Judges of Probate shall be heard and determined by the Governor and Council, until the Legislature shall, by law, make other provision.

CHAPTER IV.

Delegates to Congress

THE delegates of the Commonwealth to the Congress of the United States, shall, sometime in the month of June annually, be elected by the joint ballot of the Senate and House of Representatives, assembled together in one room; to serve in Congress for one year, to commence on the first Monday in November then next ensuing. They shall have commissions under the hand of the Governor, and the great seal of the Commonwealth; but may be recalled at any time within the year, and others chosen and commissioned, in the same manner, in their stead.

CHAPTER V.

The University at Cambridge, and Encouragement of Literature &c.

SECTION I.

The University.

Art. I. WHEREAS our wise and pious ancestors, so early as the year one thousand six hundred and thirty-six, laid the foundation of Harvard-College, in which university many persons of great eminence have, by the blessing of GOD, been initiated in those arts and sciences, which qualified them for public employments, both in Church and State: And whereas the encouragement of arts and sciences, and all good literature, tends to the honour of GOD, the advantage of the christian religion, and the great benefit of this and the other United States of America—It is declared, That the PRESIDENT and FELLOWS of HARVARD-COLLEGE, in their corporate capacity, and their successors in that capacity, their officers and servants, shall have, hold, use, exercise and enjoy, all the powers, authorities, rights, liberties, privileges, immunities and franchises, which they now have, or are entitled to have, hold, use, exercise and enjoy: And the same are hereby ratified and confirmed unto them, the said President and Fellows of Harvard-College, and to their successors, and to their officers and servants, respectively, forever.

II. AND whereas there have been at sundry times, by divers persons, gifts, grants, devises of houses, lands, tenements, goods, chattels, legacies and conveyances, heretofore made, either to Harvard-College in Cambridge, in New-England, or to the President and Fellows of Harvard-College, or to the said College, by some other description, under several charters successively: IT IS DECLARED, That all the said gifts, grants, devises, legacies and conveyances, are hereby forever confirmed unto the President and Fellows of Harvard-College, and to their successors, in the capacity aforesaid, according to the true intent and meaning of the donor or donors, grantor or grantors, devisor or devisors.

III. AND whereas by an act of the General Court of the Colony of Massachusetts-Bay, passed in the year one thousand six hundred and forty-two, the Governor and Deputy-governor, for the time being, and all the magistrates of that jurisdiction, were, with the President, and a number of the clergy in the said act described, constituted the Overseers of Harvard-College: And it being necessary, in this new Constitution of Government, to ascertain who shall be deemed successors to the said Governor, Deputy-Governor and Magistrates: IT IS DECLARED, That the Governor, Lieutenant-Governor, Council and Senate of this Commonwealth, are, and shall be deemed, their successors; who, with the President of Harvard-College for the time being, together with the Ministers of the congregational churches in the towns of Cambridge, Watertown, Charlestown, Boston, Roxbury, and Dorchester, mentioned in the said act, shall be, and hereby are, vested with all the powers and authority belonging, or in any way appertaining to the Overseers of Harvard-College; PROVIDED, that nothing herein shall be construed to prevent the Legislature of this Commonwealth from making such alterations in the government of the said university, as shall be conducive to its advantage, and the interest of the republic of letters, in as full a manner as might have been done by the Legislature of the late Province of the Massachusetts-Bay.

CHAPTER V.

SECTION II.

The Encouragement of Literature, &c.

WISDOM, and knowledge, as well as virtue, diffused generally among the body of the people, being necessary for the preservation of their rights and liberties; and as these depend on spreading the opportunities and advantages of education in the various parts of the country, and among the different orders of the people, it shall be the duty of legislatures and magistrates, in all future periods of this Commonwealth, to cherish the interests of literature and the sciences, and all seminaries of them; especially the university at Cambridge, public schools, and grammar schools in the towns; to encourage private societies and public institutions, rewards and immunities, for the promotion of agriculture, arts, sciences, commerce, trades, manufactures, and a natural history of the country; to countenance and inculcate the principles of humanity and general benevolence, public and private charity, industry and frugality, honesty and punctuality in their dealings; sincerity, good humor, and all social affections, and generous sentiments among the people.

CHAPTER VI.

Oaths and Subscriptions; Incompatibility of and Exclusion from Officers; Pencuniary Qualifications; Commissions; Writs; Confirmation of Laws; Habeas Corpus; The Enacting Stile; Continuance of Officers; Provision for a future Revisal of the Constitution, &c.

Art. I. ANY person chosen Governor, Lieutenant-Governor, Counsellor, Senator, or Representative, and accepting the trust, shall, before he proceed to execute the duties of his place or office, make and subscribe the following declaration, viz.—

"I, A.B. do declare, that I believe the christian religion, and have a firm persuasion of its truth; and that I am seized and possessed, in my own right, of the property required by the Constitution as one qualification for the office or place to which I am elected."

AND the Governor, Lieutenant-governor, and Counsellors, shall make and subscribe the said declaration, in the presence of the two Houses of Assembly; and the Senators and Representatives first elected under this Constitution, before the President and five of the Council of the former Constitution, and forever afterwards before the Governor and Council for the time being.

AND every person chosen to either of the places or offices aforesaid, as also any person appointed or commissioned to any judicial, executive, military, or other office under the government, shall, before he enters on the discharge of the business of his place or office, take and subscribe the following declaration, and oaths or affirmations, viz.—

"I, A.B. do truly and sincerely acknowledge, profess, testify and declare, that the Commonwealth of Massachusetts is, and of right ought to be, a free, sovereign and independent State; and I do swear, that I will bear true faith and allegiance to the said Commonwealth, and that I will defend the same against traiterous conspiracies and all hostile attempts whatsoever: And that I do renounce and abjure all allegiance, subjection and obedience to the King, Queen or Government of Great-Britain, (as the case may be) and every other foreign power whatsoever: And that no foreign Prince, Person, Prelate, State or Potentate, hath, or ought to have, any jurisdiction, superiority, pre-eminence, authority, dispensing or other power, in any matter, civil ecclesiastical or spiritual, within this Commonwealth: except the authority and power which is or may be vested by their Constituents in the Congress of the United States: And I do further testify and declare, that no man or body of men hath or can have any right to absolve or discharge me from the obligation of this oath, declaration or affirmation; and that I do make this acknowledgment, profession, testimony, declaration, denial, renunciation and abjuration, heartily and truly, according to the common meaning and acceptation for the foregoing words, without any equivocation, mental

evasion, or secret reservation whatsoever,
So help me GOD."

"I, A.B. do solemnly swear and affirm that I will faithfully and impartially discharge and perform all the duties incumbent on me as ; according to the best of my abilities and understanding, agreeably to the rules and regulations of the Constitution, and the laws of this Commonwealth.
"So help me GOD."

PROVIDED always, that when any person chosen or appointed as aforesaid, shall be of the denomination of the people called Quakers, and shall decline taking the said oaths, he shall make his affirmation in the foregoing form, and subscribe the same, omitting the words *"I do swear," "and abjure," "oath or," "and abjuration,"* in the first oath; and in the second oath, the words *"swear and;"* and in each of them the words *"So help me GOD;"* subjoining instead thereof, *"This I do under the pains and penalties of perjury."*

AND the said oaths or affirmations shall be taken and subscribed by the Governor, Lieutenant-Governor, and Counsellors, before the President of the Senate, in the presence of the two Houses of Assembly; and by the Senators and Representatives first elected under this Constitution, before the President and five of the Council of the former Constitution; and forever afterwards before the Governor and Council for the time being: And by the residue of the officers aforesaid, before such persons and in such manner as from time to time shall be prescribed by the Legislature.

II. NO Governor, Lieutenant-Governor, or Judge of the supreme judicial court, shall hold any other office or place, under the authority of this Commonwealth, except such as by this Constitution they are admitted to hold, saving that the Judges of the said court may hold the offices of Justices of the Peace through the State; nor shall they hold any other place or office, or receive any pension or salary from any other State or government or Power whatever.

NO person shall be capable of holding or exercising at the same time, more than one of the following offices within this state, viz.—Judge of Probate—Sheriff—Register of Probate—or Register of Deeds—and never more than any two offices which are to be held by appointment of the Governor, or the Governor and Council, or the Senate, or the House of Representatives, or by the election of the people of the State at large, or of the people of any county, military offices and the offices of Justices of the Peace excepted, shall be held by one person.

NO person holding the office of Judge of the supreme judicial court—Secretary—Attorney-General — Solicitor-General — Treasurer or Receiver-General—Judge of Probate—Commissary-General—President, Professor, or Instructor of Harvard-College—Sheriff—Clerk of the House of Representatives—Register of Probate—Register of Deeds—Clerk of the Supreme Judicial Court—Clerk of the Inferior Court of Common Pleas—or Officer of the Customs, including in this description Naval-Officers—shall at the same time have a seat in the Senate or House of Representatives; but their being chosen or appointed to, & accepting the same, shall operate as a resignation of their seat in the Senate or House of Representatives; and the place so vacated shall be filled up.

AND the same rule shall take place in case any Judge of the said Supreme Judicial Court, or Judge of Probate, shall accept a seat in Council; or any Counsellor shall accept of either of those offices or places.

AND no person shall ever be admitted to hold a seat in the Legislature, or any office of trust or importance under the government of this Commonwealth, who shall, in the due course of law, have been convicted of bribery or corruption in obtaining an election or appointment.

III. IN all cases where sums of money are mentioned in this Constitution, the value thereof shall be computed in silver at six shillings and eight pence per ounce: And it shall be in the power of the Legislature from time to time to increase such qualifications, as to property, of the persons to be elected to offices, as the circumstances of the Commonwealth shall require.

IV. ALL commissions shall be in the name of the Commonwealth of Massachusetts, signed by the Governor and attested by the Secretary or his Deputy, and have the great seal of the Commonwealth affixed thereto.

V. ALL writs issuing out of the clerk's office in any of the courts of law, shall be in the name of the Commonwealth of Massachusetts: They shall be under the seal of the court from whence they issue: They shall bear test of the first Justice of the court to which they shall be returnable, who is not a party, and be signed by the clerk of such court.

VI. ALL the laws which have heretofore been adopted, used and approved in the Province, Colony or State of Massachusetts-Bay, and usually practised on in the courts of law, shall still remain and be in full force, until altered or repealed by the Legislature; such parts only excepted as are repugnant to the rights and liberties contained in this Constitution.

VII. THE privilege and benefit of the writ of habeas corpus shall be enjoyed in this Commonwealth in the most free, easy, cheap, expeditious and ample manner; and shall not be suspended by the Legislature, except upon the most urgent and pressing occasions, and for a limited time not exceeding twelve months.

VIII. THE enacting stile, in making and passing all acts, statutes and laws shall be——"Be it enacted by the Senate and House of Representatives in General Court assembled, and by the authority of the same."

IX. TO the end there may be no failure of justice or danger arise to the Commonwealth from a change of the Form of Government—all officers, civil and military, holding commissions under the government & people of Massachusetts-Bay in New England, and all other officers of the said government and people, at the time this Constitution shall take effect, shall have, hold, use, exercise and enjoy all the powers and authority to them granted or committed, until other persons shall be appointed in their stead: And all courts of law shall proceed in the execution of the business of their respective departments; and all the executive and legislative officers, bodies and powers shall continue in full force, in the enjoyment and exercise of all their trusts, employments and authority; until the General Court and the supreme and executive officers under this Constitution are designated and invested with their respective trusts, powers and authority.

X. IN order the more effectually to adhere to the principles of the Constitution, and to correct those violations which by any means may be made therein, as well as to form such alterations as from experience shall be found necessary—the General Court which shall be in the year of our Lord one thousand seven hundred and ninety-five, shall issue precepts to the Selectmen of the several towns, and to the assessors of the unincorporated plantations, directing them to convene the qualified voters of their respective towns and plantations for the purpose of collecting their sentiments on the necessity or expediency of revising the Constitution, in order to amendments.

AND if it shall appear by the returns made, that two thirds of the qualified voters throughout the State, who shall assemble and vote in consequence of the said precepts, are in favour of such revision or amendment, the General Court shall issue precepts, or direct them to be issued from the Secretary's office to the several towns to elect delegates to meet in Convention for the purpose aforesaid.

THE said delegates to be chosen in the same manner and proportion as their Representatives in the second branch of the Legislature are by this Constitution to be chosen.

XI. THIS form of government shall be enrolled on parchment and deposited in the Secretary's office, and be a part of the laws of the land—and printed copies thereof shall be prefixed to the book containing the laws of this Commonwealth, in all future editions of the said laws.

JAMES BOWDOIN, *President* of the Convention.

Attest,
SAMUEL BARRETT, Secretary.

The Ratification of the Constitution of 1780

53. The Return of Boston, May 12, 1780

[*Boston Town Records, 1778-1783,* 129-35]

Wednesday May 10th. 9. O. Clock Forenoon—Met according to Adjournment

The Committee to whom was referred the consideration of the third Article in the Declaration of Rights—Reported the same with such alterations as they Judged most consonant to the Sense of the Town and is as follows—Viz[t].

As the Happiness of a People and the Good Order; and Preservation of civil Government essentially depends upon Piety, religion and morality; and as these cannot be generally deffused through a Community, but by the Publick Worship of God, and Publick Instructions in Piety religion and morality, Therefore to promote their happiness and to secure the good order and preservation of their Goverment the People of this Commonwealth have a right to invest their Legislative with Power; to Authorize and require all the Inhabitants of this Commonwealth to make provision at their own expence for the Publick Worship of God and for the support and maintainance of Publick Protestant teachers of Piety, Religion and Morality who have not made such provision voluntary, or who have not made voluntary provision for some other Publick religious Teacher or for the support of some other Publick Worship within their commonwealth—And the several Towns Parishes Precincts and other Bodies politick or religious societies shall at all times have the exclusive right of electing their Publick teachers and of contracting with them for their support and maintainance; provided nevertheless that the minority of such Towns, Parishes Precincts and other Bodies Politick or religious Societies shall not be bound by the voice of the Majority in their electing their Publick Teachers or contracting with them for their support, but such Minority may if they see fit elect some other publick religious Teacher and Support him And all Monies Assessed upon the Subject for the support Of Publick Worship and of Publick religious Teachers shall if he requires it be uniformely Applied to the support of the Publick Worship which he may chuse to support: provided however that such Teachers shall bonafide receive the same to his own Use Otherwise such sum shall be appropriated to the use of the Poor of any Parish or religious society that such Subject shall chuse if he makes his Election within twelve Months, and if not it shall be applied to the support of the Poor of the Parish or Precinct in which said Moneys were raised. And all Religious Sects and Denominations Whatsoever, demeaning themselves Peaceably and as good Subjects of the Commonwealth shall be equally under the Protection of Law—And no Subordination of any one

Sect or denomination to another shall ever be established by Law

The foregoing Report having been read, it was moved, and Voted that a Question previous to the Report, being Acted upon. Viz[t]. Whether there shall be any thing further Added to the 2[d]. Article in the Declaration of Rights, which relates to Religion—And the Question being accordingly put—Passed in the Affermative, by a great Majority

The said Report being again taken up Paragraph by Paragraph—and amended the same was Accepted by the Town

It was moved and Voted that when this Meeting shall be Adjourned it be to 4. O.Clock P:M:

Moved that a Committee be appointed to bring in an Article in addition to the Article in the 43 Page—but the Motion was withdrawn

Adjourned to 4: O.Clock P:M:

4: O:Clock : P:M: Met according to Adjournment

It was moved and carried that the foregoing Clauses be added to the Report of the Committee on the 3[d] Article in the Declaration of Rights Viz[t].—The foregoing however is not to be so construed as to Nullify or infring any express voluntary Contract that hath been entered into between any Person or Persons, or any Town Parish, Precinct or Body of Men on the one Part and any Teacher or Minister of Religion on the other

The aforegoing Report of the Committee of the Committee [*sic*] on the 3[d]. Article, which had been accepted paragraph by paragraph—was put in the whole as amended—when it appeared that Four hundred and twenty were for accepting the Report—and one hundred and Forty against Receiving it

A Motion was then made that if the amendments proposed by the Town cannot be obtained by their Delegates, that they then shall be and hereby are Instructed to Vote for the 3[d]. Article in the Declaration of Rights, as it stands in the Form laid before the People—rather than the Article, should be lost at the next Meeting of the Convention—And the Question being put—it appeared that two hundred and seventy seven were in faviour of the Motion, and one hundred and forty against it

On a Motion, Voted, to appoint a Committee to draw up the reasons for the proposed Alterations in some Articles of the Frame of a Constitution presented by the Convention; and to draught Instructions to our Delegates in the said Convention

Voted, that Perez Morton Esq[r].
M[r]. Samuel Eliot
William Tudor Esq[r].
M[r]. John Sweetser
M[r]. Thomas Walley
be a Committee for the Purpose aforesaid

Adjourned to Fryday next. 3 O: Clock P: M:

Fryday May 12. 3 O.Clock P: M met according to Adjournment

M[r]. Morton had leave to withdraw his dissent to the passing the Article which relates to the mode of electing Senators

The Preamble to the Constitution or Form of Government for the Commonwealth of Massachusetts, again read—whereupon the Question was put—Viz[t]. Whether the Town do approve and accept of the Same——passed in the Affermative

The Committee appointed to draw up reasons for the proposed alterations in some Articles of the Constitution or Form of Goverment laid before the Town, and also to draught Instruction to our Delagates in the Convention—Report as follows—Viz[t]. Gentlemen

The Town of Boston have Convened in a legal Meeting to consider the Constitution or Forms of Goverment agreed on by the Convention, & by them proposed to the People for their Approbation, rejection, or amendment, having had the same repeatedly read proposed to a discussion of the Several Articles theirein contained and having recommended amendments in the 16th. Article of the Declaration of

Rights, in the 7th. Article of the 2d. Chapter in the 4th. Section of the 2d. Chapter & in the 7th. Article of the 6th. Chapter unanimously voted to accept said Constitution or Form of Goverment with the Amendments, the third Article in the Declaration of Rights excepted, provided by the most Strenious endeavours of their Delegates the said Amendments can be procured, otherwise to accept the said Articles as they were agreed to by the Convention, But the 3d. Article in the Declaration of Rights was refered to futer consideration; the meeting then consisting of eight hundred and eighty seven Voters —The Town then proceeded to consider the 3d. Article; which having been largely debated, was amended and Voted, 420 for & 51 against it. It was then moved and seconded, that if you could not obtain this Article as amended, you should be impowered to Vote for The 3d. Article as it originally stood rather than the Amendment should be the Means of postponing the establishment of the Constitution at the next Meeting of the Convention; as some Form was necessary to give Stability and force to Goverment. The Question being put the numbers were 277 for and 140 against it. Your utmost exertions are nevertheless earnestly enjoined to obtain the Amendments A principle of respect to a Body of Men of such distinguished rank and Ability as the Convention would not assuredly have led the Town to Assign the reasons for any alterations they might make in a system they had formed and recommended. But as the Convention have requested the doing it, it is now to be performed on a higher Principle. In general it may be Observed that the Amendments proposed were made upon the idea that they would more effectually subserve the excuse of Civil and Religious Liberty, that great object of our endeavours, and the point to which all our efforts ought to tend, The Amendment of 16th. April [Article] of the Declerations of Rights, was made upon the strongest persuation, that Liberty of Speech, as it respected publick Men in their publick Conduct, was an essential and darling right of every member of a free State upon which in a very emenent Degree the preservation of their other reights depends; that nothing spoken with design to give information of the State of the Publick should be ever subject to the smalest restraint; and that any Attempt to oppose such restraint ought to excite an alarm in the People as it infered a consciousness of demerit on the part of those Attempting That such restraint was more degrading and more Strongly marked the Slaves than ever the privation of the Liberty of the Press; and that the latter, so absolutely necessary, and therefore so justly dear to every free State could not be maintained in its full force and vigour without the former. But while we hold up the Liberty of the Press, as essentially necessary to general Freedom, as it respects publick Men and Measures we reject with Abhorrence the idea of its abuse to the injury of private Characters.—The next amendment gives Power to the Governor, in the recess of the General Court, to march or transport, the Inhabitants of this State for the relief of a Neighbouring State invaded or threatened with immediate invation. This was judged incumbent on the general Principles of humanity, and absolutely necessary upon the Principles of Policy, A threatn'd invastion may be wholly prevented by the early appearance of a respectable Military force and Invation actually begun may be easally repeled, in many Instances by an immediate Opposition. In the former case, the Lives & Property of our Friends & Neighbours may be entirely saved & Secured; and in the Latter case fewer lives may be lost In all Probability, and less Property Destroyed, Besides delay may give oppertunity to an Enemy (so disposed) to take Post, and establish himself in such a manner as would require a very great force to remove him while an early force might be adequate to his immediate expulsion. Further the withholding immediate aid, may open a passage into our own State, and to bring the War to our own doors.—It was also suggested, that the Article, of Confederation bound us to grant immediate relief, which can only be Obtained by Vesting the Governor with such power, and was therefore Voted,—The next amendements respects the time of service of the Commissary General which is proposed to be limited to the Term of Five years. This was done because it was apprehended that a change or relation of Officers was necessary, in general to the preservation of Freedom. Persons longe in Office are apt to lose that sence of Dependance upon the People, which is essential to keep them within the Line of duty to the Publick. And especially may the good of the Community be promoted by the retirements of such Persons from Office at certain fixed periods, who have been largely intrusted with Publick Money or Stores—The next Article respects that important Write of Habeas Corpus. Many Reasons might be given for the Alterations made. It was judged best to confir the Suspension of this security of personal Liberty or freedom from Imprisonments to times of War, invation and rebellion, the terms urgent and pressing occations, being too indefinite and giving scope to the most powerfull Engine of Despotism, and Slavery. It was not conceived that any cause could possibly exist in time of peace, that could justify imprisonments without allegation or charge; and the granting a power in a season of tranquility liable to such gross abuse, and which might be attend with consequences destructive of the dearest priviledges and best interest of the Subject was deemed incompatable with every Principle of Liberty. Nay it was apprehended that it might Opperate as an incentive to Despotism; and to hold up a temtation to Tyranny while human Nature is constituted as we find it was judged to be wholly inexpedient. Confineing the suspencion won in time of War, invation and rebellion, to Six Months, was supposed a proper Limetation, as every purpose of an honest Goverment might be fully answered, in that period. A larger pereod might lead to a State of forgetfullness of the unhappy Subject of Suspission, and he might Drag on a Wretched being in the Dark abode of a Dungion, or within the gloomy walls of a Prison, without a Single Ray of hope to enlighten his cell or a single Friend to chear his Desponding spirit. Thus may his dreadfull Confinement when the Reason that operated to his Commitment have been long done away. Can a Power pregrant with such mighty Evils be too Strongly guarded; Or can we be too solicetious to confine it within the narrow limits that will comport with the Publick safety?—The only Article now to be attended to is the third in the Decleration of Rights, which Asserts that Piety, Religion and morality are essential to the happiness, Peace and Good order of a People and that these Principles are diffused by the Publick Worship of God, and by Publick Instructions &c—and in Consequence makes provision for their support. The alterations proposed here which you will Lay before the Convention were designed to Secure the Reights of Consience and to give the fullest Scope to religious Liberty In support of the proposition it urged that if Publick Worship and Publick teaching, did certainly (as was allowed) defuse a general Sence of Duty & moral Obligations, and, so secured the safety of our Persons and Properties, we ought chearfully to pay those from whose agency we derived such Advantages. But we are Attempting to support (it is said) the Kingdom of Christ; It may as well be said we are supporting the Kingdom of God, by institution of a Civil Goverment, which Declared to be an Ordinance to the Deity, and so refuse to pay the civil magistrate. What will be the consequence of such refusal—The greatest disorders, if not a Dissolution of Society. Suspend all provision for the inculation of Morality, religion and Piety, and confusion & every evil work may be justly dreaded; for it is found that with all the Restraints of religion induced by the Preaching of Ministers, and with all the Restraints of Goverment inforced by civil Law, the World is far from being as quiet an abode as might be wished. Remove the former by ceasing to support Morality, religion and Piety and it will be soon felt that human Laws were feble barriers opposed to the uninformed lusts of Passions of Mankind. But though we are not supporting the kingdom of Christ may we not be permitted to Assist civil society by an addoption, and by the teaching of the best set of Morals that were ever offered to the World. To Object to these Morrals, or even to the Piety and Religion we aim to inculcate, because they are drawn from the Gospel, must appear very singular to an Assembly generally professing themselves Christians. Were this really our intention, no Objection ought to be made to it provided, as in fact the case that equal Liberty is granted to every religious Sect and Denomination Whatever, and it is only required that every Man should pay to the support of Publick Worship In his own way. But should any be so Conscientious that they cannot pay to the support of any of the various denominations among us they may then alott their Money to the support of the Poor—It remains only to fix the time when this Form of Goverment shall take place; But having had large experience of your Ability and Zeal in the course of the very lengthy Session of Convention, the last Winter we very Chearfully leave the Determination of this point to that prudence, Judgement and Integrity, which have so strongly marked your conduct in this Department and to the united Wisdom of the whole Body.

The foregoing Report of the Committee having been read and considered—the Question was put—Viz[t]. "Whether the same shall be accepted, by the Town"—Passed in the Affermative, almost unanimously

The Resolves of the Convention, passed the 2[d]. March having been read and considered—whereupon

Voted, almost unanimously that the Selectmen of this Town be directed to transmit to the Secretary of the Convention the doings of this Town relative to the Form of Government agreeable to the Resolves of Convention; in order, to the Secretary of Convention laying the same before a Committee to be appointed for the purpose of examining and Arranging them for the Rivision and consideration of the Convention at the Adjournment; with the Number of Voters on each side of every Question, in order that the said Convention at the Adjournment may Collect the general sense of their Constituents on the several parts of the proposed Constitution; and if it do not appear to be two thirds, of their Constituents in faviour thereof, that the Convention may alter it in such a manner as that it may be Agreeable to the sentiments of two thirds of the Voters throughout the State, also

Voted, almost unanimousley the Delegates of this Town be and hereby are impowered at the next Session of the Convention; to agree upon a time when this Form of Government shall take Place without returning the same again to the People: Provided that two thirds of the Male Inhabitants of the Age of twenty one years and upwards, Voting in the Several Towns and Plantations Meeting, shall agree to the Same, or the Convention shall conform it to the Sentements of two thirds of the People as aforesaid

A Motion made, that this Meeting be now dessolved

And the Meeting was accordingly dissolved.

54. From the Return of Ashby (Middlesex County), 1780

[Massachusetts Archives, CCLXXVII, 3]

We Object against Those words in the second Article; (the publick piece)——

We also Object against the Whole of the third Article;—The reasons for our exceptions against those words—the publick piece) in the second, and for our rejection of the whole of the third Article, are as follows.——

Reason the 1st that all the Liberty and security which any religeous Society can resonably desire, is granted by the Legeslature, in the second Article, without the words (the publick piece) which are there incerted, that said second Article stands clear and intelageble without these words —the publick piece)—

Reason 2 The third Article is inconsistant with the second for the second Article alows of no restraint upon any one as to their persons, Liberty, or Estates, except in them words, objected to as above——

The third Article lays a restraint: for those who cannot Concientiously or Convenantly attend upon any publick teachers are under restraint as to their Estates & so injurd as to their Liberty and property——

Reason 3 Religeous Societys as such have no voice in Chusing the Legeslature, the Legeslature therefore have no right to make Law binding on them as such; every religeous Society, as such, is intirely independant on any body politick, the Legeslature therefore have no more right to make Laws Binding on them, as such, then the Court of Great Britton have to make Laws binding on the Independant states of America——

Reason 4 as religeous Societys, and bodys politick, are bodys distinct an independant of each other, they have not aright therefore to make Laws binding on each other; how amaising absurd it would be for a number of persons in a Town to form into a religeous Society and in that Capacity make Laws or authorise others to make Laws binding on the Town as a body politick——

Reason 5 that which is of greatest importance ought not to be subordinated to that which is least the well being and prosperity of religeous Society as such, is of greater importance, then that of politick bodys as such, the reason therefore which is given in the third Article for investing the Legeslature with authority to make Laws binding on religeous Societys as such is inconsistant and against the piece and welfare of the State——

Reason 6th. The Rivers of blood which has ran from the Veins of Marters! and all the torment which they have indured in the flames! was ocationed by the authority of Legeslature over religeous Society in consequence of the authority of the Legeslature or the authority arising from the authority of the Legeslature, the Feet of Paul & Silas where made fast in the stocks, the three Children Cast into the Furnace of fire, Daniel into the Lions Den, and many other such instances might be inumerated——

Reason 7th. the third Article says the people of this common wealth have a right to invest their Legeslature with power to make Laws that are binding on religeous Society as (as we understand them) which is as much as to say we will not have Christ to reign over us that the Laws of this Kingdom are not sufficient to govern us, that the prosperity of his Kingdom is not eaqualy important with the Kingdoms of this world and that the Ark of God stands in need of Uzza's band to keep it from falling to the ground, butt lett us attend sereously to this important Truth that I will build my Church upon this Rock, and the Gates of Hell shall not prevail against it, now where resides this power in Christ only? or in the Legeslature?——it may be Objected against the Reasons here given that it leaves people two Louse and does not ingadge them to there duty & therby all religion will fall to the ground and this Objection indeed is very plausable because it may flow from an outward zeal for a form of Godliness without the power butt is it not founded upon this Supposition that men are not sufficiently ingadged to the practice of their Duty unless they doe somthing that God never required of them——

He that made us reasonable Creatures and Conferd upon us the Blessing of the Gospell has by this frame and situation laid us under the strongest Obligation to the practice of Piety, Religeon, and Morality that can posibly be conceived, & if this wont impress our minds to doe our Duty nothing will

55. From the Return of Braintree (Suffolk County), 1780

[Massachusetts Archives, CCLXXVII, 63]

Declaration of Rights

Ar. 24th add, *excepting only manifest breaches of natural Law (which in old Countries have obtained the name of common Law) & which are not sufficiently provided against by any written Law; which Cases, if any such there shall be, tried in a Court of Equity, which Court shall be established, as soon as may be, after the Establishment of this Constitution.*

Ar. 25th add, *excepting, only, Cases of Treason against the State, not provided for by any written Law.*

Reasons for the two last additions. All persons living under the protection of the Laws of any civil Society, are bound, by natural Law (upon which all other good Laws are built) to refrain from all things injurious to such Society whether Such Injury is, or is not, a breech of any Written Law. The inventions of wicked men have been frequently employed in devising means to evade written Laws; & in young States they have more frequently Succeeded, than in Old; for as States advance in Age, they from time to time, improve their Statute Law,—providing against such Mal-doers,—& transplanting (so far as human frailty will permit) into their Written Codes, the body of natural Law; but from a consciousness of the imperfection of their Codes, the best Governments have provided Courts of Equity, to Soften the rigour of Written Law, & to Act upon Such parts of natural Law, as have not been rendered Sufficiently clear & plain in their Statutes.

Without such additions, as aforesaid, will not all that has been done by this State, relative to Confiscations &c be revoked, in effect, & great Confusions ensue? And how can such confiscations be justified, but *only* upon the foot of Natural Law?——

56. From the Return of Rehoboth (Bristol County), 1780

[Massachusetts Archives, CCLXXVI, 35]

The Objections Against haveing a Governor &c as Reported & accepted—Your Committe Report that as the Town Have Rejected A Governor Lieut. Governor & Senate we think the whole of the Remainder is Rejected in Consequence thereof

We therefore Give our Reasons for Rejecting a Governor Senate & &c is from our Being of Opinion that our Safety &

happiness Esentially Consists in Being Governd by one house of Representatives which shall be Stiled the Great & Genaral Court of the Comonwealth of the Massachusetts to be Elected Annually. Whose Rules & Regulations Shall be Simeler to that of the Honourable Continental Congress And the House of Representatives to Annually Elect all the Executive officers & all Other Publick Officers Except Judges of Probate of Wills & Register of Deeds which ought forever thereafter to be done in Each Respective Town & all milatary Officers to be chosen Agreable to the Proposed form of Goverment. & the Judges of the Supreme Judicial Court to hold their Office During their good Behaviour & no Legislative Officer to be an Judicial Officer & no Judicial Officer to be an Executive Officer &c. all which Objections & amendments we find Absolutely Nesecary for Enjoying a free well Regulated Goverment

57. The Return of New Marlborough (Berkshire County), 1780

[Massachusetts Archives, CCLXXVI, 15]

At a Legal Town meeting of the Inhabitants of New Marlborough on May the 11th 1780 warned in Pursuance of a Resolve of the Convention of this State Dated March 2 1780. for laying before the Inhabitants of the Several Towns & Districts of the State, the Constitution or Frame of Government Purposed to be adopted in said State——

The inhabitants Present Taking the Constitution into their Serious Consideration, Passed upon the whole with the following objections (viz) In Chapt. first Section Second article Second, and Section third article Fourth, all that is Contained in the above articles making money an Essential Qualification for a Voter was objected to by 54. In favor of the above said articles 4—as being Contrary to the first article in the Bill of Rights which we agree with The next objection is Chapt 1st Section 2d the Senate. Chapt 1st Section 3 House of Representatives. Chapt. 2d Section 1 Governor and in Chapt. 2. Section 2d Lt Governor, all the last mentioned articles are objected to for that Such Large Sums of money is made a Nessesary Qualification for the above said offices as Renders Inconvenient in many Respects and dangerous in Some, the Last mentioned articles yeas 8 Nays 29——

Objection 3d In Chapt 2 Section 1st Article 9th for that the Remotest Parts of the State by the Govener and Council cannot be fairly & Justly Represented without the Sufferages of the People by their Representatives or the officors of the County in General—yeas 1 Nays 42.——

Objection 4 Chapt 6 article 3d Nays 57. this article objected to for that the Legislative have Power to alter the Qualification to office as they shall see fit. which we think amounts to afull Power to make the Qualifications such that theire cannot be more than one, and Prehaps no Representative in some Countys——

Objection 5 no yeas Nays 53 in Chapt 6 article 10th this article objected to for that the Time Perfixed for altering or Revising the Constitution, ought not to be more than five years—In Chapt 6 article 2 after mention of the officers of Harvard College, all Settled ministers of the Gospel of all Denominations, ought to be Inserted in addition thereto—the Question being Put upon the whole of the Declaration of Rights and Frame of Government with the foregoing objections it Passed Yeas 63 Nays 1 our Deligate instructed to agree with the Convention upon atime when the Constitution Shall Take Place

58. From the Return of Mansfield (Bristol County), 1780

[Massachusetts Archives, CCLXXVI, 33]

[The town voted 50 to 0 against property qualifications to vote for senator and 26 to 0 against such qualifications to vote for representatives.]

The propperty required as a quallification for Electors of Senators this Town are humbly of Oppinion is unjust; Notwithstanding in assigning the Numbers, Reference is to be had to the proportion of Taxes each District pays; and therefore in the address of the Convention page 11th are called Representitives of propperty, which we allow they are, but notof propperty only; for we conceive the Senate ought to Represent persons as well as propperty, and that the Second Branch Represents propperty as well as persons for sure both branches make but one General Court, and each Branch ought Equally to consult the Safty, Prosperity, and the happiness of the whole; and if so evry male inhabitant of the Common-Welth of the age of Twentyone years and upwards being of understanding suficient to mannage the Common and ordinary affairs of life and is a Good subject, we think should be a Voter for senator, or senators, in the Town where they have their usual residence and are Taxed (unless by law Excused:) and propose an amendment to be made to said art. accordingly. . . .

For here we finde the same quallification of propperty Required for a Voter for a Representative as is proposed by the Convention for the electors of the Senate; We are very sorrey to differ in oppinion from the Honorable Convention in a matter of so grate Importance as that of determining, who shall, and who shall not have a voice in the choice of a Representitive: Doubtless there are, and ever will be some in the Commonwelth who pay little regard to the Rights of propperty as is hinted at in the address Page 12th this we readily Grante, but on the other hand, how many young men Neither Profligates Nor idle persons, for some years must be debared that priviledge? how many sensable, honest, and Naturly Industerouss men, by Numberless Misfortins Never Acquire and possess propperty of the value of sixty pounds? and how many Thousands of good honest men, and Good members of Society who are at this day possessed of a comfortable Interest, which before the publick debts of the Commonwelth are discharged, will not be possessed of a soficiency to quallify them to vote for Representatives if this article takes place as it now stands; We readily allow as we said before that there are and ever will be some who pay little regard to the rights of Propperty: But shall it from thence be argued, that thousands of honest Good members of society shall be subjected to laws framed by Legislators, the Eliction of whom, they could have no voice in? Shall a subject of a free Commonwilth, be obliged to contribute his share to to publick Expences, to give his personal servis, or an equivilent, when Necessary, see bill or Rights Pag 10th and be excluded from Voting for a Representative; This appears to us in some degree, Slavery. on these Considerations, with others which might be mentioned We Reject said article as it now stands: and do propose to have sutch alteration, or amendment made to said article, whereby. Evry male person being Twentyone years of age and upwards being a Good subject of the Commonwelth, and Resident in any peticular Town for the space of one year, in sutch Town, have a Right to vote for a representative, or Representatives for said Town, Provided also that he has paid taxes in the same Town (unless by law excepted)

59. From the Return of Dorchester (Suffolk County), May 16, 1780

[Massachusetts Archives, CCLXXVII, 67]

May the 16th 1780

The Town of Dorchester being Convened in Legal Meeting to Consider the Constitution or Form of Goverment, having recommended an Amendment in the 4th Article of Section 3d Chapter 1st are happy in giving their Reasons for it, on so high a Principal as that of a Request from the honourable Body, who agreed upon the same.——

Said Article having been read & Debated, the following Amendment was proposed & Voted viz That the Articles of Estate & Income be omitted in the Qualification of a Voter for Representatives.——

This Amendment made upon the strongest Persuation that the Article as proposed by the Convention, infringes upon the Rights & Liberties of a number of usefull & respectible members of Society; which number we believe is daily increasing & possibly may increase in such proportion, that one half the People of this Commonwealth will have no Choice in any Branch of the General Court, & who are at the same time liable (by the 4th Article of Chapter 1st Section first) to pay such a proportion of the Publick Taxes as they shall Judge reasonable; and the members of the said Court being all men of Considerable Property, may be induced to lay too great a proportion on the Polls, & by that means ease their Estates & bring a heavy burden on those who have no power to remove it.——

And being fully convinced that Taxation & Representation ought to be inseperable, & that the Property & Estates of the People will be sufficiently guarded by the Senate who represent the same, we see no Reason of sufficient weight to Debar any Person Qualified as in the Article amended provides, from Voting in Choice of Representatives.——

60. From the Return of Springfield (Hampshire County), 1780

[Massachusetts Archives, CCLXXVI, 66]

As to the second Article in the first Section of the second Chapter, they are constrained to express their disapprobation of the Same providing that no Person shall be eligible to the Office of Governour unless he declare himself to be of the Christian Religion—As the People of this Commonwealth are generally, if not universally, of the Protestant reformed Religion, they apprehend it would be Matter of Great & General Concern that any Person might ever be elected to this Office over them or their Posterity, who should not be of the Protestant Religion; and they are of Opinion this ought to be provided for in the most express Terms; and that the same Provision, Alteration or Amendment, should be made in the Declaration to be made by the Lieutenant Governor, Councellors, Senators & Representatives,

& in the Form of the Oath to be taken by all Officers under the Government—

To the second Article, in the third Section, in the same Chapter, [Chapter I] they object—It is calculated to give the several Towns a Right of sending so many Members to the Gerneral Court, as (if exercised) will at present make the House of Representatives a a very unwieldy Body; to the Disadvantage of a regular Transaction, & reasonable Dispatch of Business; & will be productive of heavy & needless Expence. And as in such Case the Number will be constantly increasing, this Inconvenience & Expence will be also increasing, until the one be enormous & the other insupportable.—If to avoid these Difficulties, some Towns should decline the Expense of these Rights in their full Extent, others would Probably improve them, & the Representation would by that Means become more unequal in Fact without effectually answering the End proposed. And as it is probable, by Reason of their different Situations, that many of the more distant Towns will generally omit the full Exercise of these Rights, & that those at or near the Center of Government will exercise them in their full Extent, it may always be expected, on this Plan, that the latter will have more than an equal Proportion of Influence in the Conduct of Publik Affairs in general—And as it is provided thereby, that Sixty Members shall make a Quorum of the House, they think it may be justly feared, that in some future Time less virtuous than the present, they may avail themselves of these Advantages of Situation & Numbers, by an easy, speedy and unexpected Collection, to determine interesting & favorite Matters, not altogether to the general Satisfaction or Benefit of the State: and that the Provision made for paying out of the Publick Treasury, the Expences of Travel of the Members, will not sufficiently secure against it— —They are therefore of Opinion that each and every Town, even the largest, should be expressly limited to a certain moderate Number of Representatives, which they should not exceed; that this should be so done, that the Number should be reduced, its Increase duly restrained, & the Mischiefs or Danger aforesaid prevented—

61. From the Return of Middleborough (Plymouth County), 1780

[Massachusetts Archives, CCLXXVII, 40]

Chapter II, Section I

article: 9th and: 10th we object against the governor & Council or any other man or ordor of men. in any place office or power whatever. as having any Kind of Right by any means Whatsoever. to Nominate or appoint any one Officer that shall have Even the Least Degree of Power over the people in Common: Either Legislative Judicial Executive or any other way—if Each and Every man in Common have Not a Right to Vote for Each and Every Officer; under which they must or Shall at any Time or by any means Subject themselves: we ask how it Came to pass that any one man or Number of men Should be possessed of a Right to Chuse Officers: for other men: as we Do Not understand it to be Consistant with the Right of Nature: But the Reverse and Every way inconsistant with the Sense of the 5th article in the Bill of Rights: as it is most Certain that Every part of publick Business that is Conducted out of its proper Line will produce Some publick Evil: and that as the Chusing of the greatest part of publick Officers out of its proper Chanel will have a Tendency to fill the State with the most Corrupt, Vitious, and Sordid Set of Officers: therefore productive in its Consequences of the greatest Evil we Say that Every man ought at Least to have as good a Chance in Voteing for Every Officer placed over him as he has by this form of government. in Voteing for Captains and Subalterns——

62. From the Return of Barnstable (Barnstable County), 1780

[Massachusetts Archives, CCLXXVII, 48]

Voted 2[d] that it is the Opinion of this Town founded upon the Law of Nature and Common Sense & the Reason of things that no more of the Natural Rights of a free people ought to Be Given up to the governing power than is absolutely and Esentially necessary for the good government of the whole and as we can at present see no reason to the Contrary: it is the opinion of this Town that the Judges of the inferiour Courts and Justices of the Peace for Each County ought of Right to be Elected by the free Suffrages of the people of said County in the Same way & manner (and if that may be agreable) on the Same Day the Senators are Chosen and on their good Behavior to Continue in Office 5 or 7 years Before a new Election takes place: the number of Justices for Each Town in a County to be assertained by a County meeting held for that purpose: or in Such manner as is provided for assertaining the number of Representitives which Each town may not Exceed——we have Carefully attended to the Objection: in the Adress Page 15—But we apprehend: the People at Large Especially in the Remoter Countys in the State have Infinitely more to fear from the Banefull influence of the ambitious and artfull men with Some future Governor & five Councillors who are not Likely to be acquainted with the personal accomplishment of those he may recommend to those Important offices—besides it ought allways to be Remembered that the Same pernitious influence may be used in favor of a governors Election: and Perhaps urged by the unworthy men in order to Give his Recommendations the greater weight with a Governor—Consequently these offices in the Civill Department are in the Greatest Danger of Being filled with persons the most unworthy which may Prove a Grevious Injury—Rather than a blessing to the Community & fit to answer Little or no Valluable Purpeses to Society. We cant at present apprehend more need to be urged on the Subject than Just To mention that it appears To us if the matter Rested with the people of a County. (who Generally Know thire worthyest men they will be in no Danger under these Circumstances to be unduely Influenced to their own apparent Injury—it is also the Opinion of this Town that as in Some Cases no appeal is to be had from the inferior To the Supream Court that the Justices of the inferior Courts ought not To Sit as Legislatures——

63. From the Return of Belchertown (Hampshire County), 1780

[Massachusetts Archives, CCLXXVI, 40]

5 With Regard to the Justices of the superior Court we should think it much preferable to the proposed Plan, that they be Commissioned only for three years—at the End of which their Commission may be renewed, unless some reasonable ob-

jection be made against it—By this means a bad one may be removed with less Trouble & Observation, and (the sallery being fixed and sufficient) there is sufficient Encouragemants for Men of Ability & Entegrity, and a greater stimulus to good Behaviour.

(This Refers to Declaration 29 & Chap 3 Art 1)

None for it as in Book but 72 with this alterration

6 It is our Opinion that Justices of the Inferior Courts should be taken out of the Justices of the County & Commisioned for three years only at one time for Reasons similar to those given in the preceeding Article none for as in Book but 73 with this alterration

7 For similar Reasons we apprehend that the Attorney General Sollicitor General & Judges of Probate ought not to be Commissioned for longer than three years.

None for as in Book but 73 with this alterration

8 For the Reasons given Chap 3 Art 3 we are of Opinion that seven years is vastly to long for a Commission for a Justice of the Peace—that this Commission ought to be but for one year—and that there ought to be no more Justices in any Town than the Town has Liberty to send Representatives—and that they ought to be recommended to the Governor & Council for a Commission (annually) by a majority of the Votes in every Town of those Persons who vote for Representatives, as they may be presumed to the best Judges of their Qualifications

None for as in Book But with 61 with this alterration

9 It is our opinion that the sherif of Each County ought to be annually elected at the Time & in the Manner that the Councellors & senators are, & that there is equal Reason for it.

none for as in Book 61 with this alterration

10 It is our opinion that military officers ought to be annually elected—to the End that those who are unfit for their tasks may be eesily dropped, & such as are worthy as they come on this tasc elected & that by this means the militery Power may be more easily kept in a proper subordination to the Civil Authority

None for as in Book 61 with this alterration

64. The Return of Pittsfield (Berkshire County), 1780

[Massachusetts Archives, CCLXXVI, 18]

At a Legal Meeting of the Inhabitants of the Town of Pittsfield duly Qualified on Monday the Eighth Day of May 1780. for the purpose of Considering, approving or disapproving the Constitution sent out to them by the Convention, the Number of Voters being Eighty, the Address, Declaration of Rights & Constitution being read to them at large.

To take the Same into Consideration Article by Article

And every Article in the Declaration of Rights was Unanimously accepted Exept on Disentrint to Article 3^d^. And one to Article 10th.

As was the Constitution also, Exept 15 Dissentrints to the 4th Article in the first Section of the first Chapter, And one to the 2^d^. Article in the Second Section in Said Chapter. And one to the 2^d^. Article in the First Section of the 2^d^. Chapter.

And being Called upon by the Moderator to Exhibit their reasons, some of them desired time, upon which the Meeting was adjourned to the 17th of Said Month.

And met according to adjournment at which time no reasons were offered, and not one Disentrint appeared——

65. Pittsfield Instructs its Delegate to the Ratifying Convention, May 17, 1780

[Massachusetts Archives, CCLXXVI, 18]

Pittsfield, May 17th 1780

To Col James Easton,

Sir,

As you are chosen a Delegate to represent us in State Convention to be holden at Boston on the 8th Day of June next ensuing to receive & examine the Returns of the several Towns & places within this State relative to the Constitution sent forth for their Approbation or Disapprobation in which we expect you'll meet with little Difficulty as we apprehend more than two Thirds of the State will approve of the same. Such being the Case, as the Reins of Government are so relaxed & this County in particular so long deprived of all Law you are strictly required to endeavor that the Constitution take place as soon as possible which we hope will not exceed the month of August next.——

If we are disappointed in our Expectations & there is great Variance in the Returns made from the several Towns within the State to that Degree that you shall be obliged to send it out for a Revision we expect you do not dissolve yourselves till such Time as one is formed & accepted.

Thomas Allen
Wm Williams } Committee
Jno Brown

Reactions to Ratification

66. Theophilus Parsons: The People Would Have Accepted a More Conservative Constitution, August 3, 1780

[Theophilus Parsons to Francis Dana, Aug. 3, 1780, Dana Papers, Massachusetts Historical Society]

". . . Our Constitution is settled. The Convention made some unhappy alterations in the Report of the Comee. Several Gentlemen of the Comee deserted the few worthies in the debates in convention, not from conviction but through fear that the constitution would be too perfect for the acceptance of the People—But they were mistaken, & were not sensible of it till it was too late. The People accepted the Report of the Convention without the alteration of an iota, though objections were made to every article. I now forward to you the report of the Convention—with the number of voters thro' the State as they were on each article—. . . The People discovered themselves to be steady sensible judicious and fond of a respectable Government. Their votes and instructions were in general shrewd and generous—The greatest objections were to those articles which were calculated as it was thought to please the People—viz the Governour's Negative—Militia—&c Had the Convention been wise and united, we might have had *a perfect constitution.* The People would have accepted one, and the palliated articles discovered that many of our wise ones did not know the real sentiments of the People—*There was no danger in proposing too perfect a constitution.*"

67. The Officers of the Massachusetts Line Approve the New Constitution, November 12, 1780

[Address from the General and Field Officers of the Massachusetts Line, to the Honorable the SENATE and HOUSE of REPRESENTATIVES, of the Commonwealth of Massachusetts, in General Court assembled, November 12, 1780, *Independent Chronicle,* Dec. 8, 1780]

On such an uncommon occasion as the establishment of a new constitution, it becomes every constituent part of the community to express their sentiments on a matter so interesting to their future prosperity.

Upon this principle, the undersigned officers of the troops of Massachusetts, in our own names, and in the names of our brethren in the field, conceive ourselves obliged to declare, that we highly respect and approve, in general, the new constitution of the Commonwealth of Massachusetts.

We are at a loss to find terms sufficiently expressive of our veneration and gratitude for that illustrious Convention, who prepared the form of government, in which the spirit of the ancient free republics is so admirably preserved, and adapted to the manners of the present day.

We form the most auspicious omens of its free operation and prosperity, from the liberality of sentiment which pervaded the State in so chearfully receiving it.

Having thus declared our ideas of the new system of government, and of the happiness we anticipate in residing under its protection, we cannot but feelingly regret, that it should have been thought improper to admit us to a declaration of our sentiments, on a subject with which our future welfare is so intimately connected.

It would be uncandid to suppose, that our countrymen considered our being in the field a crime which should deprive us of our unalienable rights: We impute it to an inadvertent omission, rather than a deliberate design. We are obliged to wound our pride and consciousness of service, in preference to impeaching the justice of our country.

We consider ourselves as citizens in arms for the defence of the most invaluable rights of human nature; and we beg attention to our assertion, that no honors of the field, however splendid, or pecuniary rewards, however great, would induce us to suspend, for a moment, our rights as citizens; and we conceive ourselves bound to say, that, if one is to be the consequence of the other, we shall be constrained to transfer the defence of our country to persons who may hold such rights in less estimation.

Although we apprehend that we have been injured in this important transaction, yet we beg permission to express our firm reliance on your honorable legislature, as our fathers and guardians. We perfectly believe, that your attention to the rights of the members of the Commonwealth, will ever be so universal as to comprehend that part of them who are necessarily absent in arms, to obtain and secure, for themselves and their countrymen, the equal rights of citizens.

The inflexible determination of America, even in the most critical situations, never to submit to Great Britain, but to form free governments, in which the human mind might dilate and expand to the utmost, have animated us to persevere through the vicisitudes and difficulties of the war. Indeed, it is impossible to return under the dominion of a power, which has given such numerous and flagrant proofs of unjust ambition and vindictive rage.

We are made peculiarly happy by the late acts of Congress, establishing an army for the war, without an alternative. These resolutions fully evince that no change of sentiment has taken place in the minds of the people,—but, that roused by the ill effects of former temporary expedients, we are determined to adopt the only system that can promise a speedy and honorable peace.

If the legislatures of the respective States will vigorously carry into immediate effect the resolutions of Congress, the enemy will be deprived of their only well grounded hope of conquest; and be obliged to relinquish the attempt to acquire an object in which they have profusely lavished their blood and treasure.

Surely the people of America, who deliberately refered their happiness to the decision of arms, rather than submit to an arbitrary power, cannot hesitate, for an instant, to prefer such rational measures as will successfully terminate the contest, to a mode expensive and hazardous, and which, if continued, must issue in the destruction of our liberties.

Instead of any demur, we believe the wisdom of the requisitions of Congress will appear so evident, that all classes of men will press an immediate compliance with them. And if, in place of creating obstacles, the offspring of diffidence, the patriotism of 1775 should revive, all fancied difficulties would be overborne, and the process become easy to obtain the full number of men required.

Allow us to suggest, that no method appears to us so equal and consistent with the spirit of a free republic, of which every person ought to assist in the defence, as to establish classes throughout the community. We presume this mode, if fully investigated and fairly tried, will be found to be more equal and effectual, and less expensive, than any other that can be devised.

Let the number required from each State be apportioned on the respective counties and towns, each town to class its men according to the numbers it is to furnish. The men to be delivered to the proper officer by the day prefixed, or the deficient class obliged to be draughted indiscriminately; the certainty of which would probably operate so as to produce competent motives to some person to engage voluntarily.

The classes to be made as nearly equal as possible in point of property.

As an obligation on the classes to send proper men, and whose fidelity can be relied on, they should be obliged to supply the places of such as were refused by the inspecting officer, and all deserters.

The Commonwealth that shall make this arrangement, will, in all circumstances, be able to exert its strength, support its armies, and force the enemy to respect its energy.

Suffer us to assure your honorable legislature, that a full determination to compleat your battalions, and properly supply them, would greatly inspirit the brave men in the field engaged for the war, and stimulate them to the highest exertions for the honor and interest of their country.

We speak with the freedom of men, who, from the earliest stages of the contest, have had the honor to assist in the defence of the liberties of our country. We have too high an opinion of your wisdom, to suppose you can be offended with us for a manifestation of that spirit which is so diffusive throughout the constitution.

Camp, at Totowa, 12th November, 1780.

68. The General Court Praises the Constitution, November 7, 1780

[Answer of a Committee of both Houses of Assembly of Massachusetts to the speech of his Excellency the Governor at the opening of the Session, November 7. 1780, *Independent Chronicle*, Nov. 16, 1780]

May it please your Excellency,

We the Senate and Representatives of the people, who constitute the Free and Independent Commonwealth of Massachusetts, in General Court assembled, beg leave to address your Execellency, on your accession to the high and important office of Chief Magistrate.

With grateful hearts we acknowledge, with your Excellency, the goodness of the Great Lord of all, in the steps of his providence which have led to the present happy revolution, and afforded to this people an opportunity of framing a Constitution of civil government, upon the liberal and permanent basis of freedom and independence, and with such powers and barriers, as have a necessary tendency "to secure the existence of the body politic, to protect it, and to furnish the individuals who compose it, with the power of enjoying, in safety and tranquility, their natural rights and the blessings of life."

A government thus constituted, well administered, and supported by the people; being at certain periods regretable to them who are the fountain of honour, the last resort of power, and the express guardians of their own lives; liberties and properties, cannot fail to command respect, and answer the ends of its institution.

It is our peculiar felicity to find that such a constitution, originating with the people who are to live under it and formed by delegates of their own choice, has met with so general and cordial a reception; and that the first elections have been conducted with the most perfect order and harmony, but more expecially that the virtues and patriotism of our constituents have led them to the free and unbiased choice of a gentleman to fill the highest office in the commonwealth, whose native and political attachments to their civil and religious rights, early and uniformly conspicuous, have been so illustriously distinguished by both the first honors of the supreme council of these United States, and by the earliest proscription of the British government.

As it is essential to a free Republic, that it be a "government of laws and not of men," so the principles and views of your electors are fully confirmed, when by your Excellency's speech from the chair they are incontestibly ascertained, that far from being elated by the honors you have so justly merited and received, your Excellency regards the station to which you are now advanced, although an honorable, yet as an arduous and extensive sphere of usefulness, and that you realize a proportionate weight of obligation and duty.

As the powers vested in the Chief Magistrate are ascertained, limited and restrained by the constitution, so are they sufficiently competent to the purpose of commanding respect to government, and obedience to the laws, and for calling forth the utmost energy of individuals for the necessary service and protection of the Commonwealth. While, therefore, you continue to discharge, with fidelity, the duties incident to your exalted nation, govern according to law, execute justice with clemency and duly exert your civil and military power for maintaining the rights of the subject, you shall never fail of support.

While the people over whom you are called to preside, descended from republican ancesters, well informed in the principles of government, and animated by a generous and ardent zeal for the rights of men and citizens, with a laudible jealousy, regard the conduct of their rulers, we trust, they will find yours uniformly consistent with the constitution.

We are happy in being able to assure your Excellency, that our constituents, dispossed as they now are and ever have been, to good order and a peaceful subjection to laws of their own making, will ever cheerfully exert themselves to support a constitution which ascertains to them personal security, liberty, and property; and to render the arduous services of those who rule well, as easy to themselves and as conducive to the great ends of government "as the lot of humanity will admit". While, from our long experience of your Excellency's firmness on the one hand, and from their affection and confidence in you on the other, we flatter ourselves that your administration will exemplify in all periods of the commonwealth, that its utmost power may be called for and exerted in a perfect consistency with the happiness of the subject.

We beg leave further to assurance your Excellency, that relying, under GOD, upon the firm support of our constituents, no efforts or assiduity of ours shall be wanting to fulfill [?] the part assigned us by the constitution. Happy should we be, could we perform it to these expectations, and to the satisfaction of our own minds.

But in order thereto we shall immediately enter upon the consideration of the important purpose for which we are convened—and especially those which your Excellency has recommended to our attention.

Sensible that no one valuable object of government can be either compleately attained or enjoyed unless the defence of the State is first sufficiently provided for, and that every regulation of internal police, which does not terminate in or fecilitate the accomplishment of this grand object, must be posponed to it; our first and principle attention shall be paid to the army—which, by the most vigorous and decisive measures, we are determined to compleat for the war, and accomodate so far as our proportion of man and supplyes shall extend, without a moment's delay and at any expense—resting no longer on those temporary levies and occasional provisions which have only tended to distress the people, enhanced the expences, and protest the period of the war.

And we doubt not, that the result of the general commission on this most interesting subject, instituted by the last General Assembly under the late constitution, executed as we trust it will be by the people of those States, will be such as shall enable the good people of America, cemented as we are by indisoluable connection, and aided by the forces of our powerful magnaminous Ally, to bid perpetual defiance to the utmost power and policy of our enemies.

The militia of the Commonwealth, upon which its more immediate security depends, we shall endeavour to place upon such an establishment, and under such regulations and provisions as that we may be able either to repel invasion, or to cooperate with the army of the States or of our Allies on any emergency, be it even so sudden or unexpected. Taking the necessary measures for their pay and subsidence as occasion may require, and forming such arrangements in the civil or staff department, as that the purchases and distribution of the public stores may be placed in suitable hands, and conducted, both in the army and in the militia, upon just principles, and to proper effect.

The General Court will also take effectual order for the protection of our seacoasts; and of that navigation and commerce, with the freedom and extent of which the opulence and strength of the Commonwealth is most intimately connected, from the insults, interruptions and depredations of the enemy. While we shall guard with all possible vigilance against a clandestinely carried on by flags of the truce with the subjects of that insidious and cruel power with which we are at war—now shall impolitic and false delicacy of admitting prisoners of distinction to go at large, make a part of that liberality with which, as citizens of the world in times of profound peace, we might be inclined to treat those, to whom considered as enemies, although we should shew every office of humanity, consistent with the public safety and with the comfort of our friends in Captivity, yet whose residence with us in times of war, except in confinement, may be and often has been very injurious.

In order to the accomplishment of the grand object of war and of victory, we assure your Excellency that we will critically examine into the fate of our finances, and place them, in addition to what has been already happily effected; upon so respectable a footing as that the public faith shall be fully restored and established; and are very happy in finding that notwithstanding the infamous practise of our enemies to ruin our cause by counterfeiting and depreciating our currency, the real debt of the Continent does not amount to more than half the sum which is annually expended by them in support of the war against us, in addition to the load of many millions of national debt.

While on this head we sincerely regret with your Excellency that in the course of events many of the creditors of Government, among which are unhappily a great number of widows and orphans, and of that patriotic and valuable order of men the clergy, and or our brethren in arms, had been injured in their property, as well as in consequence of the rapid depreciation of our currency: As the late assembly have taken up the case of the latter, so the present are going on to perfect their relief, while urged by all the principles of justice, honor and humanity, they will do every thing for the redress of the former which can be devised and effected.

Convinced that the means of supporting the war to any period, are, under the auspices of Heaven, within our own power, we shall, by such reforms in the mode of taxation as shall be found necessary, draw forth the large resources of the commonwealth in such just proportions, as we have reason to think have not heretofor been properly attended to, which will add to the satisfaction and chearfullness with which our constituents will contribute of there property to the public service, and ascertain to us seasonable and adequate supplies.

Nor can we admit a doubt that the same genius of liberty which at first inspired, still animates the freemen of Massachusetts, and that not "an ability will be suffer to lay dormant or be misapplied, not a necessary measure be left unexplored, or just one unattempted, nor a nerve unexerted" until, from the wisdom of our councils and the vigor of our aims glory and peace shall crown the contest.

The civil matters which your Excellency has been pleased to recognize, are subjects of real and interesting concern.

Deeply impressed with a sense of the importance of religion to the happiness of men in civil society to maintain its purity and promote this efficacy, we shall protect professors of all denominations, demeaning themselves peaceably and as good subjects of the Commonwealth, in the free exercise of the rights of conscience; and shall exert ourselves to carry the wise and equitable provision of the constitution for these salutary purposes into the fullest effect—and as one necessary measure, shall revise the laws and make such additions to or amendments in them as may be necessary and consistent with personal liberty, for the due observance of that day which the Supreme hath consecrated to his more immediate worship and service.

Inasmuch as knowledge and virtue are essential to the preservation of freedom in a State, we shall be happy in affording the highest marks of attention and respect to all Seminaries of Literature, and yielding them all the support they may need, and which it becomes the Representatives of a wise and free people to afford—especially our University at Cambridge, founded by the wisdom and virtue of our ancestors, approved by long experience of its utility, and honoured by the many illustrious characters which have adorned our country, and who imbibe the first principles of science at that pure and copious fountain.

Nor can the schools throughout this Commonwealth be permitted to continue under such inattention and discouragement as they have for many years suffered, to the irreparable injury of the present and future generation, and to the indelible disgrace of a free government. We shall therefore hold ourselves obliged to form proper establishments for restoring them to their primitive dignity and usefulness.

It gives us singular pleasure to find the Society of Arts, &c. lately founded in this Commonwealth, dignified and enriched by the addition of many respectable literary characters, and promising such happy improvement. . . Institutions, which have a tendancy "To cherish the interests of literature and sciences, to extend and improve commerce, to promote agriculture, arts, trades, and manufactures, and a natural history of the country," are by the Constitution intituled to, and cannot fail to find the patrionage and protection of the Government.

We beg leave to assure your Excellency that we shall make it our sincere endeavour, both by precept and example, to countenance and inculcate obedience to the laws, with the principles of religion, patriotism, "Humanity, and general benevolence, public and private charity, industry and frugality, honesty and punctuality in dealing, sincerity, good humour, and all social affections, and generous sentiments among the people."

And as the dignity and reputation of the Commonwealth, as well as the interest of the subjects, demand the independence both of the Chief Magistrate and of the Justices of the Supreme Judicial Court, so it shall be among our first Acts of Legislation, to provide and establish permenant and honorable salaries for each.

May it please your Excellency,

With all the liberality and candor, unanimity and harmony which can consist with the due exercise of the powers and rights vested in the several branches respectively, We shall now proceed to the business of the session, and shall forthwith attend to the revision of the laws and to the framing such new Statutes as may be requisite for accomplishing the important purpose of our election; and shall at all times pay that respect to the communications and recommendation[s] of your Excellency, and give the dispach to the public business which the safety and happiness of the commonwealth may require.

69. Samuel Adams: "This great Business was carried through with good Humour among the People."

[Samuel Adams to John Adams, Philadelphia, July 10, 1780, Harry Alonzo Cushing, ed., *The Writings of Samuel Adams* (New York, 1908), IV, 199-200]

MY DEAR SIR

I wrote to you several Times when I was at Boston, and receivd your Favor by the Marquis de la Fayette. Another, to which you referrd me, has not yet come to hand. This Letter will be deliverd to you by Mr Searle, a Member of Congress for the State of Pennsylvania. He will be better able to inform you of the State of things here, than I can, who after twelve Months Absence from this City, returnd but a few days ago. The People of Massachusetts have at length agreed to the Form of a civil Constitution, in Nothing varying from a Copy which I sent to you by a Son of our Friend General Warren. This great Business was carried through with much good Humour among the People, and even in Berkshire, where some Persons led us to expect it would meet with many Obstructions. Never was a good Constitution more wanted than at this Juncture. Among other more lasting Advantages, I hope that in Consequence of it, the Part which that State must take in the War, will be conducted with greater Attention and better Effect. Who is to be the first Man, will be determind in September, when if our News papers rightly inform us, the new Government is to take Place. The Burden will fall on the Shoulders of one of two Gentlemen whom you know. May Heaven lead the People to the wisest Choice. The first chosen Governor may probably have it in his Power to do more good or more Hurt than any of his successors. The french Fleet is not yet arrivd. Perhaps their long Passage may turn out for the best. An earlier Arrival might have found us not altogether prepared to cooperate with them to the best Advantage. I now think we shall be ready to joyn them. One would think the Exertion which America might make with such Aid, would rid us of British Barbarians. I hope this will be a vigorous and an effective Campaign. I left Massachusetts exceedingly active in filling up their Battalions by Drafts, besides raising 4000 Militia for the Service.

Mr Laurens arrivd here from the Southward a few Days past. He will speedily embark for Holland to prosecute a Business which you are not unacquainted with. Adieu my dear Sir.

Y^r^ affectionate Friend